WORKING ACROSS MODALITIES IN THE ARTS THERAPIES

Working Across Modalities in the Arts Therapies: Creative Collaborations offers an in-depth insight into cross-modality and transdisciplinary practice in the arts therapies. Including contributions from drama, music, dance movement and art therapists, as well as professionals from related disciplines, it vividly demonstrates how the alchemy of these collaborations produces innovative interventions and new approaches to working with clients.

Compelling examples of collaborative practice cover a variety of client groups, ranging from Syrian refugee children and women with eating disorders, to homeless war veterans and sex offenders. Together, the authors make the case for the effectiveness of cross-modal and transdisciplinary approaches when working with otherwise hard-to-reach and complex populations.

This book is a guide to good practice and an invaluable resource for both experienced arts therapists and those new to the field. It will also be of benefit to healthcare and education professionals, arts practitioners, and anyone with an interest in the subject.

Tasha Colbert PGDip, RDMP, UKCP, is a registered dance movement psychotherapist who has practiced for over fifteen years with a variety of client groups in the NHS, education and private practice. She lectures on dance movement psychotherapy programmes in the UK and internationally, and facilitates various continued professional development (CPD) trainings. She is an experienced clinical supervisor and psychotherapist with a private practice in West London.

Cornelia Bent MA, HCPC, BAMT, is a UK-registered music therapist who has worked for over ten years with a wide range of client groups in a variety of settings, including the NHS, education and charity sector. Within her current clinical practice in adult mental health, she often collaborates with other arts psychotherapists, contributes clinically to music therapy research trials and presents at conferences internationally.

WORKING ACROSS MODALITIES IN THE ARTS THERAPIES

Creative Collaborations

Edited by
Tasha Colbert and Cornelia Bent

LONDON AND NEW YORK

First published 2018
by Routledge
2 Park Square, Milton Park, Abingdon, Oxon OX14 4RN

and by Routledge
711 Third Avenue, New York, NY 10017

Routledge is an imprint of the Taylor & Francis Group, an informa business

British Library Cataloguing in Publication Data
A catalogue record for this book is available from the British Library

Library of Congress Cataloging in Publication Data
A catalog record for this book has been requested

ISBN: 978-1-138-65642-0 (hbk)
ISBN: 978-1-138-65643-7 (pbk)
ISBN: 978-1-315-55988-9 (ebk)

Typeset in Bembo
by Integra Software Service Pvt. Ltd.

CONTENTS

List of contributors *vii*

Foreword *xiii*

Introduction *xvi*

PART I

Cross-modality practice and research in the arts therapies **1**

1 Not what it says on the tin: A family awareness group in a high
security hospital 3
Alex Maguire & Martina Mindang

2 Moving Colour: Combining dance movement psychotherapy
and art psychotherapy in a NHS community women's group 15
Claire Burrell & Marika Cohen

3 Staying connected: Combining music therapy and dance
movement psychotherapy in an acute mental health setting 30
Tasha Colbert & Cornelia Bent

4 Facing rupture and nurturing a creative space: A dramatherapy
and art therapy group on an acute ward in a medium secure
forensic hospital 42
Cathy Goodwin & Alison Ramm

5 Ambivalence, boundaries, edges and expansion: Relatedness and
collaboration in a dance movement psychotherapy and music
therapy group for adults with learning disabilities 55
Céline Butté & Diana Whelan

6 Stretch marks: An exploration of a joint dramatherapy and music therapy group 69
Gillian Downie & Robin Wiltshire

7 An innovative collaboration: Combining art and music therapy interventions for adults with learning disabilities 81
Megan Charles & Judith Sanoon

8 Holding hope: Rehabilitation of Syrian refugee children through art, music and dance movement therapy 95
Seda S. Güney, Leyla Akca Atik & Danny S. Lundmark

PART II
Transdisciplinary practice and research in the arts therapies **109**

9 Regaining balance through family art psychotherapy 111
Katie Wilson & Yvonne Rose

10 A transdisciplinary approach: Working with individuals in a sex offender treatment programme 126
Kate Rothwell & Laura Henagulph

11 'The boy who cried wolf': A collaborative approach to long term segregation 139
Emma Allen

12 Leftovers: Exploring body image 152
Camilla F. Matthews

13 Almost paradise: A creative arts collaboration helping US veterans recover from homelessness 165
Lisa Peacock

Acknowledgements *178*
Index *179*

CONTRIBUTORS

Leyla Akca Atik, MPS, LCAT, completed her graduate degree in art psychotherapy in the USA. She was employed at University Settlement, a New York-based social service establishment, as a team-coordinator to help Hurricane Sandy survivors by offering crisis counselling and emotional support. She was a coordinator, providing art therapy workshops, after the 2011 earthquake in Van, Turkey. Following the Soma Mine Disaster, she provided on-site psycho-social support to adults and young people. In 2014 she helped develop and implement Project Lift. As Clinical Director of the project, she conducts creative art therapy workshops with Syrian refugee children, and provides training in the field.

Emma Allen, MA, HCPC, is a UK registered art psychotherapist, sand-play therapist, clinical supervisor and a published author. Emma has been working full time at Rampton Hospital – one of the three high secure hospitals in the UK – since 2009, and has over ten years' experience of working in NHS settings. Emma is currently working part time at Rampton, and is a senior lecturer in the MA Art Psychotherapy programme at the University of South Wales.

Cornelia Bent, MA, HCPC, BAMT, is a UK registered music therapist who completed her training in Austria. Over the past ten years she has worked with a wide range of client groups in a variety of settings including the NHS, education and charity sectors. In her current clinical practice in adult mental health, she often collaborates with arts psychotherapists from different modalities, as well as other health professionals. She has been a lead clinician in a number of research studies and has presented at conferences. She regularly supervises students on trainee placements.

Claire Burrell, PG(dip), RDMP, is a registered dance movement psychotherapist who has practiced for over twelve years. Her current clinical practice is in adult mental health in the NHS, where she delivers dance movement psychotherapy inpatient and community services. For many years she has run movement-based therapy groups for asylum seekers and refugees, and has considerable experience working within therapeutic communities. At Roehampton University she contributes to the Dance Movement Psychotherapy MA programme, offering supervision to trainees. Her practice has evolved through dance performance and investigation into dance improvisation, and her own creative process is documented through her interest in making short films.

Céline Butté, MA, PGCert PHE, Dip Creative Supervision, Sensorimotor Psychotherapy level I, RDMP, UKCP, has practiced as a dance movement psychotherapist for fifteen years. She offers dance movement psychotherapy within a day centre for people with learning disabilities and in the context of her private practice. She is a qualified supervisor with the London Centre for Psychodrama, currently teaching on this programme, and contributes to the MA in dance movement psychotherapy at the University of Roehampton. Céline was a member of the ADMP UK Council, a UK delegate and Treasurer of the European Association of Dance Movement Therapy.

Megan Charles, MA, HCPC, BAAT, completed her MA in art therapy at the University of Hertfordshire, following an undergraduate degree in psychology. Megan currently works as an art psychotherapist at a residential unit for adults with long-term mental health problems, as well as working as a freelance art psychotherapist for the NHS and third sector organisations. Additionally, Megan has been setting up a social enterprise, developing open studio groups for older adults living in supported and sheltered accommodation with the support of the School for Social Entrepreneurs.

Marika Cohen, MA, HCPC, is a senior art psychotherapist specialising in adult mental health. This has involved acute, community and perinatal NHS settings. Her journey in the NHS has been varied, through clinical and managerial roles. Although originally from Finland, she has now established both her personal and professional life in the UK. She studied art at Camberwell College of Arts, and later completed an MA in art psychotherapy at Goldsmiths, University of London.

Tasha Colbert, PG(dip), RDMP, UKCP, is a registered dance movement psychotherapist with fifteen years' experience in various settings including the NHS, education and charity sectors, and has had the opportunity to collaborate with other arts psychotherapists on a number of occasions. Tasha lectured on the MA Dance Movement Psychotherapy course at Derby University for three years, and continues to teach dance movement psychotherapy (DMP) internationally. She is currently co-ordinating a DMP programme in Romania, and facilitates various continued professional development (CPD) trainings in the UK. She is also an experienced clinical supervisor and psychotherapist, with a private practice in West London.

Gillian Downie, MA, UKCP, BADth, HCPC, is a dramatherapist, supervisor and gestalt psychotherapist. Her dramatherapy experience over the past sixteen years includes working in schools, mental health services, prison, and private practice at the Gestalt Centre Wales. She is a CAST trained clinical supervisor and particularly enjoys group work. She facilitates regular CPD events on issues such as shame, narcissism and attachment. She is a tutor on the Psyche and Soma training, a sixteen-month course for registered practitioners. Gillian plays the clarinet, loves drumming and movement and is a member of The Golden Thread Playback Theatre Company.

Cathy Goodwin is a qualified dramatherapist, and practiced at South London and Maudsley NHS Foundation Trust, working with older adults. For the past six years Cathy has been working with a team of arts therapists in secure mental health services within the NHS. Alongside clinical practice, Cathy is a visiting lecturer at Roehampton University, teaching on the MA Dramatherapy programme, and is a trained supervisor in Creative Arts Supervision Training (CAST).

Seda S. Güney, MA, RDMP, is an ADMP UK registered dance movement psychotherapist who trained in London and is currently based in Istanbul. She established and developed the first official DMP service in a psychiatric hospital in Istanbul. Alongside adult mental health, she works with children and adults with special needs, people with physical disabilities and with the elderly. She has performed with and taught at AMICI Dance Theatre Company, and has led dance workshops across Europe. Responsible for developing and delivering trainings in trauma rehabilitation for refugee children, Seda is also a board member of Arts Psychotherapies Association in Turkey.

Dr Laura Henagulph, MA (Oxon), DClinPsych, is a chartered senior clinical psychologist. Until recently, Laura worked within East London NHS Foundation Trust in forensic learning disability and forensic active rehabilitation; she now lives and works in Bermuda. Laura has a background in psychodynamic approaches, especially mentalisation-based therapy. Her main area of expertise is working with personality disorders.

Danny S. Lundmark, MT-BC, graduated from Berklee College of Music with a degree in music therapy. He received his Music Therapist – Board Certified (MT-BC) credentials from the American Music Therapy Association, and is a professional member of the World Federation of Music Therapy. He specialises in working with child development, psychiatric care and trauma rehabilitation. He is currently living in Istanbul, Turkey, providing music therapy services to a variety of institutions.

Alex Maguire, MSc, PG(dip), MT, HCPC, is a music therapist in a high security hospital in the UK, working with high dependency and intensive care patients. He has presented his work at numerous conferences and is a contributing author to the book *Forensic Music Therapy*. The hospital choir, which he co-founded, was commended in the Arts and Health Awards 2013, and this work is shortly to be published. He has contributed to *The Forensic Arts Therapies Anthology in Research and Practice* (FA Books) and is currently writing a music therapy case study for the book *Violent States* – Creative States (JKP).

Camilla F. Matthews, MA, BAAT, HCPC, UKCP, IGA, is an art therapist, psychotherapist, group analyst and a qualified group analytic supervisor. She has many years of experience within social services and the NHS working with trauma, personality difficulties and eating disorders. She is currently the manager and senior clinician of a personality disorder unit and has a private practice providing psychotherapy, supervision and training for individuals and groups.

Martina Mindang, PG(dip), HCPC, BAAT, HEA (Fellow), is an art therapist. Since qualifying in 1996 she has worked within the NHS mental health services in adult community care, acute admission and high secure services. Her special clinical interest is creative approaches to psychological recovery from violence, on which she has presented at international conferences and seminars as well as contributing to the books *Forensic Arts Therapies* – *Anthology of Practice & Research* (Free Association Press) and *Violent States* – *Creative States* (JKP). Martina is a registered clinical supervisor, private practitioner and lecturer on the MA Art Psychotherapy Programme at Roehampton University.

Lisa Peacock, MA, RDT, is a registered dramatherapist with the NADTA (US) and BADth (UK) who works with veterans, adolescents and children who have experienced trauma. She is pursuing her PhD in dramatherapy at Anglia Ruskin University in Cambridge, UK. Trained in art therapy, narrative therapy, authentic movement, and dance movement therapy, she is the founder and director of the Vet Art Project and the Women Warriors Project, and a contract psychotherapist with the Wounded Warrior Project. Peacock is an author and was a Chicago Dramatists Resident Playwright for ten years and a book editor.

Alison Ramm worked for many years as an artist in schools, with community groups and in mental health settings. She trained as an art therapist at Queen Margaret University, Edinburgh and worked with inpatients and outpatients in Adult Mental Health in NHS Scotland. In 2013 she began to work in forensic settings, in a medium secure hospital. She has worked in education with primary school children, and she contributes lectures and workshops to art therapy training programmes in the UK.

Yvonne Rose, MSc, BSc, UKCP, qualified as a systemic family psychotherapist in 2013. She has completed an MSc in Child Family Mental Health, BSc/Diploma in Social Work and an Advanced Diploma in Person Centred Counselling. Following specialising in child protection, she later returned to work therapeutically, initially with the NSPPC and then community CAMHS, where she developed an interest in attachment while setting up a service to support the placements of children and young people who were fostered. Currently, Yvonne is gaining further training as a systemic supervisor while drawing on narrative therapy ideas as a systemic family psychotherapist, working in CAMHS Tier 4.

Kate Rothwell, PG(dip) Art Therapy MAACP, PG(dip) NHS Leadership, HCPC, UKCP, is Head of Arts Therapies working in the Forensic Directorate at the East London Foundation Trust and core creative therapist at HMP Grendon. With over 25 years' experience working in forensic settings, Kate convened the Forensic Arts Therapies Advisory Group from 2009–16 and is editor of the Forensic Arts Therapies Anthology of Practice and Research. Kate previously lectured on the MA Art Therapy training at the University of Hertfordshire, and has a private practice working with children, adolescents and adults. Kate supervises arts therapists across a range of services.

Judith Sanoon, LGSM (MT), trained as a music therapist at the Guildhall School of Music & Drama under Juliet Alvin in 1979–80. Her first experience of cross-modality working was in the early 1980s, when she co-ran a group for dementia patients with a dramatherapist in a large psychiatric hospital in Essex. Judith now works with adults with learning difficulties in residential homes as well as in a mainstream school, with young children – who naturally work across modalities.

Diana Whelan qualified as a music therapist in 2003 at Anglia Ruskin University. She has worked with adults with learning disabilities for the past thirteen years and currently works in the field of adult mental health. Diana's clinical and research interests include the integration of arts modalities in therapeutic practice and working with the legacies of trauma. She has completed further trainings with the Sesame Institute for Drama and Movement Therapy and the Sensorimotor Psychotherapy Institute. Diana is also a senior lecturer in music therapy at the University of Roehampton, and a Fellow of the Higher Education Academy.

Katie Wilson, MA, BAAT, HCPC, worked as a theatre designer before qualifying as an art psychotherapist in 1996. After three years working in Tier 4 CAMHS, she currently works within a community team. Katie is also an associate lecturer at the northern programme for art psychotherapy. In this role she has facilitated supervision and developed training with the BAAT Special Interest Group for art psychotherapists working with children and families. She has recently piloted an art psychotherapy project for teenagers and young adults with cancer. Katie has a special interest in attachment work and is developing her skills in dyadic art psychotherapy.

Robin Wiltshire, PG(dip), HCPC, BAMT, has been practicing as a music therapist for the past fifteen years. He has experience of providing individual and group music therapy across a range of services including adult learning disabilities, acute mental health and palliative care. Robin is a trained psychodynamic clinical supervisor and maintains a small supervision practice. He regularly performs with The Golden Thread Playback Theatre Company as their musician.

FOREWORD

This book takes us on a fascinating journey through the overlap between the arts therapies professions. It describes work in art therapy, dramatherapy, dance movement psychotherapy and music therapy. As a community in the UK we have become increasingly aware of the positive impact of the arts for health, and we can trace our own relationships with different art forms – music, dance, art and drama – through our lives. Here, we can read how the benefits of these art forms are harnessed in skilled therapeutic work led by professionals across the arts therapies disciplines. This welcome book presents a deep exploration of the central themes in transdisciplinary and cross-modality work in arts therapies practice.

'It is in the overlap where disciplines meet that practitioners really begin to be creative' (Twyford, 2008: 60). The idea of cross-modality is one that is familiar to arts therapists, perhaps to music therapists in particular, from the writings of Daniel Stern on affect attunement. This concept describes the creative use of different modalities of expression by care givers, to meet an aspect of the feeling state of their infant, who learns that internal states of feeling can be shared (1998: 142, 151). Stern also noted the 'central role of vitality forms in establishing contact with the patient and working with them' (Stern, 2010: 141). These ideas of cross-modality are central to our work as arts therapists in supporting service users to rebuild a sense of self, reconstruct lost or damaged relationships and reconnect with their lives and communities. The arts therapies are unique in their ability to offer playful and accessible interventions that allow profound emotional pain and challenges to be approached and addressed. These are therapeutic journeys which are often too difficult and anxiety-provoking to attempt, using other approaches. Winnicott wrote 'It is play that is the universal, and that belongs to health: playing facilitates growth and therefore health' (1971: 41). In order to play one must feel safe; 'playing can only occur in a setting where there is a feeling of ease, of security, of not having to be vigilant, being free of pressing other needs' (Stern, 2001: 145).

The power of the arts to frame and contain, and the idea of cross-modality as contributing extra resilience to the work, allows a robust and safe therapeutic environment to be provided. As we read in this book, the triangular nature of engagement in different art forms, often with two or more therapists, allows for the containment of complex material and extreme distress.

We read of the gritty, real-life nature of this work in the chapters that follow. The experiences of service users are distressing and often lead to the use of behaviour that challenges families, staff and the environment. In these chapters we read about the way in which the careful, planned use of the arts therapies is used to draw into therapeutic contact people who may find it very hard to access traditional health support. We read of pioneering work that weaves together different approaches to provide bespoke treatment for groups of service users. This level of therapeutic containment through combined approaches provides long-term and preventative support for those with enduring conditions (NHS England, 2014). In this way, whilst, as noted in this volume, collaborative work can be seen by some services to be expensive, it may paradoxically save funds through its preventative action. Good outcomes for service users are indicated when professionals work closely together.

The arts therapies professions are established but still young, perhaps entering their adolescence. In the UK our regulatory standards require us to work in partnership with colleagues, and to understand the need for this and its impact on our practice (HCPC, 2013). The theory and practice of collaborative and transdisciplinary work has gradually been developed, with music therapy publications such as Fearn and O'Connor (2003), Twyford and Watson (2008) and most recently Strange et al. (2017). *Working Across Modalities in the Arts Therapies* provides a vivid picture of the latest clinical developments in the field.

Working with others in the therapy room, as well as collaborating outside the room, requires that we understand and manage the similarities and differences in modalities and practices – and the challenges that these differences pose. The challenges posed by these creative collaborations include projections and transferences: powerful experiences that, if not reflected upon and worked through, can lead to destructive processes impacting upon the therapeutic work. One vital thread of this volume is an exploration of different resources for support and development that can be used by therapists who are working in cross-modal and transdisciplinary ways. Collaborative supervision and open reflection are essential to work through any parallel processes, and, as the authors note, these structures help to strengthen the team and develop skills for future work.

This book is a cause for celebration. It documents therapeutic stories that will help us to learn about our own disciplines and those in related fields, and I recommend it to a wide range of health professionals. It presents a diverse picture of collaborative clinical work, and provides creative ideas for the continued development of practice. The boundaries of collaborative work are broadened, with chapters about innovative approaches in areas such as homelessness, family therapy, sex offending, eating disorders, work with veterans and refugee work. Working collaboratively means not that core skills are set aside, but that they are built upon, and the narratives in this book show the deep learning and development that results, both for service users and professionals.

Tessa Watson

References

Fearn, M.C. and O'Connor, R. (2003). The Whole is Greater than the Sum of its Parts: Experiences of Co-working as Music Therapists. *British Journal of Music Therapy*, 17(2), pp. 67–75.

HCPC (2013). *Standards of Proficiency. Arts Therapists*. [online] Available at: https://www.hcpc-uk.org/assets/documents/100004FBStandards_of_Proficiency_Arts_Therapists.pdf [Accessed 12 Dec. 2016].

NHS England (2014). Chapter Two – What Will the Future Look Like? A New Relationship with Patients and Communities. *Five Year Forward View*, NHS England, pp. 10–17.

Stern, D.N. (1998). *The Interpersonal World of the Infant*. London: Karnac Books.

Stern, D.N. (2001). Face-to-Face Play. In: J. Jaffe, B. Beebe, S. Felstein, C. Crown and M.D. Jasnow, eds., *Rhythms of Dialogue in Infancy: Coordinated timing in development. Monographs of the Society for Research in Child Development, Vol 66*, 1st ed. Belford: Ann Abor Publishers Ltd. MI.

Stern, D.N. (2010). *Forms of Vitality: Exploring Dynamic Experience in Psychology, the Arts, Psychotherapy, and Development*. Oxford: OUP.

Strange, J., Odell-Miller, H., and Richards, E. (2017). *Collaboration and Assistance in Music Therapy Practice*. London: Jessica Kingsley Publishers.

Twyford, K. (2008). Collaborative and Transdisciplinary Approaches with Children. In: K. Twyford and T. Watson, eds., *Integrated Team Working. Music Therapy as Part of Transcisciplinary and Collaborative Approaches*, 1st ed. London: Jessica Kingsley Publishers.

Twyford, K. and Watson, T. (2008). *Integrated Team Working. Music Therapy as Part of Transcisciplinary and Collaborative Approaches*, 1st ed. London: Jessica Kingsley Publishers.

Winnicott, D.W. (1971). *Playing and Reality*. London: Routledge.

INTRODUCTION

Our aims

This book was inspired by a shared commitment to collaborative work within the arts therapies, and aims to fulfil the need for a deeper understanding of cross-modality and transdisciplinary work. It is intended to be a guide to good practice as well as an inspiration to practitioners to reach out from within their own modality or discipline, share skills and discover new ways of working. Aiming to illustrate how the alchemy of creative collaboration can produce innovative interventions and new approaches to working with clients, it will be of equal interest to those with no experience of cross-modality and transdisciplinary work who are thinking of embarking upon a collaborative project, and experienced practitioners who wish to develop this aspect of their practice.

While the book's theme has to some extent been explored in books on music therapy and collaborative practice (Twyford and Watson, 2008; Strange et al., 2017), isolated chapters (Davies, 2015; Davies and Richards, 2002; Gale and Matthews, 1998; Twyford and Watson, 2007; Vickers and Watson, 2002; Watson, Bragg and Jeffcote, 2004), and journal articles (Best, 2000; Cardone, Marengo and Calisch, 1982; Cohen, 1983; Zagelbaum and Rubino, 1991), it remains under-represented in arts therapies literature. Seeking to redress this imbalance, the aim of the book is to delineate, support and extend the field of interdisciplinary work within the arts therapies and between other psychological and health care disciplines. Its broad clinical base will be of value to clinicians working in a range of sectors.

Terminology

For the purposes of this book, 'cross-modality' and 'cross-modal' refer to instances where arts therapists working in different modalities collaborate with one another, while 'transdisciplinary' is used where an arts therapist collaborates with a practitioner from a different discipline such as psychology or systemic family therapy. However, both cross-modal and transdisciplinary practice should be distinguished from inter-modal or integrative arts therapy. These have their own trainings, tend to focus on the interrelatedness of the arts, and are generally delivered by a single therapist trained to use a variety of art-forms therapeutically, rather than specialising in one modality.

The arts therapies

Emerging in the mid-twentieth century as distinct approaches with their own methodological and theoretical frameworks, the arts psychotherapies are currently recognised and registered as four separate professions: art therapy, music therapy, dance movement psychotherapy and dramatherapy. While each profession has developed its own unique identity, they share certain common beliefs, values and ways of working. The arts therapies are most commonly defined as follows:

> Art therapy is a form of psychotherapy that uses art media as its primary mode of expression and communication. Art is not used as a diagnostic tool, but as a medium to address emotional issues which may be confusing and distressing. It is used with individuals, families and groups of all ages.
>
> *(British Association of Art Therapy, 2016)*

> Music therapy facilitates positive changes in emotional wellbeing and com-munication through engagement in live musical interaction between client and therapist. In music therapy, therapists draw upon the innate qualities of music to support people of all ages and abilities and at all stages of life.
>
> *(British Association of Music Therapy, 2016)*

> Dance movement psychotherapy (DMP) recognises body movement as an implicit and expressive instrument of communication and expression. DMP is a relational process in which client and therapist engage creatively using body movement and dance to assist integration of emotional, cognitive, physical, social and spiritual aspects of self.
>
> *(Association of Dance Movement Psychotherapy, 2016)*

> Dramatherapy is a form of psychological therapy in which all of the performance arts are utilised within the therapeutic relationship. Dramatherapists are both artists and clinicians, and draw on their trainings in theatre/drama and therapy to create methods to engage clients in effecting psychological, emotional and social changes.
>
> *(British Association of Dramatherapists, 2016)*

The arts therapies share a psychotherapeutic approach, which distinguishes them from other professions such as speech and language therapy and occupational therapy. To avoid confusion with such non-psychotherapeutic approaches, some practitioners prefer to use the terms 'psychotherapy' and 'psychotherapist', in place of 'therapy' and 'therapist' respectively. The Association for Dance Movement Psychotherapy UK (ADMP UK) has officially changed its title to reflect this. The equivalent art, music and dramatherapy associations continue to use the term 'therapy'; however, many practitioners use the terms 'therapy' and 'psychotherapy' interchangeably. In the UK, practitioners working in the National Health Service (NHS) more commonly use the term 'arts psychotherapies', to make evident the psychotherapeutic nature of their work. With such a variety of terms in current use, each chapter reflects its authors' preferred terminology.

The challenges and benefits of collaboration

Arts therapists often express a wish to collaborate, creating a place where core disciplines can be brought together, developed and synthesised into new methodologies in the interests of providing a deeper and broader experience for their clients. This can be complex to implement in public sector institutions, where there may not be a range of arts therapies or related disciplines available, or it may not be considered cost effective to have two therapists facilitate a group. This book highlights instances where arts therapists have been fortunate enough to have had the opportunity to collaborate.

Collaboration brings challenges as well as rich experiences. Managing power-dynamics between facilitators, tricky transference issues and the potential for 'splitting' by the group all add a layer of complexity to the work. From a psychodynamic perspective, it has been noted that there is a danger that clients might manoeuvre two therapists into rivalry, and unresolved tensions between the therapists only heighten the risk of this happening (Mintz, 1963: 39). This highlights the need for effective co-supervision, as well as time for debriefing after sessions, in order to examine how themes such as competition, power and trust can play out in the co-working relationship. One makes moment-to-moment decisions when co-working, such as when to lead and when to follow, and the success of this 'dance' often depends on the ability to pick up on non-verbal cues from each other, and the willingness to reflect on any misunderstandings that might arise.

There are many benefits to co-leading in group therapy, such as the therapists being able to model healthy interpersonal interactions, and the potential to increase their observation range within the group. It has been suggested that, no matter how skilled an individual group therapist may be, important cues, particularly non-verbal ones, can be missed (Breeskin, 2010: 5). Also, a therapist's anxiety may be reduced by co-facilitating, particularly with challenging or high risk groups (Yalom and Leszcz, 2005). Co-leading often involves taking different positions and roles within the group, and this offers different perspectives on the group process. These roles may change at different times, and can prevent one or another therapist from being 'sucked in' to the group process and losing perspective (Woodward and Carvisiglia, 2005).

Co-working in individual therapy is most common in forensic settings, and is an approach often chosen to minimise risk and increase the safety of all those involved. This approach also provides some of the benefits evident in co-led group therapy, such as the opportunity to work with re-parenting dynamics. Having two therapists can provide fertile ground for a re-working of internal parental models into something more balanced and supportive.

Research has shown that participants in co-led group therapy rate higher satisfaction than with single-therapist led groups (Kivlighan and Miles, 2012) Historically, group therapists have expressed a preference for co-leadership, and there has been widespread use of this model since the 1960s (Friedman, 1973; Paulson, Burroughs and Gelb, 1976; Yalom and Leszcz, 2005). However, within government-funded institutions, the pressure on the arts therapies to be cost-effective may mean that there are fewer opportunities for co-leadership, even when this is the preferred model.

Effective co-working takes time to develop, and depends on a range of factors such as personal compatibility, openness to difference, flexibility of thinking and approach, and a willingness to be comfortable in the 'not knowing'. Best suggests, 'Collaborative work can expose differences in views, beliefs and methods of working' (Yalom and Leszcz, 2005: 197). Furthermore, to work with someone from a different modality may bring up insecurities in the therapist, which need to be worked through in supervision in order to avoid being acted out in the co-working relationship.

There is a shared understanding and knowledge inherent in working with another arts therapist, albeit from a different modality – such as the power of the arts to contain and be a vehicle for self-expression. This may be missing when working with a practitioner from a separate discipline, although working with professionals from psychotherapy and psychology will inevitably involve some shared theoretical knowledge and understanding. Respect for each other's modality or discipline, confidence in one's own working model and a willingness to learn from one another are all essential components of effective cross-modality and transdisciplinary practice. Being able to recognise the uniqueness and limitations of one's own approach is also important when collaborating (Wilson and Cooppan, 2005). The contributions in this book represent instances where collaborations have been successful, despite the inherent challenges that such work brings.

Who this book is intended for

Working Across Modalities in the Arts Therapies: Creative Collaborations is intended for students and professionals within the field of the arts therapies worldwide. Reaching across professional boundaries, its intended readership extends to a range of other disciplines, including psychology, psychiatry, psychotherapy and those working in social care and the voluntary sector. It will also be of interest to arts practitioners working within the community and criminal justice system.

How the book is structured

The book is divided into two parts:

Part I is dedicated to cross-modality practice in the arts therapies. The chapters in this section present examples of clinical practice and research where arts therapists from different modalities have co-facilitated short- or long-term therapy groups. We have included a range of collaborative combinations – for example, art and music, dance movement and art, drama and music – giving the reader an insight into what can take place in the 'space between' different art forms, and how this provides clients with varied forms of expression. Chapters are clustered according to client groups, ranging from mental health service users, adults with learning disabilities and refugee children.

Part II presents transdisciplinary practice and research in the arts therapies. Represented are examples of collaborations with a dialectical behaviour therapy (DBT) facilitator, a systemic family therapist, a therapeutic yoga teacher and psychologists. Clinical contexts are diverse, and include forensic clients, women with eating disorders, family therapy clients and homeless veterans.

The contributions

Contributors to this book comprise qualified and experienced arts therapists from all modalities – dance movement psychotherapy, music therapy, dramatherapy and art therapy – as well as professionals from the fields of psychology and systemic family therapy. Contributors draw on a variety of theoretical frameworks informing their practice.

There follows an overview of the entire book, chapter by chapter.

Part I – Cross-modality practice and research in the arts therapies

In Chapter 1, 'Not doing what it says on the tin: A family awareness group in a high security hospital,' Alex Maguire and Martina Mindang describe a long-term art and music therapy group for men with severe and enduring mental disorders. The chapter gives a fascinating insight into the fragmented internal working models of these men, and the way in which the therapists address converging and diverging narratives within the group. The authors describe the challenges they faced in encouraging a sense of relationship and managing difficult transference issues, and reflect on the value of the co-working relationship to contain the therapeutic process.

In Chapter 2, 'Moving colour: Combining dance movement psychotherapy and art psychotherapy in a NHS community women's group,' Claire Burrell and Marika Cohen give a sensitive account of their cross-modality work in a group which offers an exploration of dance movement and art-making to women coping with the impact of long-term mental illness. The authors reflect on how running the group allowed for a 'layering and filtering' of experiences, through the interplay of the two arts mediums. They demonstrate how offering mixed modality support can enhance arts therapies interventions, providing a variety of tools to enhance the development of verbal and non-verbal expression.

In Chapter 3, 'Staying connected: Combining music therapy and dance movement psychotherapy in an acute mental health setting,' Tasha Colbert and Cornelia

Bent present service users' experiences of a cross-modality group, and share their findings from a qualitative research project that explored the therapeutic benefits of a combined approach. The authors share their observations and reflections on the collaborative process, their rationale for cross-modality working, and the interplay between music and movement. From the findings they suggest that synchronous access to both modalities provides alternative modes of expression that can be useful to clients experiencing a sense of 'stuckness' or inhibition in one modality, and how this can facilitate greater spontaneity and engagement in the therapeutic process.

In Chapter 4, 'Facing rupture and nurturing a creative space: A dramatherapy and art therapy group on an acute ward in a medium secure forensic hospital,' Cathy Goodwin and Alison Ramm describe a cross-modality art and dramatherapy group in a forensic setting. The authors reflect on the challenges of retaining their creativity, and the difficult countertransference feelings they faced in working with people experiencing psychosis. They imaginatively present how the archetypal figure of Hermes as a metaphor helped them to make sense of the work, and how the mythological 'hero's journey' represented hope and the possibility of change and renewal. They go on to describe how they used different elements from their respective modalities to validate the experiences of the patients and foster creative energy and inspiration.

In Chapter 5, 'Ambivalence, boundaries, edges and expansion: Relatedness and collaboration in a dance movement psychotherapy and music therapy group for adults with learning disabilities,' Céline Butté and Diana Whelan present a multi-faceted piece of collaborative clinical work and research with a group of adults with learning disabilities. The chapter skillfully explores the authors' experiences of co-working as a music therapist and dance movement psychotherapist, with the assistance of three volunteers experienced in the modalities of art, dance movement and music therapy. The theme of meaning-making in the context of the group is discussed; shedding light on different aspects of holding, 'coming and going', change and letting go, and asks how these may be understood therapeutically.

In Chapter 6, 'Stretch marks: An exploration of a joint dramatherapy and music therapy group,' Gillian Downie and Robin Wiltshire give an account of a cross-modality group that aims to offer clients with a learning disability a sustained and safe way of expressing and exploring feelings. Through vivid case vignettes, they reflect on how bringing together dramatherapy and music therapy created a new way of working, supporting clients to *stretch* when one of the modalities served as familiar support and the other presented as a challenge. Describing their collaboration, they elaborate on the way it developed aspects of themselves and brought them to understand the differences in their modalities.

In Chapter 7, 'An innovative collaboration: Combining art and music therapy interventions for adults with learning disabilities,' Megan Charles, an art therapist, and Judith Sanoon, a music therapist, describe their journey in collaborative working at a residential unit for adults with learning difficulties and mental health issues. They describe how budgetary constraints led them to job-share, and how the needs of the residents gave rise to an alternating format incorporating both media. The impact on three residents is illuminated through detailed vignettes describing their individual therapy, group therapy and their experiences of the joint group. They highlight themes unique to the joint music therapy and art therapy group, and discuss the benefits and drawbacks of working in this way.

Part I concludes with Chapter 8, 'Holding hope: Rehabilitation of Syrian refugee children through art, music and dance movement therapy'. The authors Seda S. Güney, Leyla Akca Atik and Danny S. Lundmark give an engaging account of a collaborative arts therapies project undertaken with Syrian refugee children. The therapists describe how they used the Skills for Psychological Recovery model as a framework for structuring the sessions, alongside music, dance movement, drama and art therapy interventions. They advocate a multi-modal approach for supporting recovery from trauma, and refer to research supporting this work. The chapter describes how their collaboration provided containment and other benefits to participants, exposing them to new experiences and ways of learning.

Part II – Transdisciplinary practice and research in the arts therapies

Chapter 9, 'Regaining balance through family art psychotherapy,' sees Katie Wilson and Yvonne Rose illuminate the benefits of combining art psychotherapy and family systemic therapy through a moving clinical vignette. The authors explore and discuss a process originally developed as a pragmatic response to working with a teenage girl and her family, and their therapeutic needs. They explain how this approach supported the family's creative exploration, and played an important role in providing a facilitating environment where feelings could be experienced and reflected on through playful encounters.

In Chapter 10, 'A transdisciplinary approach: Working with individuals in a sex offender treatment programme,' Kate Rothwell and Dr. Laura Henagulph open by discussing the rationale for creative and transdisciplinary work with patients who find it hard to tolerate groups, and often find themselves excluded by others. Compelling case examples highlight the challenges of working with patients with a learning disability on a sex offender treatment programme in a forensic context. Facilitators include an art therapist and psychologist, as well as consultants, speech and language therapists, occupational therapists and nurses, in a joined-up approach that adheres to core principles while accessing skills unique to each discipline. The authors make the case for the effectiveness of this approach in adapting to the needs of the client group while ensuring the safety of practitioners.

Chapter 11, 'The boy who cried wolf': A collaborative approach to long-term segregation,' by Emma Allen, presents a unique example of a forensic art psychotherapist working jointly with an assistant psychologist in a high security hospital, providing sessions for 'Daniel,' a patient in long-term segregation, including periods of seclusion where sessions took place 'through the hatch'. The chapter discusses the background and the rationale leading to the decision to work collaboratively using joint dialectical behaviour therapy and art psychotherapy, along with how risk was managed. Emma writes about her experiences of joint working, and includes an interview with her male co-therapist, providing an insight into the necessity and complexities of this approach, and its implications within a high security environment.

In Chapter 12, 'Leftovers: Exploring body image,' Camilla F. Matthews gives an evocative account of a body image group conducted and researched by an art therapist and psychologist. The author outlines the process of creating the programme with her psychologist colleague, utilising a range of techniques including mindfulness, mask-making and body-tracing. She describes how group members moved from literal depictions of their bodies to more metaphorical images associated with childhood memories. She describes how the women's artwork came to depict an increased integration of 'good' and 'bad' elements, transcending what began as polarised extremes. The chapter explores how the programme progressed, presenting evidence that group members had 'met their internal worlds' through a variety of media that allowed them to hold effective internal dialogues.

In the final chapter, 'Almost paradise: A creative arts collaboration helping US veterans recover from homelessness,' Lisa Peacock describes a collaborative therapeutic community model of care in the American Midwest – combining dramatherapy, art therapy, music therapy, writing and poetry therapy, mindfulness of breathing, therapeutic yoga, healing retreats and psycho-social support plans – to help veterans recover from homelessness. Through interviews with her co-workers, she brings to life the ethos and aims of the project. The author also presents an overview of what the project was able to offer, and reflects on some of the challenges and benefits of working with this collaborative model of therapeutic care.

In summary

The diverse and vivid examples of collaborative practice presented here showcase imagination, innovation and creativity across the arts therapies and related professions. Together, the contributions make the case for how cross-modal and transdisciplinary approaches offer effective ways of working with otherwise hard-to-reach and complex groups. The scenarios presented in this book demonstrate how the decision to collaborate has often arisen from the necessity to create a new therapeutic approach that better meets the needs of clients.

Collaborating with other professionals can create a rich learning ground, promoting new understanding of one's own and others' practice, and how different modalities and disciplines relate to one another. This type of work provides the opportunity to broaden practice by learning to adapt to and value theoretical, practical and political differences (Best, 2000: 210).

At its best, cross-modality and transdisciplinary work can be stimulating, refreshing and enriching for practitioners and clients alike. In a co-working relationship there is also an opportunity to provide support to one another in a way that can help with managing the emotional impact of the work (Twyford and Watson, 2008).

In many ways, this book demonstrates how the arts therapies have become established in a variety of settings and with different populations. It perhaps suggests a greater confidence within the arts therapies that they can join forces with other clinicians to create innovative approaches. By demonstrating what cross-modality and transdisciplinary work may look like in practice, we hope this book will make a valuable contribution to the field, and be a source of stimulus and inspiration to practitioners and trainees alike.

References

Association of Dance Movement Psychotherapy (ADMP) UK (2016). Admp.org.uk. [online] Available at: http://www.admp.org.uk/ [Accessed 17 Dec. 2016].

Best, P. (2000). Theoretical diversity and clinical collaboration: Reflections by a dance/movement therapist. *The Arts in Psychotherapy*, 27(3), pp. 187–211.

British Association of Art Therapy (BAAT) UK (2016). Baat.org.uk. [online] Available at: http://www.admp.org.uk/ [Accessed 17 Dec. 2016].

British Association of Dramatherapists (BAD) UK (2016). Badth.org.uk. [online] Available at: http://www.badth.org.uk/ [Accessed 17 Dec. 2016].

British Association of Music Therapy (BAMT) UK (2016). Bamt.org.uk. [online] Available at: http://www.bamt.org.uk/ [Accessed 17 Dec. 2016].

Breeskin, J. (2010). The co-therapist model in groups. *The Group Psychologist*, 20(1), pp. 5–6.

Cardone, L., Marengo J. and Calisch, A. (1982). Conjoint use of art and verbal techniques for the intensification of the psychotherapeutic group experience. *The Arts in Psychotherapy*, 9(4), pp. 263–268.

Cohen, B. (1983). Combining art and movement therapy group: Isomorphic responses. *The Arts in Psychotherapy*, 10(4), pp. 229–232.

Davies, A. (2015). Co-therapy and working with others. In: A. Davies, E. Richards and N. Barwick, eds., *Group Music Therapy: A Group Analytic Approach*, 1st ed. East Sussex: Routledge, pp. 139–148.

Davies, A. and Richards, E. (2002). *Music Therapy and Group Work*. London: Jessica Kingsley Publishers.

Friedman, B. (1973). Cotherapy: A behavioral and attitudinal survey of third-year psychiatric residents. *International Journal of Group Psychotherapy*, 23(2), pp. 228–234.

Kivighlan, D. and Miles, J. (2012). Group dynamics: Theory, research, and practice. *American Psychological Association*, 16(1), pp. 1–13.

Mintz, E. (1963). Transference in co-therapy groups. *Journal of Consulting Psychology*, 27(1), pp. 34–39.

Paulson, I., Burroughs, J. and Gelb, C. (1976). Cotherapy: What is the crux of the relationship? *International Journal of Group Psychotherapy*, 26(2), pp. 213–224.

Strange, J., Odell-Miller, H., and Richards, E. (2017). *Collaboration and Assistance in Music Therapy Practice*. London: Jessica Kingsley Publishers.

Twyford, K. and Watson, T. (2007). Multidisciplinary working and collaborative working in music therapy. In: T. Watson, ed., *Music Therapy with Adults with Learning Disabilities*, 1st ed. Hove: Routledge, pp. 121–132.

Twyford, K. and Watson, T. (2008). *Integrated Team Working: Music Therapy as Part of Transdisciplinary and Collaborative Approaches*. London: Jessica Kingsley Publishers.

Vickers, L. and Watson, T. (2002). A music & art therapy group for people with learning disabilities. In A. Davies and E. Richards, eds., *Music Therapy and Group Work Sound Company*, 1st ed. London: Jessica Kingsley Publishers, pp. 133–146.

Watson, T., Bragg, A. and Jeffcote, N. (2004). Working together: Integrated multi-disciplinary practice with women. In: N. Jeffcote and T. Watson, eds., *Working Therapeutically with Women in Secure Mental Health Settings*. London: Jessica Kingsley Publishers, Chapter 7, pp. 91–107.

Wilson, S. and Cooppan, D. (2005). Music and occupation: Collaborative work between a music therapist and an occupational therapist in an acute mental health setting. In: *BAMT Conference – No Man Is an Island: Group, Partnerships and Teams in Music Therapy*. London: BAMT Publications, p. 80.

Woodward, A. and Carvisiglia, G. (2005). Teaming up in therapy: Art and music therapist co-working an art therapy group. In: *BAMT Conference – No Man Is an Island: Group, Partnerships and Teams in Music Therapy*. London: BAMT Publications, p. 84.

Yalom, I. and Leszcz, M. (2005). *The Theory and Practice of Group Psychotherapy*, 5th ed. New York: Basic Books.

Zagelbaum, V.N. and Rubino, M.A. (1991). Combined dance/movement, art and music therapies with a developmentally delayed psychiatric client in a day treatment setting. *The Arts in Psychotherapy*, 18(2), pp. 139–148.

PART I

Cross-modality practice and research in the arts therapies

1

NOT WHAT IT SAYS ON THE TIN

A family awareness group in a high
security hospital

Alex Maguire & Martina Mindang

Introduction

In this chapter, we relate the narratives of the Family Awareness Group, run in a
high security hospital with men who have committed violent crimes. This was a
cross-modality group facilitated by a music therapist and art therapist, together with
a third professional of various disciplines. We discuss the creative collaboration
between therapists in this slow-open group over six years, presenting the themes
that emerged, and noting parallels between the lives of the men and the clinical
setting. We also illustrate the therapeutic relationships forged in the group, through
a clinical vignette. We conclude with our reflections on this kind of work.

Our experience in this group was often one of struggling to establish and
maintain a sense of ordinary domesticity, given the patients'[1] own chaotic, traumatic
family histories. The group came together in an extraordinary setting, that of a high
security hospital. Although most group members reported that the experiences of
their own families were at odds with the accepted idea of what makes a 'good
family', they were nevertheless prepared to defend their families to the last, despite
the vicissitudes and separation they had experienced. For these 'family' members,
used to a high expressed emotion within interpersonal relationships (McCreadie
and Phillips, 1988), the experience of the Family Awareness Group challenged the
idea of what 'family' can be about, and offered an opportunity to look at what tests
the ordinary, consistent and predictable (if alien) values of the group.

We attempted to provide what Yalom termed the 'corrective recapitulation of
the primary family group' (Yalom, 1995: 13–15), wherein the dysfunctional patterns
or roles the patients play or adopt in the group can be challenged and changed by –
in this case – playful and symbolic use of art and music. Via the pro-social act of
adopting a position in the group, attending regularly and committing to the group

rules, the group fostered a therapeutic space safe enough for 'serious play'. In this way, we hoped to encourage a sense of relational security, and offer an experience of tolerable intimacy amongst members, which had both been absent from their families of origin.

This chapter also considers the role of the high secure environment in this endeavour. Paradoxically, for this group of men it was only within the safe embrace of such a 'brick mother', a term Henri Rey used to describe the Maudsley Hospital and its concrete containment (Rey, 1994), that the experience of 'family' could be described and shared with others who may have had similar experiences. One of the group members described how being physically incarcerated had provided a sense of emotional liberty for his complex family: 'We can all say we love each other now, because we are separated; my brother is in a cell next to my mother's boyfriend, my little brother is in hiding because of what I have done, and I am in here.'

Family history and the Family Awareness Group

A problematic family background is often present in the histories of patients in high secure care, and frequently highlights some of the long-term antecedents to offending. The men who became Family Awareness Group members were no exception, with histories of interpersonal violence and trauma in their families. Prior to admission, each member had committed a violent offence against another person, including serious assaults and homicide.

It was in response to such a need for work on 'family' that this high security hospital had long provided group and individual psychotherapy, raising an awareness of the impact that past experiences have on our understanding of mental health and acts of violence. Group dynamics can be thought about in terms of processing the difficulties of being either part of or separated from a complex or difficult family, and provide an opportunity for considering current relationships with peers and authority figures. We hoped that through group acknowledgement of early disturbed or volatile family dynamics (leading to disturbed or volatile mental states), the men might be helped to transcend this cycle in the formation of new, healthier relationships.

This non-manualised group was the first Family Awareness Group to run for longer than nine months, and the use of arts psychotherapies approaches was in response to the fact that offender patients' beliefs about family are highly defended, and consequently difficult to articulate. Family is seldom spoken about due to a real fear for their safety, and because it represents an idealised 'other' to the incarcerating authority. In earlier, directed groups it was noted that the men often invented their family situation, complete with cast, set and plot.

In those nine-month groups, patients were only beginning to volunteer authentic information about their families as the groups concluded. A decision was made to run the group as a slow-open group, which we hoped would allow for a period of 'gestation' and the development of trust, growth and disclosure, prior to the men completing the group.

Modalities and rationale for co-working

The offender identity is one for which it could be said that one's family is 'sacred', and it is understood that 'no man may speak of another's mother'. In reality this code, although sentimentally represented in the media, serves as a sound piece of advice in the offender community; withholding information about their own families protects not only themselves, but their families too.

The arts therapies approach provided alternative media within which complex and emotional material, with the overall theme of relationships, could be addressed in a way that felt safe and potentially productive. Patients were encouraged to share their experience of 'family' – its impacts, secrets, traumas, comings and goings, consequences, resiliences, and beginnings and endings – without necessarily naming names or using words. In their own time, unspeakable traumatic experiences could be both acknowledged and shared in the group. Patients experienced, between them, extensive memory loss, considerable substance misuse and episodes of dissociative states of mind. These are linked both to psychopathology (Hayes et al., 1996), and to a need to disavow the emotions associated with disturbing thoughts and memories.

We hoped to provide a 'container' (Bion, 1962), or a state of 'holding' (Winnicott, 1945), as we strove to use our media to hold the unconscious phenomena as they manifested in the group dynamic. The non-verbal creative processes of music and art were to be a container in and of themselves. Within this framework, the patients were encouraged to reveal only what they wished to, so ameliorating the pressure, to simply 'release' their distress before they were ready.

Therapeutic approach

Patients were encouraged to share their family structures and wider social networks, using musical instruments and art materials as well as discussion. The materials and instruments were objects for reflection, providing a non-directive structure and adding an experiential dimension to the group. Particular anxieties about being required to share 'private' material in this work were addressed in the process of becoming a group, and were further held by the psychotherapeutic boundaries of the sessions.

A feeling of curiosity, articulated by a free-associative approach to the media and the material, was proffered by the facilitators from the outset, although, as will be seen, this was neither always welcomed nor accepted. The idea that as a group we were a type of 'family' was often strongly resisted.

Sessions ran for an hour and a quarter on a weekly basis, with patients brought to and from the sessions by dedicated escort staff, maintaining the physical boundaries of the group. Over its lifetime the group moved location four times due to external pressures, eventually settling in the art therapy room, where it stayed for its last four years. Each group started with a brief check-in, and a chance for patients to reflect on the preceding week. They were given as much notice as possible if a session was to be cancelled, and feedback was provided to the patients' clinical teams via a Care Programme Approach report, or by more direct liaison with the ward if needed. Preparation for new arrivals and leavers was made in collaboration with the group and clinical teams over a number of weeks, although abrupt endings did occur when patients were discharged from the hospital.

The art materials and musical instruments were provided each week, so even if the music therapist was absent, the instruments were still there. All facilitators were expected to handle and use the creative objects to model sharing, creative experimenting and getting-it-wrong-to-get-it-right. Thus the art therapist played instruments, the music therapist made images and the third therapist did both, seeking symbolic form through holding of the therapeutic space.

A group in this setting can only ever run with at least two facilitators. Having a third facilitator in this group was not only for the sake of continuity, but was also a response to the need for considerable 'thinking power', where these patients and their families (and associated projections) were concerned. The role of third therapist was initially taken by a forensic psychologist, then a psychodynamically trained clinical nurse specialist, followed briefly by a psychiatric nurse and, for a time, a trainee art therapist. All facilitators had an equal and active role in the group and contributed according to their competencies.

The facilitators encouraged the thought that they might represent the 'parents' of the group. This concept was particularly challenging to one long-term member, who had been abandoned by his mother at an early age and later been coerced by his father into sharing sexual partners. He often attempted to recreate his family dynamic by undermining the female art therapist, and looked to the male music therapist for approval of this way of relating (as discussed later in the chapter). When enacted in the group setting, this dynamic could be thought about by all facilitators together.

Overview

Play is an important activity through which patients can gain awareness into their authentic emotional selves. However, the Family Awareness Group was characterised from the outset by the patients' struggle to play and be creative, indeed even to pick up or take any interest in the art or music materials. The facilitators wondered if group members were in part immobilised by the fear of their own destructive capabilities, fuelled partly by fiercely protective instincts when it came to family, and partly by a learned sense that family secrets are simply not to be shared with strangers.

Early sessions were characterised by a refusal to acknowledge, create or 'do' artwork, except begrudgingly to appease the therapist, yet we observed that they would bite, mould, pinch and worry their cardboard cups, stopping just short of spilling the contents. At the same time there was a stubborn refusal to make a mess of any kind. We were witnesses to the impoverished creative ability that can result when normal development is hampered in victims of trauma, as energy is spent in warding off further vulnerability (Case, 2010).

To mark the departure of a facilitator, a group piece was made, consisting of individual handprints joined together – at this stage it seemed okay to make a group piece about holding hands, but not to make actual physical contact. We reflected that touch had become taboo for these men, even touch of the materials. The group wondered out loud what kind of life these hands of theirs had had up until now, and what they had done over the years. During this reflection, one member looked at the clock and folded his hands under his armpits, as if the loving acts had been overshadowed by violence, and the instruments of those acts needed to be hidden. 'Why did you say that?' He said, 'It goes without saying – you don't have to make something of out of everything.'

In supervision, we discussed how the room felt as if it was populated by 'silent babies'. The group often began in what felt like a cruel silence, the blank paper and silent instruments untouched like quiet and foreboding objects. Accordingly, we began to place the art and music materials closer and closer to the patients; firstly to a place where they would have to leave their seats to use them, then just out of arms' reach, and eventually beside them where they sat. We introduced Plasticine for its tactile and forgiving properties – not only is it a mutative material, but capable of being 'broken' and then reformed. Part of our endeavour was to help our group release the uninhibited child within, and to discover a true sense of being, to animate the 'silent babies'.

An unwritten rule arose – 'only a member of the family can be critical of it' – and this was paralleled in the group. Although this 'family' was deeply self-critical, it was also fiercely defensive of its existence at times of institutional threat or change. However, internal denigration was forcefully articulated: 'what's the value in keeping this group's rubbish? It doesn't add up to anything. . . . it's boring, morose, like a damp blanket, nothing can catch fire... I won't join in because I'll only spoil things', and a review of the group's folder of artwork showed that its contents were made up principally of many small pieces, fragments which were either seemingly unrelated objects or repeated images.

If one definition of family is that of a caring group within which a child is engaged and 'held' so that trust and safety can be nurtured, this picture did not emerge of members' families, as for them families don't 'do what it says on the tin'. These men had developed antisocial behaviours from having been deprived of any such holding environment in childhood, and these behaviours were maintained by deeply held and ongoing feelings of insecurity.

The group examined itself and found it to be a family that hates itself – it was a 'family with murder in it – like the Addams family, everyone hates them'. The members displayed a cruel sibling rivalry in their keenness to let fellow members go, often feeling that they didn't belong in the group in the first place: 'I bet he never went shoplifting with mum or was beaten by dad or had to take sides.' Once, when considering new members, the group grimly suggested an initiation ceremony – there was no warm welcome for 'new' babies here – and the facilitators were correspondingly seen as careless breeders without any consideration for the existing brood. The group wryly noted that there was 'no licence required' to have children.

Over the years, these comments were further contextualised, as the room became slowly populated by 'violent fathers', 'useless mothers', 'needy sisters', 'alien brothers', 'unasked-for children' and 'stolen sperm'. The group made statements such as, 'family is overrated. I lived with violence and drug addiction, I was never safe in my family, I am not safe in these places [groups] but I am safe on my own'. There were long periods of what felt like group paralysis, particularly when the group was dealing with loss, and bitter scorn was heaped on any absent facilitators.

The group members did, however, tentatively start to use the materials to create what could be considered small transitional objects (Winnicott, 1973), such as might help a child feel safe and secure when beginning the process of mature dependence (Fairbairn, 1952), but used here with adults facing their own kind of transition.

Over time, small but significant objects were made (Fig. 1.1) while unobtrusive and tentative music provided a pattering accompaniment. The small Plasticine objects were made, yet not 'owned', by their creators. Instead, they 'belonged to the group', and were put out and cleared away at the beginning and end of each session by the facilitators. They became like condiments at a meal, family souvenirs or knick-knacks which were ever-present during quasi-domestic exchanges such as 'Who would employ me now?' and 'What girl would have me with these scars?' These objects were inspected, handled, repaired and replaced by the men. The damaged or perished artwork was symbolically rescued, and survived in a damaged state (Schaverien, 1992).

Over time, there was a shift away from guilt and embarrassment at having touched something towards a tentative acknowledgement of creating something meaningful, like rolling-out and making a dolphin from Plasticine, leading to a discussion on the subject of captivity. Statements began to have a sense of agency: 'I am doing some primal pictures at the moment, aren't I?' or 'This tree is a one-off, I think it looks well thought-out', and permission emerged to discuss one another's work: 'Those bricks must have taken a long time to do.'

As the group progressed, the men often chose to sit where their favoured instruments had been placed. The use of instruments was not limited to their sound-making potential – beaters were covered in Plasticine, in effect buried, then discovered at a later date. Instruments were also sometimes combined to make

FIGURE 1.1 Plasticine objects: maximum height 5cm (h) x 6cm (w); various colours

kinetic sculptures, becoming multi-modal – both sound-producing tools and symbolic artefacts (Sloboda, 1997). At this stage, the group members were seeing beyond the instruments' intended uses, proffering temple gongs as begging bowls or vessels for raffle tickets or group suggestions. Eventually, group dynamics were commented upon more favourably: on those who had left the group, 'They may have left some of their soul behind'. Body language was noted and could be commented on without offence, creativity and change could be admired – 'It's not about the room, it's the people in it that count'.

Towards the closure of this group, the music therapist made a reference to Philip Larkin's 'This Be the Verse'[2] (with its iconic opening lines: 'They fuck you up, your mum and dad'), and one member, Matthew, who had been in the group since the beginning, took the printed text back to the ward with him. He, like other members of the group, could fully relate to its excoriating critique of parenting. Its presence in the group was like a gift, and the group seized upon the lines: 'They fill you with the faults they had and add some extra just for you. But they were fucked up in their turn.'

Having been in the group for a while, the men started to tell more fully-rounded, authentic family stories. We began to hear not only of their unresolved pasts, but also of current relationships, of good stepdads, helpful girlfriends, able half-sisters, and a sister who was 'good at art'. In particular, we began hearing of affection between siblings, and we used expressions cards, depicting family scenarios – one man brought in a photograph of his courageous brother.

By the end of their participation in the group, we heard more reflective statements, such as 'Maybe what I have taken from this group is patience', and 'I haven't always been well enough to remember between groups'. And finally, to a new member, 'We give each other a space to talk if we need to'.

Family, in all its complexity, could be described and shared more freely. The men took ownership of what they had made of their lives so far, and, more concretely, what they had made in the group. At the group's ending, a collective decision was made to roll all the small pieces of Plasticine together into a huge, heavy ball, which was passed around from hand to hand and shaped by all, together with comments about its weight (Fig. 1.2).

Clinical vignette – The band

Whilst often maintaining a superior, stand-offish stance, which was enhanced by adopting a sunken slouching pose reminiscent of a racing-car driver, Matthew did at times shake off his lethargy and take centre-stage. This typically happened when the talk turned to money – he had aspirations to affluence – but happened especially when the subject of music was raised. Matthew had been in the music business when younger, and the metaphor of 'the band' was one of the few with which he readily identified. This fantasy always involved the male music therapist, and, correspondingly, the demotion of the female art therapist to the position of 'the backing singer', 'the groupie who wears the t-shirt', etc.

FIGURE 1.2 Plasticine ball: 13.5cm (h) x 13cm (w) max; various colours

Such sexualised transferences were repeated over many sessions. Whilst uncomfortably inappropriate (Greenson, 1973), they were crucially not colluded with by either the idealised male facilitator, nor the group members, who responded with appropriate discomfort and silence as they found themselves marginalised or excluded from this wished-for intimacy with the 'father' facilitator. Matthew later described the complicated relationship he had had with his father, and the utter rejection he had experienced from the women in his family.

The 'band' idea frequently emerged during one of the occasional musical interludes, when Matthew would join the music therapist in a rhythmic interaction, making knowing and often admiring glances in his direction, suggesting that 'we knew we were together', in an exclusively private encounter characterised by specialness. This had the quality of an almost homoerotic musical exchange, with ideas traded like secrets while the rest of the group carried on their humdrum activities, unaware of this blissful union.

Matthew's idealisation of the therapist was viewed as a transference of his earlier transgressive relationship with his father, where the parent-child dyad had been confused with the peer-to-peer position, and perverted by the alleged sharing of sexual partners. The confusion of identities – which was further amplified to the point where Matthew felt 'we should be brothers', and that the music therapist and he should adopt a uniform ('goatees and neckerchiefs') – found its apotheosis in

Matthew's wishful thinking that that music therapist 'should be a black guy'. Despite his own strong Caribbean roots, Matthew found it impossible to see himself as black, and often derided West Indian culture. It was as if Matthew saw the music therapist as a healthy version of himself with whom he effortlessly merged, the boundary between them erased as it had been with his father.

Matters came to a head when Matthew demanded to know how many instruments the music therapist played. This question, and the therapist's perceived avoidance of answering it, took on massive proportions, as Matthew persisted in both repeatedly asking the question and resisting all attempts to explore what might lie behind it – what he might do with the response, what it might mean to him, and what that would make the therapist in his eyes. These were things too difficult to contemplate, things which would belie their companionship in music, make clear their separateness, and leave Matthew alone as an individual. It led to a terrible impasse, with Matthew physically turning his back on the music therapist in subsequent groups. The other facilitators and fellow group members, commenting on the action of the group as usual, noted that Matthew was now making derogatory references. They verbalised his feelings of being unfairly treated, while holding the boundaries. It was only after a number of weeks of angry silence that Matthew's pain seemed to subside, and he was able to acknowledge, 'Aw, you're okay really', and the relationship could resume in a new, more mature and boundaried form.

This was a painful and important separation – a difficult move towards a depressive position (Klein, 1946), as was shown by Matthew's many later references to our 'falling out'. Matthew spent many sessions seeking out, handling and placing the upturned thumb piano (mbira) on his own stomach, as if it was a kind of comforter, full belly or, indeed a child of his own. (It was later revealed that he was already a father.)

Discussion

In line with the hospital's aims of facilitating engagement and mental health recovery, group members were encouraged to recognise the impact that a mental disorder had had on their relationships. The art and music therapy approach provided the men with the possibility of working with their internal and external distress, and this could be said to have succeeded to varying degrees. Over time, the patients' actual experiences of family were shared, and ordinary 'domestic' situations were created and managed in the Family Awareness Group 'family', allowing the group some degree of access to an authentically bearable sense of family intimacy.

In order to continue as a slow-open group for over six years, the Family Awareness Group moved to four different therapy spaces, and was facilitated by a combination of clinicians. This seemed to mirror the patients' own experiences of being moved from one care environment to another. All members of the group had dysfunctional family histories and disturbing early experiences, including forced childhood relocations and familial rejection. With such obvious parallels, we felt it important that the group co-facilitation was consistent, and that the art materials and musical instruments remained constant and present throughout the life of the group, wherever it was situated.

The group's aim was to represent a 'good enough' family, offering a sense of trust and safety, but that of course could only be realised over time. The Family Awareness Group endured, survived and adapted, and at a time when the service came under pressure to deliver time-limited interventions, it came under much scrutiny. Like the patients who were fiercely disturbed by the failings in their early families yet just as fiercely defensive of them, so the facilitators fought to continue the group despite a shifting resource landscape. In fact, the men became increasingly accommodating of the need for the group to move location in order to continue, and treated each new therapeutic space as if it were a new home, an experience, with which they were highly familiar.

The art and music therapy co-working approach was attuned to noting and assessing very early damage to the patients' capacity to trust and 'play', locating early pre-verbal disturbance in the patients' capacity to think creatively. Through recreating lived group experiences, we attempted to encourage a sense of autonomy in the context of attachment, and a shift in the patients' fears of both creative and destructive forces, from concrete to symbolic enactment.

At the outset, the cross-modality approach was recognised as facilitating the emergence of an authentic family narrative. However, the outcomes of this approach to working with family experience were not fully anticipated at first, and the goals and aims of the group responded dynamically to both group composition and the shifting local and national clinical agenda. For example, the Family Awareness Group operated at a time of huge investment in numerous cognitive behavioural therapy approaches, and the free-floating un-manualised nature of the group seemed at odds with other group approaches in the hospital. Our frequent geographical moves – as if we were being evicted and made homeless, trailing from one room to another with our Plasticine objects, drums, shakers and members in tow – were underlined in the statement of one patient, that this group also 'doesn't do what it says on the tin'.

Indeed, the art media often 'stayed inside the tin'. There were sessions in which any suggestion to use the materials was rebuffed, leaving the art therapist feeling like a 'trolley dolly' with no takers, and the music therapist like a lone busker, and there were few moments where the group spontaneously worked together towards any kind of mixed media artwork. When the materials were used, it was more often as if in tiny islands of creativity, maintaining distance between us. Use of the arts media was mono-thematic, and took place in isolated duos, as if each of us could only trust one person at a time. At times, it felt just too dangerous to play, or talk of metaphor; symbolism was denigrated, and any suggestion of possible interpretations was hotly refuted.

One benefit of the cross-modality approach was that the materials and sounds could become objects on which to focus while remembering family experiences, just as a 'good enough' family might gather around a fire or a meal. At times, they could take on a talismanic quality – at one point, the group was portrayed by a participant as a kind of cult, with rules and corresponding punishments for their infringement.

Conclusion

In object relations terms, it is difficult not to see the group as an on-going attempt to move towards a depressive position (Klein, 1946). The group facilitators often felt under attack – accused on the one hand of preciousness, and on the other hand of attacking what its members held most dear: their 'sacrosanct' families. This was not an easy group – the urgency of survival worked against group cohesion, and individual members fought to maintain their 'splendid isolation'. Paranoid-schizoid thinking, with its associated projections and splitting, was a weekly feature of the sessions. Unbearable feelings of helplessness were frequently projected into the therapists, which in turn led to a lack of agency in our own art forms; we found we needed each other for support, and to combine our understanding of the underlying issues in the group – helplessness, mistrust, anger, paralysis and disintegration. Dependency, as a defence against the fear of engagement in the therapeutic task, was rife, and often involved a splitting of the facilitation team (Bion, 1961).

Matthew had a good clinical outcome, the group having been a constant psychotherapeutic support through many ward and clinical team changes during his journey through high secure care. The Family Awareness Group had accompanied him while he came to terms with the gravity of his offence, his status as a patient, and the implications of his mental illness diagnosis, as well as through a deeply depressive period in which he attempted suicide, and finally his emergence as a person accepting of 'mature dependence' (Fairbairn, 1952). Indeed, before moving to lesser secure care, Matthew began to foster a non-competitive parental relationship with his now adult son. In this new relationship, he was present but 'off-stage', and demonstrated sensitivity to its boundaries in order to sustain it and allow it to flourish. This was much more like the parenting modelled within the group than that of his own lived experience.

The authors would like to thank the Family Awareness Group members for their permission to write up this cross-modal therapeutic intervention. We would also like to thank and acknowledge our colleagues, other co-facilitators and supervisors.

Notes

1 Please note: The term 'patients' is adopted by the authors as the term preferred by the group participants at the time. Every effort has been made to protect the identity of persons referred to in this text, whose real names have not been used.
2 Extract taken from 'This Be the Verse' from *The Complete Poems*. (c) Estate of Philip Larkin and reprinted by permission of Faber and Faber.

References

Bion, W.R. (1961). *Experiences in Groups*. London: Tavistock.

Bion, W.R. (1962). *Learning from Experience*. London: Heinemann.

Case, C. (2010). Representations of Trauma, Memory-Layered Pictures and Repetitive Play in Art Therapy with Children. *Art Therapy Online: ATOL*, 1(1), pp. 1–28. Available at: http://ojs.gold.ac.uk/index.php/atol/article/view/212/227 [Accessed 22 January 2016].

Fairbairn, W.R.D. (1952). *Psychoanalytic Studies of the Personality*. London: Routledge.

Greenson, R. (1973). *The Technique and Practice of Psychoanalysis*. London: Hogarth Press.

Hayes, S.C., Wilson, K.G., Gifford, E.V., Follette, V.M. and Strosahl, K. (1996). Experiential Avoidance and Behavioral Disorders: A Functional Dimensional Approach to Diagnosis and Treatment. *Journal of Consulting and Clinical Psychology*, 64(6), pp. 1152–1168.

Klein, M. (1946). Notes on Some Schizoid Mechanisms. *International Journal of Psychoanalysis*, 27, pp. 99–110.

McCreadie, R.G. and Phillips, K. (1988). The Nithsdale Schizophrenia Survey. V11. Does Relatives' High Expressed Emotion Predict Relapse? *The British Journal of Psychiatry*, 152(4), pp. 477–481. doi: 10.1192/bjp.152.4.477.

Rey, H. (1994). *Universals of Psychoanalysis in the Treatment of Psychotic and Borderline States*. London: Free Association Books.

Schaverien, J. (1999). *The Revealing Image: Analytical Art Psychotherapy in Theory and Practice*. London: Jessica Kingsley Publishers.

Sloboda, A. (1997). Music Therapy and Psychotic Violence. In: E. Welldon and C. Van Velsen, eds., *A Practical Guide to Forensic Psychotherapy*. 1st ed. London: Jessica Kingsley Publishers, Chapter 16.

Winnicott, D.W. (1945). *Primitive Emotional Development. Through Paediatrics to Psychoanalysis: Collected Papers, 1958*. London: Tavistock Publications.

Winnicott, D.W. (1973). *The Child, the Family, and the Outside World*. London: Penguin.

Yalom, I. (1995). *The Theory and Practice of Group Psychotherapy*. 4th ed. New York: Basic Books.

2

MOVING COLOUR

Combining dance movement psychotherapy and art psychotherapy in a NHS community women's group

Claire Burrell & Marika Cohen

> Very little grows on jagged rock
> Be ground
> Be crumbled
> So wild flowers will come up
> Where you are
> You have been stony for too many years
> Try something different
> Surrender.
> *(Jelauddin Rumi, thirteenth-century Sufi poet)*

Introduction

The Moving Colour women's arts psychotherapies group proposed an 'exploration of dance movement and art making' to women coping with the impact of long-term mental illness. It was delivered through an arts psychotherapies service based within an inner London National Health Service (NHS) Trust. In this chapter we will present our reflections on how running this cross-modality group allowed for both a layering and filtering of experiences, exploring both connectivity and fragmentation. We will validate how offering dual-modality support can enhance the potential for arts psychotherapies interventions, providing adaptable ground to nurture evolving experience.

Combining dance movement psychotherapy and art psychotherapy, we collaboratively facilitated the sessions. A constant dialogue underpinned our work as we navigated the mixed-medium approach, drawing from our experience within the same arts psychotherapies team. Claire's dance movement psychotherapy practice has evolved out of a career in collaborative dance performance and investigation into dance improvisation. The exploration of movement remains central to her clinical work, where ideas of locating embodied narratives are enhanced through combining mixed-medium approaches. Marika's art psychotherapy practice is rooted in her work in psychodynamic services within the NHS, and shaped by her interest in layers, colour and mixed media in her own creative process.

Meeting the need to develop an arts psychotherapies space for women, the group provided a single-gendered environment that allowed culturally inclusive access to arts psychotherapies, and provided safety and containment to vulnerable women. As many of these women had begun to engage in some form of arts psychotherapy during hospital admission, the group also provided continuity of care, enhancing transitions between inpatient and outpatient settings.

With an awareness that this transition from inpatient to community is often a challenging period for those who have complex mental health needs (recommendations published by NICE guidelines 2014: 26; and DH, 2012) the use of recovery-focused care offered continuity and stability during this period. The recovery model in mental health care broadly enables people, despite their ongoing symptoms, to reclaim their lives by restoring their sense of authority, purpose and hope. This personal journey is often linked to self-empowerment and experience of social inclusion (DH, 2012; Shepherd et al., 2008).

So, from within these transitional parameters, the Moving Colour group aimed to nurture an expansion of resources through introducing two forms of embodied exploration. Offering ten spaces in secondary care to creatively explore personal and interpersonal experience, the work was framed in three blocks of twelve weekly sessions throughout a year. Alongside a regular feedback process, the group therapy was supported by periodic individual reviews, providing the opportunity to reflect and consider subjective pathways within the wider group frame.

Practising in an arts psychotherapies service with a history of trialing cross-modality work, we had already begun to establish shared working patterns, shifting in and out of each other's therapeutically held spaces. By further developing the cross-modality practice, we were hoping to enhance its psychotherapeutic potential by attuning our sense of the layering and filtering process occurring through the interplay of the two arts media. As the sessions progressed, the women themselves reflected on this process, describing how the transition from one creative medium to another had been surprising. In anonymous group feedback it was commented how 'moving it to something else and changing it a bit, rather than leaving it there' had been helpful, perhaps highlighting a sense of flow, which allowed for evolution of process and growth in the path to greater self-awareness, and in time a resonating of consciousness.

Dr. Natalie Rogers, psychotherapist and founder of the Person-Centred Expressive Therapy Institute in California, speaks of her own mixed-media approach in her book *The Creative Connection: Expressive Arts as Healing*. She writes: 'The creative connection describes the process of allowing one art form to influence another directly. Using various expressive arts in sequence heightens and intensifies our journey inward. When we start by expressing ourselves through movement and sound – moving in response to our feelings – and then immediately to colour or clay, our art work changes. Frequently what we then create comes from the unconscious. We may be surprised by what appears' (Rogers, 1993: 43).

Within the group's process, shifting between images and movement, many examples of this connectivity (and disconnection) emerged as the women layered and filtered their experiences. We describe their process below, sharing examples of the artwork they made to highlight their journey.

The unfolding shape of the group

The sessions began with us all seated in a large circle, where, following a general check-in the women were invited to locate their inner sensation by naming a colour which they resonated with that day. Starting with movement exploration guided by the dance movement psychotherapist, the women were encouraged to gently bring awareness to individual body parts, and then to the experience of moving the body as a whole. Movement improvisation followed, in which imagery – sometimes guided – arose through a process of themes and ideas emerging in the group. Included in each session was the process of shifting relationally within the work; perhaps first focusing on the self, then connecting to the self in relation to other, and then finally to the experience of moving as part of the whole group. As the dance unfolded, opportunity was given to notice the diverse relational responses arising through these changes of perspective and evolving interactions.

Such improvised practice encouraged play, expanded by the use of props (multi-coloured scarves and ribbons, large fabric cloths, elastic stretch bands) and percussive instruments, during which the dance movement psychotherapist maintained a central capacity in holding the group. Concurrently, the art psychotherapist actively participated in the work in what may be called a peer position role, modelling her own subjective experience of improvised play and reflective narrative within the group's process. Halfway through the session the art psychotherapist would invite the women to further explore their process with a full range of art materials (paper, paints, clay, pastels, pencils, felt tips, collage material). As the shift in modality took place the women were supported to either continue following their emerging narrative or bring in something else, perhaps yet unexplored, which could then be embodied through the image-making process. To employ the full potential of the space and to concretely mark the shifting roles of the co-facilitators, the room was reconfigured by bringing the tables and art materials into the centre of the room. In this phase, the process of relationally shifting that is described above was evoked around the art table. As individual themes emerged and expanded, the artwork either mirrored – or defined itself as separate from – the work of others. With the process expressed in the images, such connectivity was echoed in cross-table conversation as wider collective themes were shared.

Here the art psychotherapist non-directively held the space, paying attention to the wider perspective and boundaries, as well as being available for individual exchanges when they arose in the image-making process. At the same time, the dance movement psychotherapist would position herself alongside the participants, contributing to the image-making exploration and at times offering reflections from this perspective. Bringing participants back into a seated circle at the close of the session created a contained environment within which the artworks could be viewed, providing an opportunity to individually share and collectively summarise the wider perspective and common themes. As each session reached its conclusion, the women were guided through movement exploration, further embodying the images held in the group. Time and space were taken to allow the process to settle in the body, to further connect or disconnect from the imagery that had emerged, in preparation for the transition back into everyday life.

The fostering of personal narratives within the group frame

The importance of improvisation and play

The work supported a process-based ethos, embedded in the experience of allowing oneself to follow an emerging narrative with curiosity – rather than seeking to define meaning, problem-solve or validate achievement. Emphasis remained focused on the creative potential of the individual and the journey they undertook within the established safety of the group environment. Giving space to the improvised process in both the dance and the art-making experience allowed freedom of choice in the moment – taking the next step, making the next mark. Together with the encouragement of a non-judgemental stance, this nudged the group towards the edge of the unknown, nurturing new pathways and patterns of behaviour. Tufnell and Crickmay (1990: 46) describe how 'Improvisation provides us with a means to excavating [sic.] layers of experience, sensation, character, feeling that we normally rush through or suppress – to travel deeper into an ever enlarging and changing moment.'

Within the framework of the group, the women were able to enter a relaxed body/mind state. Here the therapists fostered the women's capacity to discover or rediscover the parameters of play; engaging with others in this way enhanced the women's trust, and nurtured the potential for new ways of being and relating. Winnicott (1971: 63) stated: 'It is in playing and only in playing that the individual child or adult is able to be creative and use the whole personality, and it is only in being creative that the individual discovers the self'.

Locating embodied exploration within collective experience

While the development of greater embodied awareness is credited as a benefit of dance movement psychotherapy, the embodied experience is inherently central to all arts psychotherapies practices. Art psychotherapist Schaverien (1999) describes the embodied image in the context of the holding environment of art psychotherapy: rather than seeing the image as playing a solely descriptive – essentially diagrammatic – role, she suggests that the image-making process, inclusive of its physicality, can 'take precedence over the original idea', leading the picture to evolve and 'reveal previously unconscious' material (Schaverien, 1999: 87). In this way, the emerging embodied artwork enables the 'unspoken' to enter the group space, not just for the individual but for the group as a whole.

As creative enquiry unfolded, participants were encouraged to give themselves permission to be in touch with what they may have been unwilling to feel. Working with kindness and compassion, they nurtured the vulnerable aspects of themselves, as unheard, unfelt feelings came to the surface. As the unknown was faced collectively, trust and intuition developed, and harboured a sense of self anchored within the group dynamic.

In this way the women explored moving between an internal and external gaze, echoing, mirroring and defining both their connectivity and separateness. Challenged and encouraged to expand, they found playful ways to locate and honour their stories, and perhaps to experience themselves differently. By committing to the group process, the relatedness of their expression brought a renewed sense of hope, establishing foundations from which change and transformation could arise. Jill Hayes (2013) describes how a clearer image of one's own emotional landscape is enhanced through the interrelations exchanged within the wider landscape of the group context. She writes: 'It is through the development of awareness of organic connectivity via the living body that our sense of life is changed' (Hayes, 2013: 79).

As the group progressed, participants validated their sense of belonging established through the co-creation of ritual meaning and metaphor, in the developing owner-ship of the group's emerging culture. Some described finding a sense of 'love' in a 'sacred' ritualistic experience that connected their dances and image-making beyond personal meaning to transpersonal connectivity.

Shifting positions in the dual facilitation process

Enabling the group

As well as providing opportunities for change and transition to occur, the co-facilitation process and the shifting of leadership roles within the mixed-modality frame could arguably also trigger a parental split in the transference interplay (Dalley, 1993; Dudley, 2001). However, by working in this way, we experienced how 'the co-therapy relationship allows for group members to project different roles onto each of the therapists, which can be tested out and worked with' (Meekums, 2000: 118). As the dynamics of the group evolved, so did our working patterns, and, through attuning our positional responses, we felt that the structure of the work was enriched, enabling us to contain and hold the work more flexibly.

As the group alternated between the two modalities, and the therapists exchanged roles, they shifted in their proximity in relation to the holding of the group, perhaps modelling Winnicottian ideas in terms of their positioning in the group in relation to the developmental stages of the work undertaken by the women. It was Winnicott's (1971) framing of 'Theory of Play' (Winnicott, 1971: 47), and concept of 'potential space' (Winnicott, 1971: 41; Davis and Wallbridge, 1991: 57–61) that our shifting positions in the dual facilitation process initially resonated with, as we attuned to the stages described as 'playing with mother' and 'playing alone whilst in the presence of mother' (Winnicott, 1971: 47–52). In general terms, we reflected on how a more directive, inter-relational approach to dance movement psychotherapy provided access to the to and fro of the 'playing with' dynamic whilst the art psychotherapy modality allowed for the extension of more independent, witnessed play to unfold.

The group provided a flexible frame for the diverse stages of recovery that the women explored, and offered multi-focal support to a group of women whose internalised stage of developmental attachment varied. By taking a range of positions within the group, we hoped to facilitate an environment in which participants could benefit from visiting and revisiting their own experiences of relatedness. The benefits of shifting the therapeutic stance, to match and mismatch the relational dynamic, are highlighted by dance movement psychotherapist Penny Best, who encourages us as practitioners to heighten our awareness of how we engage our clients in therapeutic processes through attuning ourselves to the 'embodiment of core relational elements' which she introduces as: 'being with, going against and influencing' (Best, 2009: 1–12).

Stepping into an unknown area of exploration with a spirit of creativity provides challenges for us all. As therapists, we felt that, by adopting a non-expert stance in the creative process of our non-specialist medium, we enhanced the women's potential to travel an unfamiliar, improvised path, perhaps through 'swimming alongside' (Best, 2009: 1–12). The non-expert stance, modelled by the therapists, invited the women to mirror these shifting roles as they explored the potential of their own positions and relationships within the group dynamic.

Additionally, the cyclical holding of the dual-modality group enabled repetition. The gradual expansion of rhythmic and spatial patterning resounded through movement exploration and the emerging artwork meeting the women's need to revisit and repeat their emerging patterns. We are reminded by Jill Hayes that 'being with the coherence and consistency of organic pattern inspires trust that something with creative potential is moving through us' (Hayes, 2013: 97). Held by the therapists in both modalities the women could allow themselves to experience external and internal patterns in re-resonating frames. As the patterning unfolded slowly, relocated in dance, image, sound and word, the experience had time to be felt, seen, acknowledged and embodied.

Enabling the therapists

The challenge of inviting group members to 'try something new' was mirrored in our own process as therapists, as we explored in a spirit of curiosity how our own practice might be expanded in a dual-modality forum. Both therapists reported feeling 'freed up' engaging more playfully in their non-expert medium, enabled by the secure holding of their co-facilitating colleague. With this flexibility to play alongside the group, the therapists honoured a methodology located in human narrative and in 'being one's self', reflecting the essence of the work.

How to include this subjective component (the therapist's own material), and how much to share, reveal or hold, became fertile dialogue in our post and pre-session conversations. Within a rich texture of possibilities, decisions were made as to whether to consciously bring this material to the foreground – to name it – or simply witness it while holding it in the unconscious process of the group. To use the material in this way, investing in the group's creative process while sustaining a degree of therapeutic stance, required fine tuning, encompassing not only listening to self, other and the collective process, but also making a commitment to intuitive trust. Trusting the co-facilitative relationship under the leading therapist's direction allowed the emerging process to move in new, unknown directions.

Undoubtedly, the dual-modality interplay contained a tension, a struggle between two places; a push and pull, recognisable in the transition from one art form to another, allowing newness to unfold. Over time the group gained substance and shape. With familiarity, the two halves of the creative process, art and movement, merged into a whole. For us as therapists, this enriching experience embedded a deeper understanding of each other's working practice, which had benefits for the wider arts psychotherapies team in terms of client referral pathways and supervisory practices, as well as leading to a more creative and flexible response to its clients' needs. The team's cross-modality supervision group provided a pliant space to unpack, nurture and give language to our clients' experiences. As therapists, we had encouraged each other to think outside the box, enabling a widening of resources in our own creative tool kits. Additionally, we noted a greater openness and flow between directive and non-directive processes, and a rethinking of 'where' to meet our clients. We valued the fact that our work enabled us to experience not only different styles and models of practice, but different ways of shaping the process, using familiar and less familiar tools.

Client themes: presentation of case material

The mixed-diagnostic group provided support to women who had had experiences of schizophrenia, bipolar disorder, personality disorder, chronic depression and anxiety. Alongside the symptoms of their illness and side effects of their medication, many were also coping with underlying or associated trauma deriving from experiences such as domestic violence, sexual abuse, the impact of first or second generation migration, having children in care, and alcohol misuse. Most struggled with their sense of isolation, their ability to be in a group, and with talking about how they felt. They often experienced diminished self-awareness, a lack of confidence and poor self-esteem, and some described an inaccurate body image. Confidence in their treatment process and recovery was also sometimes lacking, and they would frequently point to family pressures in relation to their mental health. Many expressed difficulties with their ongoing current relationships, as well as with their own children and families. All of this impacted on their ability to explore autobiographical narrative.

Below, we follow the paths of three women – of similar age from different cultural origins and backgrounds – as they moved through the group. All three were familiar with one creative modality or another, and were open to the possibility of experiencing something new.

Ms A: holding the unspoken

Ms A joined the Moving Colour group, bringing with her a measure of confidence in the art medium, having used it as both a creative and expressive outlet in the past. She had previously engaged in individual art psychotherapy, but was new to working with other modalities or to engaging in a group process. Initially, she allowed little space for improvisation or group interrelations, expressing her sense of being already 'filled up' and endorsing the richness of her emerging compositions.

Social and familial isolation resonated through her initial attempts to relate to others. Engagement through art acted as a way in, a way to be known through, and offered a less threatening way to connect with others (Fig. 2.1).

Early on Ms A brought a sense of 'in between', as layers of cultural inheritance unfolded – themes of guilt, rejection and shadow filtered through her experience of living in a second generation migrant community. She found herself in the process of establishing a new identity and rejecting the values of previously familiar and cultural traditions, where she had often appeared marginalised as the scapegoat, and the images that resulted would frequently hold this wider landscape in relation to a more newly revealed experience of self.

'The Scapegoat rules the realms of the shadow, its borderline always a cut off from personal or universal love: its governor is projection, and its subjects identified as blame, rejection, repression, guilt and helplessness' (Bartel and Ne'eman, 1993: 135). Through the need to separate ourselves from what is ours and what is

FIGURE 2.1 Confrontation

FIGURE 2.2 Emerging faces

projected onto us by our parental and cultural families, the scapegoat 'relates to the individual, the social and the universal condition' (Bartel and Ne'eman, 1993: 135). In this way Ms A's embodied images provided a platform and containment for more difficult feelings and experiences to be accessed and worked through as a group. Ms A's ability to stay with the rawness of her experience offered richness in the darkness (Fig. 2.2).

As Ms A's confidence in the group grew she also began to honour the more isolated, vulnerable parts of herself, experiencing in dancing the opportunity to offer space for others to relate. As play began to emerge in movement improvisation, she allowed the spaces in between to manifest in her images and be validated.

Ms B: connectivity and disconnection

In the mixed-media group, Ms B endorsed her preference for using the movement-based language of dance movement psychotherapy. Early on in the work, sharing her experience of being 'stuck in the head', she anxiously described a state cut off from her wider embodied physicality (Fig. 2.3). Wanting to stay with the reassuring experience of self-locating through movement, she would often close her eyes, retreating as if to sustain an internal focus and prioritise her need to locate a safe place, establishing a sense of home within her own body boundaries.

As Ms B explored further, she struggled with her sense of embodied reality and spatial orientation. She described this disempowered somatised experience as a difficulty to 'get back in the driving seat', and expressed frustration at feeling unable to restore an embodied intention in her capacity to move forward. Symptoms of schizophrenia responded well to working with creative processes through body-based interventions, 'modifying dysfunctional self-perception ... and addressing

FIGURE 2.3 Magma

common psychopathological features such as boundary loss, somatic depersonalisation and body schema disturbances' (Röhricht et al., 2011: 198).

Ms B struggled, however, to describe her embodied exploration, to consider herself in relation to a wider perspective. She struggled to validate either her current life or previous experience – a story of immigration and relocation, separation and reclamation in respect of subjective and collective identity. In the sessions, she was encouraged to externalise her embodied narrative by filtering it through the image-making process, and despite her initial reluctance to use art materials, diagrammatic images emerged that connected to her initial body-based expansion and provided a more concrete platform from which to share a dialogue of her experience.

Through the process of framing the body in the image-making narrative, Ms B began to visualise, identify and relate to her experience of connectivity and disconnection. In several images – perhaps evoking a sense of both internal and external landscapes she emphasised the importance of fragmentation in the amalgamation of marks she had composed, and, as if to endorse the importance of the separateness of identity, remarked, 'look – they are disconnected' (Fig. 2.4).

Whilst continuing to remain more comfortable with movement-based exploration, Ms B acknowledged the surprising aspects of self that emerged in the artwork. Her capacity to be in the collective process strengthened as eye contact and conversation was entrusted to the group. Alongside the acknowledgement of other, of relatedness and of co-creation, a wider landscape evolved a landscape which held a sense of both her past and potential future experiences.

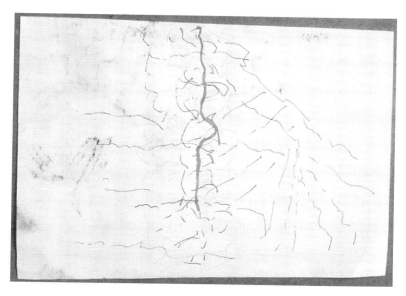

FIGURE 2.4 Connectivity and disconnection

Ms C: separation and belonging

Initially, as Ms C began to move in the group, there was a sense of her needing to be alone in her evolving dance; a separateness from the interactive group process that manifested in her movement material, as she focused on defining a safe personal space. In early sessions, her highly symbolic movements had a reverential, spiritual quality, upward-reaching gestures giving a sense of seeking to be seen by a higher presence. This would typically be followed by self-soothing, comforting movements, perhaps a sway, or, becoming overwhelmed, she would cry.

Despite what appeared to be metaphorically held in the movement (Bartel and Ne'eman, 1993; Meekums, 2012), Ms C did not overtly give meaning to her felt process at this stage. Instead, silently transitioning from the danced narrative, she allowed her experience to unfold and be revealed in the art-making process. On many occasions the pictures that emerged provided a clarification of her process, manifesting the essence of the dance, concretising metaphor and shaping meaning.

Early on in her process in the group, having explored her need to define and sustain her kinaesthetic boundary in movement improvisation, Ms C drew an image of a 'man in a bottle'. Presenting the image to the group, she placed it on the floor, moving it beyond arm's length and stating that the man in the bottle would 'be unable to get out'. Establishing some distance from what the image held, Ms C entrusted the group to witness her action. Sustaining the separateness of her own body boundaries, she was empowered through the image to express her projection of humiliation and shame, establishing a shift in the position of power.

Over time, she was able to re-use and define this process, relocating and exploring her self-experience within the group frame. She continued to shape

FIGURE 2.5 Break the chain

metaphors for important emerging themes, such as letting go of the burden of the past, which she linked to an exploration of weight, experiencing heaviness and lightness. Recognising how past trauma manifested in her present life, Ms C began to locate repeating patterns and consider how cyclical experiences might be transformed (Fig. 2.5). She questioned her sense of being held back, exploring in movement an expression of 'stuckness'.

Ms C's artwork often featured the reoccurring image of a chopped-down tree trunk, seeming to acknowledge her sense of arrested development. In time the harshness of the image gave way to the potential of new shoots, blossom suggesting the delicate beginnings of new growth. In parallel, as Ms C extended her movement range, her confidence improved in the interpersonal nature of dancing amongst others. Establishing a more grounded stance, she anchored herself relationally, enhancing her ability to work with others and experiencing an intentional concept of weight which gave rise to purpose and strength.

Towards the end of her journey in the group Ms C spoke of her experience of finding inner peace, describing her connection to movement improvisation as sacred and validating of her participation in the group as a whole. The final image that we share locates her expression of belonging to the group process, defining the inter-relational nature of her experience (Fig. 2.6). Whilst holding our defined boundaries, we had shared experience, acknowledging the colours that defined us and those which we held in common.

Group feedback

Anonymously collected feedback from the group reflected how the women had found the sessions 'relaxing' and helpful in 'increasing their awareness of others';

FIGURE 2.6 Interconnected

they had also been 'creative, energising and empowering'. One woman wrote, 'Confirming your feelings creatively in the artwork after enjoying the dancing is really fun and interesting, and most of all, the sharing of it, that helps us all'.

Another wrote, 'It is important to feel met and listened to; listening can be done through ears, hands and various mediums. I have learnt a great deal about how art making and moving colours are opportunities for mindfulness and communication.'

And finally, 'This group has been intuitive and replenished my spirit flow. Through dance and many other things I have been able to be open and received an inner peace, and through sharing my experience felt a sense of belonging.'

Conclusion

The dual-modality process allowed for and enhanced the development of verbal and non-verbal narratives. Through the layering and filtering processes, the subjective metaphor re-resonated through the exploration of diverse media. The double frame provided the opportunity to 'try again', to try something differently, and to give oneself permission to yield and become again.

It is true that each arts psychotherapy modality is unique, characterised by its own set of skills and techniques, and only by deeply exploring each modality can we understand the specific qualities of the languages which define it. The expertise of an arts psychotherapist, trained in a modality-specific field, brings a deeply creative and embodied practice to the relational interplay of therapeutic encounter. This combination of in-depth specialisms is distinct and different from the more general broadness of other integrative and expressive arts model approaches. Collectively, all arts psychotherapists share an understanding of creative process, engage in embodied practice and share the foundation of psychotherapeutic theory.

It is also true that the organic nature of self-expression does not distinguish between separate forms in the moment of inspiration. The body is inseparable from the rhythm it moves to and the landscape it moves through. And in this there is of course drama, aesthetic image and politics at play. We are in dialogue with our environments and respond to all that they contain with resonance and dissonance, continually using multidisciplinary languages to shape meaning and express our evolving, lived experience. Perhaps, as we move forward, we attempt to fully integrate our expression in a moment 'where colour, form, movement rhythm, image, sound, time, space and energy are not categorised and separated but perceived as necessary parts of the same kaleidoscopic game' (D'Agostino, 1996).

In the course of writing this chapter we have questioned what we mean by a layering and filtering process. Is it layering as in repairing a surface, or as in establishing foundations? Are we creating striate of differing colours, a range of possibilities? Is filtering sifting to eliminate unwanted matter, clarifying core components? Or perhaps allowing the soil to crack, and fresh water to irrigate new paths? Is there therefore a sense of connecting and disconnecting? Perhaps even a sense of coming together and coming apart? Could coming apart be releasing, allowing more space between tissues that have been held so tightly together for so long? Here, perhaps we can return to Rumi, as he touches on the nature of solid ground and fragmentation, encouraging yielding, that newness might unfold and give rise to new form and colour.

References

Bartel, L. and Ne'eman, N. (1993). *The Metaphoric Body: Guide to Expressive Therapy Through Images and Archetypes*. London: Jessica Kingsley Publishers.

Best, P. (2009). Swim Alongside, Block the Way and then Seduce: Building Blocks of Relationship. In: S. Scoble, M. Ross and C. Lapoujade, eds., *Arts in Arts Therapies: A European Perspective*, 1st ed. Plymouth: University of Plymouth Press, pp. 1–12.

D'Agostino, O. (1996). Sound Movement Image: Perceiving Art and the Healing Body. Unpublished workshop programme for 1996 – proposing combined workshops incorporating dance, music, visual arts and energy rebalancing techniques.

Dalley, T. (1993). Art Psychotherapy Groups. In: K.N. Dwivedi, ed., *Group Work With Children and Adolescents: A Handbook*, 1st ed. London: Jessica Kingsley Publishers.

Davis, M. and Wallbridge, D. (1991). *Boundary and Space – An Introduction to the Work of D.W. Winnicott*. London: Karnac Books Ltd.

Department of Health (2012). *Supporting Recovery in Mental Health*. London: Centre for Mental Health. [online] Available at: http://www.nhsconfed.org/Publications/Docum ents/Supporting_recovery_in_mental_health.pdf# [Accessed 19 Oct. 2016].

Dudley, J. (2001). The Co-Therapist Relationship – A Married Couple? *Inscape*, 6(1), pp. 12–22.

Hayes, J. (2013). *Soul and Spirit in Dance Movement Psychotherapy: A Transpersonal Approach*. London: Jessica Kingsley Publishers.

Meekums, B. (2000). *Creative Group Therapy for Women Survivors of Child Sexual Abuse, Speaking the Unspeakable*. London: Jessica Kingsley Publishers.

Meekums, B. (2012). Kinaesthetic Empathy and Movement Metaphor in Dance Movement Psychotherapy. In: D. Reynolds and M. Reason, eds., *Kinaesthetic Empathy in Creative Cultural Practices*, 1st ed. Bristol: Intellect.

NICE (2014). Psychosis and Schizophrenia in Adults: Treatment and Management. NICE Clinical Guideline 178. [online] Available at: http://guidance.nice.org.uk/CG178/NICE Guidance/ pdf/English [Accessed 19 Oct. 2016].

Ogden, T.H. (2004). On Holding and Containing, Being and Dreaming. *International Journal of Psychoanalysis*, 85(6), pp. 1349–1364.

Rogers, N. (1993). *The Creative Connection: Expressive Arts as Healing*. Palo Alto: Science and Behavior Books.

Röhricht, F., Papadopoulos, N., Holden, S., Clarke, T. and Priebe, S. (2011). Clinical Effectiveness and Therapeutic Processes of Body Psychotherapy in Chronic Schizophrenia – An Open Clinical Trial. *Arts in Psychotherapy*, 38(3), pp. 196–203.

Schaverien, J. (1999). *The Revealing Image: Analytical Art Psychotherapy in Theory and Practice*. London: Jessica Kingsley Publishers.

Tufnell, M. and Crickmay, C. (1990). *Body Space Image*. Cornwall: Hartnolls.

Winnicott, D.W. (1971). *Playing and Reality*. London: Tavistock/Routledge Publication.

3

STAYING CONNECTED

Combining music therapy and dance movement psychotherapy in an acute mental health setting

Tasha Colbert & Cornelia Bent

At our first meeting we immediately discovered a shared enthusiasm for collaboration. As a dance movement psychotherapist (DMP), Tasha had for three years co-led therapy sessions – with a speech and language therapist, dramatherapist and music therapist – for people with learning disabilities; while as a music therapist, Cornelia had collaborated with dance movement psychotherapists during her own training in Austria. Such enriching experiences had opened up new ways of working, which we were each keen to explore further.

The seeds sown in that first meeting led to us setting up and running a three-month pilot project for inpatients in an acute mental health setting, combining music and dance movement psychotherapy, our respective disciplines. In an environment that can be chaotic, with low service-user and staff motivation, feedback suggested that participants found the group a beneficial adjunct to treatment. Encouraged by this positive response, we went on to set up a regular ongoing open group, which went on to run for over two years, consolidating our cross-modal approach.

To further investigate service users' experience, we conducted a small research project with the aim of identifying any therapeutic benefits of engaging in a cross-modality arts psychotherapy group, and determining whether such an approach supported recovery and transition from hospital to community. Data was collected from a modest sample of exit interviews with participants that had returned to the community, following the close of therapy. The ongoing group and subsequent research project – together with our reflections – form the basis of this chapter. All participants gave consent for their contributions to be included, using pseudonyms.

Presented below are a selection of narratives from exit interviews, together with our own findings. We reflect further on our rationale for creating a cross-modality group and our personal experiences of collaboration, and make observations on the interplay between music and movement in a therapeutic setting.

Rationale for a combined approach

Music and dance have been interconnected through time, together playing a central role in traditional and ancient ritual (Phillips-Silver, 2009). Our observations have shown that, as children, we move seamlessly between the arts, and we suggest that combining modalities in the arts psychotherapies can help us reconnect to our innate creativity across different art forms (Colbert, 2009).

As single-modality arts psychotherapists, we sometimes incorporate art media other than our own, in order to better meet the needs of the clients we work with (Jones, 2005). With this in mind, we were interested in exploring what the benefits of having two arts psychotherapists from different modalities might be, in the context of acute mental health. While cross-modality work is common in areas such as learning disabilities and child and adolescent services, at time of writing there is little literature to be found on a combined music therapy and dance movement psychotherapy approach, within an acute mental health setting.

Cattanach suggests that dual-modality groups may support client engagement in arts psychotherapies, as well as enable meaningful intrapersonal and interpersonal connection (Cattanach, 1999). It has been well documented in child development literature that the responsiveness of the caregiver to the infant's nonverbal expressions – through matching sound, rhythm and movement – plays an important role in supporting children's emotional and social development (Stern, 1985; Bowlby, 1969; Loman and Sossin, 2009). Many mental health patients have experienced developmental trauma, something that can cause the individual to lose the ability to be 'in tune' with those around them. When these interpersonal rhythms are damaged, a sense of isolation and disconnection is often the dominant experience. Music and movement both involve rhythm, and we know that joining in a shared rhythm with others can be grounding and help to restore a sense of connection (Van der Kolk, 2014). By combining music therapy and dance movement psychotherapy, service users would have the opportunity to explore both media in the same space, discover their own preferences, and experience the emotional and social benefits of engaging in rhythmic improvisation.

Context

Within this inpatient setting the service user population was necessarily transient, with service users typically passing through hospital for anything between two weeks and four months at a time, and on rare occasions longer. Given this context, an open-group structure was deemed appropriate. A maximum of six participants per session were able to safely take part, given restrictions on available space in the hospital. The group was offered in the arts psychotherapies/occupational therapy department, on an ongoing weekly basis, and was open to inpatients from two acute wards, as well as to outpatients for a maximum of six months post-discharge. The decision to offer service users the choice to continue attending post-discharge came from our understanding that the transition from hospital to community can be a difficult time, when service users are vulnerable to relapse. In a containing therapeutic space, service users in the midst of this transition could reflect on the challenges that being back in the community brings, as well as benefit from a space to express their hopes and fears and receive support from the group. Once service users left the group, we were able to offer them a pathway into various community arts psychotherapies groups for those who wished to continue engaging with the process.

Fears and beginnings

Reflecting on our apprehension about working together with music therapy and dance movement psychotherapy in the same space, Tasha's fears were that the movement process would get 'lost and taken over' by the music. 'Music is such a powerful medium, and sound fills the space. I was afraid that my identity as a DMP would be compromised.' Cornelia had similar concerns that the movement process would 'overwhelm me and that I would get too involved in the movement process, and lose my music therapist identity. I also wondered what my role was going to be, whether I could reflect on the movement process, and what was okay or not okay about how I moved in the space'. Interestingly, pre-group discussions were primarily concerned with making sure each medium was given enough space in the sessions. Even in our preparation of the room, we were both concerned to create enough physical space for our discipline – Tasha moving the bulky chairs out of the way to create space for movement, and Cornelia ensuring adequate room for the instruments. Perhaps as a way of containing our fears, we began by creating a structure to the sessions that ensured an even balance between music and movement interventions. Over time we became more flexible, allowing one medium or other to dominate for a while, reflecting our growing trust in one another and in the collaborative process.

The interplay between music and movement

Initially, sessions began with a (verbal or nonverbal) 'check-in' to assess the mood and energy levels of participants, followed by a circle-activity, using a ball, to get to know one another's names, orientate participants to the group and encourage interaction. Tasha, as the dance movement psychotherapist, would then begin by leading a warm-up in a circle, using her own body to mirror and amplify participants' movements, with the aim of encouraging body awareness, extending participants' movement range, and engaging individuals in a shared group experience (Chaiklin and Schmais, 1993). At the same time, Cornelia matched the rhythm and mood of these movements on the piano, influencing how people moved in the space, which in turn influenced her music-making.

After warming up in movement, the group would be invited to choose an instrument or instruments, explore sounds and engage in musical play. This, the middle section of the session, involved bringing music and movement together in a structured improvisation. Participants were invited to choose between which of the two media they wished to start with, and to move between music and movement at any point during the improvisation. We noticed that being creative in the one art form often stimulated creativity in the other (Rogers, 1999). Towards the end of the session, the dance movement psychotherapist introduced the parachute as a way of bringing the group together in a shared activity that was often calming and centering for the group.

Tasha noticed that live music, responsive to the unfolding movement process, enabled participants to transition more fluently into expressive movement, and move with ease into a creative process – which often involved moving with props and creating music together. As a dance movement psychotherapist, this contrasted with her experience of working with recorded music, which is intrinsically unable to respond to unpredictable changes in emotional state and rhythmic interaction, and can inhibit the natural flow of the movement process.

From a music therapist's perspective, it was a new experience for Cornelia to match movement instead of sounds, which influenced the ensuing musical inter-action and play. When matching sound, a music therapist usually focuses on the musical structure, and attunes to the musical dynamics that are present. Cornelia noticed that when matching movement, an experimental element developed in her piano playing, as she responded to changes in the qualities of movement that she witnessed.

Stepping out of our comfort zone

The co-facilitation style we used involved us each at various times leading the group, with the other therapist supporting the process from 'inside': actively taking part in music-making or movement. This would sometimes develop into one or other of us improvising in the other's therapeutic medium, for example, Tasha playing an instrument. This process is illustrated in our notes of the first time this occurred:

> *Cornelia played a rhythmic melody on the balaphon, which was picked up by the movement therapist matching the rhythm of the music with the feathers; this seemed to create a space for the participants to join in, either by playing an instrument or moving. . . . Later Tasha played the drums and Cornelia moved with material . . . our spontaneity in the moment and stepping out of our comfort zones seemed to mark an important shift in the group, influencing participants to try out something they had not done before, such as pick up a movement prop and begin moving, or start playing an instrument in a new way.*

It seemed that taking our place alongside participants as 'non-experts', role-modelling, risk-taking and allowing ourselves to make mistakes and be seen to be vulnerable, all contributed to creating a permissive environment that encouraged spontaneity in participants. We were also able to acknowledge the expertise already present in the room, especially as some of the service users in the group were experienced musicians, dancers and singers. Sessions gave a space for participants to reconnect with their talents and functional selves, often forgotten in the crisis of acute mental distress.

A deeper connection

We were often reminded of tribal gatherings where people come together to sing, dance and make music. An excerpt from our notes highlights the comparison:

> *A vocal improvisation spontaneously emerged in response to movement in the circle. This developed, as participants moved towards the centre of circle and back, while at the same time using vocal expressions that matched the energy of the movement, getting bolder and louder as the rhythm was influenced by the movement and vice versa.*

The use of voice noted here seemed to mark a willingness amongst participants to share more of themselves in the group, while the use of rhythmic and spatial synchrony reflected a cohesive stage in the group's development (Schmais, 1985). When this particular improvisation came to a natural end, we felt a sense of wonder as the group stood together in silence, breathing in sync and making eye-contact with one another, and it took some time to make the transition into verbal reflection. Once we did, the group expressed awe at what we had achieved creatively together, and a feeling of greater closeness.

Over time the structure of the sessions evolved, as regular participants became more confident to take the initiative, choosing for themselves whether to begin by playing an instrument or moving. As the session progressed, participants would shift spontaneously between engaging in movement or music improvisation without prompting from the therapists. Participants would also explore moving while playing an instrument. Taken together, these developments reflected a growing sense of ease, confidence and trust in the group, and a willingness to experiment and take an active role within the process – a marker of healthy group development (Yalom, 1983).

Methodology

Our interest in collecting participants' subjective experiences of the group – rather than relying solely on our own observations and reflections – came from a desire to gain insight into the thoughts, feelings and views of participants, to hear first-hand what their experiences of a cross-modality group had been like, and whether they had experienced any benefits from such a combined approach. We were aware that service users of mental health institutions are often marginalised, their views remaining unheard within the services that are there to care for them (Stone, 2010). By conducting exit interviews we hoped to 'give voice' to those who took part in the research. We used qualitative methodologies, including narrative enquiry and thematic analysis. Narrative enquiry allowed us to collect and analyse the accounts people gave to describe their experiences, and offer interpretations (Overcash, 2003); thematic analysis of data was used to identify and build a set of themes, enabling us to illustrate a summary of findings (Riley and Hawe, 2005).

Data collection tools

Data was collected through the form of exit interviews. Interviews lasted between 45 minutes and an hour, were audio-recorded and conducted by either the music therapist or dance movement psychotherapist. The interview comprised of nine questions, and consent forms were completed at the beginning. The service users invited to take part in this study expressed a wish to be interviewed, and seemed keen to share their views about the group. They understood that they could withdraw consent at any time. We are aware that our dual role as therapists and researchers may have influenced the way participants answered our questions. Service users taking part in the research consisted of two women and two men, aged between 22 and 50 years, with diagnoses ranging from schizophrenia to bipolar disorder. Ethnicity was 50 per cent Black African/Afro-Caribbean and 50 per cent White British.

All four participants were interviewed at the end of treatment (exit interviews), had attended the group as inpatients, and continued to attend post-discharge for a period of 3 to 12 sessions. Overall duration of attendance varied, with two participants attending for a short period of 6–8 weeks, and two for longer durations of 23 and 36 weeks.

Participants' voices

We used mostly open questions in the exit interviews, to invite reflections on experience. To give a flavour of the different ways participants responded, we have included the transcript of answers to our first question in detail:

'How have you found the combination of music and movement therapy and being able to use both modalities in the session?'

SANDRA: At first, it was intimidating for me. I did a little bit of music, but I have never done movement therapy. Sometimes I have found that one has been easier than the other, and sometimes where I feel stuck in the music, I don't feel stuck in the movement, or the other way around. I like the movement and beginning with a warm-up to help you think about what's going on in the moment, in your own body. After that, when you go use the instruments, you feel in a different place to when you started, as you might have already released some kind of tension. So when you start playing, you feel calmer already, you feel more in yourself, more in your body. It doesn't feel so uncomfortable starting to play music. Sometimes, it has also been nice when we have done movement at the end of the whole group, when we used the parachute. Maybe after playing some instruments, or hearing some discordant music, it has been nice to use the parachute at the end, to let your body let go of what you have put into the session, so I like that. Sometimes to have the option of the movement takes the pressure out of it, and in the music, I first thought it is all about how to make a nice noise, but it doesn't often work out like that, and sometimes when you [the music therapist] was playing, the movement therapist used the feathers, and that reminds me that there is nothing competitive about it in this therapy session. Being able to move as well brings up feelings of being exposed, so I like using both mediums.

ABDULAI: I personally believe that music and movement are connected somehow . . . getting involved with music and movement is such a therapeutic way of getting yourself cleansed or getting yourself healed, and there is a way towards progression to deal with your medical problem . . . music and movement are very well connected . . . and enables you to express yourself through your physicality rather than just vocally.

LINDSAY: The difference in this group has been you have the music as well, and if you are moving you are interacting with others who are not moving, and you influence one another. It's been fantastic, it's often set me up for the day – sometimes, for the rest of the week . . . it's released a lot of energy for me . . . it's helped me to feel more confident, less inhibited. I started out inhibited in the group, where I was just hiding behind an instrument instead of moving . . . and now I'm spending a whole hour moving, and sometimes I'll grab an instrument while I'm moving, instead of just sitting there behind an instrument.

JEROME: I find it good – very good, if I am honest. I like the fact that I can start with music and we end with movement ... both sections help me to feel calm. When we are doing the music, we are not really rocking out, we are just playing simple melodies, relaxing-type melodies, and at the end when we use the parachute, I also like that. I like the combination of both mediums in this session.

We summarise answers to the remaining eight interview questions below.

'Could you say a few words about how you were when you started the Music and Movement Therapy Group?'

Responses to this question varied, but common key words used were: *frustrated, angry, bored, shy, anxious, stressed,* and *apprehensive*. All participants described in their own words their feelings about their admissions. As inpatients for different reasons and for various lengths of times, they nonetheless shared common themes of anxiety and a wish to attend the group for support in their recovery, as well as simply for interest.

'In your experience, was the music and movement therapy group different from a talking therapy group for you?'

A common theme for all participants was that they saw music and movement as a form of communication distinct from verbal expression. In the group, feelings didn't necessarily need to be put into words to be heard. As Sandra reflected, 'When you are in a frame of mind where your mind can't register words or you don't want to hear anything . . . music and movement still gets through to you . . . people are listening to the way you are expressing yourself, and people are with you in that moment'.

'Has the group been helpful to you?'

Respondents responded unanimously in the affirmative.

'If so, what has been helpful about the Music and Movement Therapy Group. . . . anything you have noticed over time?'

A common theme in response to this question was of feeling less inhibited over time, allowing for greater freedom of expression. As Sandra put it, 'It feels in the session that all is welcome and it doesn't matter if it's not very nice or doesn't sound good, as it's still welcome. That's what I like about it'. Lindsay reflected, 'I've noticed that I am not worrying at all about how other people in the group might see me . . . it's a release, that's who I am inside – someone who doesn't worry too much what other people think, a bubbly person . . . but I've been locked in for a while, it feels like I've shed a layer, shaken it off'.

The interpersonal aspect of the group was also cited as being important. As Abdulai put it, 'That's the beauty of music and movement therapy, as it gives individuals a way of connecting'. Jerome commented on the quality of listening in the group as being helpful to him: 'You have to listen to what's going on, as when you listen, you start to work together as a group. That's why I remember that first group I came to, as we all made a point of listening to each other, and that made me come back.'

'What changes have you noticed for yourself?'

Three out of four of the research participants commented on changes they had noticed in themselves – such as increased confidence and reduced anxiety, a feeling of greater connection between mind and body, and the ability to be authentic – associated with an increased sense of trust and safety. For example, Sandra said, 'I don't feel so scared of other people, and feel like I can just be myself, and I am not afraid of how I am going to play or how my movement or body looks like'.

Lindsay commented that attending the group had helped motivate her to engage in exercise outside of therapy, and realise that this supported her recovery. Abdulai interpreted the question differently, and focused on the changes he had noticed over time in regards to the group process, commenting on improvements that were related not only to a sense of group togetherness, but also to his own musical play and exploration of sounds and movements.

'What would you say made the most difference for you in the music and movement therapy group?'

Sandra reflected on the value of being able to access the group post-discharge, and the support this had given her. She also named the importance of a non-judgmental environment, and how this had helped her to see that there was more than one way to engage in the process: 'I thought that there was a right or wrong way to do things, but now I see that there is not, so that's also one of the most helpful things about this group.' Abdulai spoke about his experience of meeting other people, connecting with others through music and movement, and his associations with the sounds he had created: 'You play the ocean drum and it gives you the connection with the sea and the sound of the sea and the sound of the ocean. If you play a djembe drum, it gives you a festival feeling.' Lindsay spoke about moving in response to the music, and how this had influenced her movement in the group: 'I make stronger movements, I'm more positive in my attitude.' Before Lindsay's admission into hospital, she had been attending regular dance classes and had performed professionally. She spoke about how the group had helped her consider attending classes again, related to her growing self-belief: 'I wouldn't have considered doing a dance class so soon after my recovery. It's helped me to feel more confident and less inhibited.'

'Once you have finished the music and movement therapy group, would you consider joining either a community music or community movement therapy group or maybe both?'

All respondents were keen on the idea of moving on to attend arts psychotherapies groups or arts-based activity groups in the community – which one participant described as the 'the next step in my recovery'.

'We are coming to the end of the interview. Is there anything else you would like to say before we finish?'

All participants expressed gratitude at being able to attend the group, in particular for the fact that they could access it again once in the community. Additionally, being able to express a range of feelings in a safe group context was important to them. As one participant said, 'It has felt like such a safe space to go to and express any kind of anger or unpleasant feelings, but recently also more happy feelings'. Another participant expressed her desire to share something of this experience with other service users in the community. As a trained Pilates teacher, she talked about the possibility of facilitating gentle movement sessions in a local mental health day centre, and the actions she could take to make this a reality.

Summary of findings

In analysing the data for reported benefits, we identified four main themes.

1   The value of a combined approach

   (i)   Beginning with movement before shifting to music-making was seen as a way of connecting to self before progressing to the more interpersonal act of making music together.

   (ii) Reflections were made on the value of having both media available in the same space. Moving while playing an instrument, for example, or shifting freely between movement and active music-play, brought out the participants' ability to be spontaneous, providing an alternative mode of expression when feeling inhibited or 'stuck' in one medium or another.

(iii) The presence of two arts psychotherapists, and our modelling of ways to engage with props and instruments, seemed to support an atmosphere of experimentation and co-operation.

2 Self-awareness

(i) Participants commented on a new-found awareness of their bodies through engaging in movement and music making, leading to them feeling calmer and stronger, and experiencing a release of energy. An increased awareness of the connection between mind and body was noted.

(ii) Participants reported that having both media available provided the opportunity to express a wide range of feelings.

(iii) An increased confidence and authenticity was reflected on, with participants finding that over time they were able to be 'more themselves' as a result of attending the group.

3 Trust, safety and interpersonal connection

(i) A sense of trust was experienced, allowing for greater self-expression, and the freedom to explore and experiment through both media.

(ii) The quality of the therapeutic relationship was mentioned as significant in establishing feelings of safety within the group.

(iii) The fear of others' judgements – and anxiety in relation to others – decreased as the group progressed. The 'non-judgemental' environment led to participants feeling less inhibited.

(iv) A sense of group cohesion emerged, with participants feeling a greater connection with others.

4 Transition into the community

(i) Participants reported that the group had been a source of support for them as they transitioned back into the community, and had been a contributing factor in their recovery.

(ii) Several participants reflected on how the group had helped them to consider more mainstream arts groups or other activities as part of their reintegration into the community.

Discussion and recommendations for further research

Judging by the data, participants found it valuable to work with the combination of movement and music, and experienced the group as a supportive space during the transition from hospital to community. The findings also suggest that a combined music therapy and dance movement psychotherapy approach contributed to positive developments in relationship to self and others.

Although no formal evaluation took place afterwards, we do know that three out of four participants went on to participate in community arts therapies groups, and are continuing to function in the community without further hospital admission. One participant commented on how attending the group had helped her find the motivation to engage in meaningful activities outside the group, which she considered supportive of her continuing recovery. Two of the participants went on to volunteer at a local mental health charity, offering an activity group involving movement and music. It seemed that for these individuals the group had been an empowering experience, encouraging them to share their skills with others.

We are aware that there are several limitations to this study, one being that only a small sample of participants took part in the research. In order to be able to more fully evaluate the effectiveness of such an approach, further research with a larger sample size is required (Tsiris, Pavlicevic and Farrant, 2014). One way to further evaluate a combined approach would be to conduct a randomised controlled trial comparing a combined music therapy and dance movement psychotherapy approach with a single-modality group. Our recommendations for future research include interviewing participants at point of joining, at point of leaving, and in follow-up interviews at one month, three months and six months afterwards. There is also an argument for offering a combined music therapy and dance movement psychotherapy approach to service users who present with mental distress to their GPs, to evaluate if this type of intervention can prevent further deterioration in mental health, potentially preventing expensive hospital admission. We believe there is much scope for this type of work, which would benefit from further research.

Final thoughts

We suggest that the effectiveness of this intervention was due in no small part to the complementarity of music and movement, as well as to the complementarity between us as individuals. Offering both music and movement together seemed to stimulate participants' creativity – as well as our own – as together we experimented with movement, rhythm and sound. The experience of collaborating stretched us both as practitioners, as we explored and developed new ways of working. The ability to acknowledge our fears, and be open, flexible and honest with one another, are all deemed essential factors in healthy collaboration (Watson, 2008). As Best suggests, collaboration can be a catalyst for reflection and growth, provided an attitude of curiosity rather than insecurity is fostered (Best, 2000: 197). This learning has gone on to influence and enhance our individual practices as a dance movement psychotherapist and music therapist, and left us with an over-riding enthusiasm for further collaborative projects in the future.

References

Best, P. (2000). Theoretical Diversity and Clinical Collaboration: Reflections by a Dance/Movement Therapist. *The Arts in Psychotherapy*, 27(3), pp. 187–211.
Bowlby, J. (1969). *Attachment and Loss*. London: Pimlico.

Cattanach, A. (1999). *Process in the Arts Therapies*. London: Jessica Kingsley Publishers.

Chaiklin, S. and Schmais, C. (1993). The Chace Approach to Dance Therapy. In: S. Sandel, S. Chaiklin and A. Lohn, eds., *Foundations of Dance/Movement Therapy: The Life and Work of Mariam Chace*, 2nd ed. Colombia, MD: The Mariam Chace Memorial Fund of the American Dance Therapy Association, pp. 75–97.

Colbert, N. (2009). Sunita: An Example of Dance Movement Psychotherapy with Children. *e-motion: Association for Dance Movement Psychotherapy Quarterly*, 19(2), pp. 13–24.

Jones, P. (2005). *The Arts Therapies: A Revolution in Healthcare*. New York: Brunner-Routledge Press Inc.

Loman, S. and Sossin, K.M. (2009). Applying the Kestenberg Movement Profile in Dance/Movement Therapy. In: S. Chaiklin and H. Wengrower, eds., *Life Is Dance: The Art and Science of Dance Movement Therapy*, 1st ed. New York: Routledge, pp. 237–264.

Overcash, J.A. (2003). Narrative Research: A Review of Methodology and Relevance to Clinical Practice. *Critical Reviews in Oncology/Hematology*, 48(2), pp. 179–184.

Phillips-Silver, J. (2009). On the Meaning of Movement in Music, Development and the Brain. *Contemporary Music Review*, 28(3), pp. 293–314.

Riley, T. and Hawe, P. (2005). Researching Practice: The Methodological Case for Narrative Inquiry. *Health Education Research*, 20(2), pp. 226–236.

Rogers, N. (1999). The Creative Connection: A Holistic Expressive Arts Process. In: S.K. Levine and E.G. Levine, eds., *Foundations of Expressive Arts Therapy: Theoretical and Clinical Perspectives*, 1st ed. London: Jessica Kingsley Publishers, Chapter 6, pp. 113–132.

Schmais, C. (1985). Healing Processes in Group Dance Therapy. *American Journal of Dance Therapy*, 8(1), pp. 17–36.

Stern, D. (1985). *The Interpersonal World of the Infant: A View from Psychoanalysis and Developmental Psychology*. New York: Basic Books.

Stone, B. (2010). Therapy with Seriously Distressed Clients. In: C. Lago and B. Smith, eds., *Anti-Discriminatory Practice in Counselling and Psychotherapy*, 2nd ed. London: Sage, pp. 75–85.

Tsiris, G., Pavlicevic, M. and Farrant, C. (2014). *A Guide to Evaluation for Arts Therapists and Arts & Health Practitioners*. London: Jessica Kingsley Publishers.

Van der Kolk, B. (2014). *The Body Keeps the Score*. London: Penguin Books.

Watson, T. (2008). Collaboration in Music Therapy with Adults with Learning Disabilities. In: K. Twyford and T. Watson, eds., *Integrated Team Working: Music Therapy as Part of Transdisciplinary and Collaborative Approaches*, 1st ed. London: Jessica Kingsley Publishers, Chapter 2, pp. 91–123.

Yalom, I.D. (1983). *Inpatient Group Psychotherapy*. New York: Basic Books.

4

FACING RUPTURE AND NURTURING A CREATIVE SPACE

A dramatherapy and art therapy group on an acute ward in a medium secure forensic hospital

Cathy Goodwin & Alison Ramm

> Hermes, god of crossed sticks, crossed existence, protect these feet.
>
> *Prayer to Hermes (Creeley, 2006: 183)*

Introduction

In the final moments of our project, we discovered Robert Creeley's 'Prayer to Hermes'. The poem gave us a deeper understanding of the challenging psychological landscape of an art and dramatherapy group for men who experience psychosis. Hermes, and the qualities he represents, had already become a helpful element in our cross-modality work together. Creeley describes a disorientating and alienated border-realm experience, which had a powerful resonance for us. He seems to suggest that a demanding journey needs to be undertaken, and it appears that the Greek god Hermes, messenger and god of wayfaring, provides protection and equips the traveller with the imagination and creativity that is vital to address isolation and reconnect with reality (López-Pedraza, 2010).

In January 2015 we began to co-facilitate an art and dramatherapy group for the men's acute admissions ward within a medium secure hospital. Cathy had worked as a dramatherapist in the unit for five years, and Alison, an art therapist, had been part of the arts psychotherapies team for three years. Art therapy was already well established on the ward: a weekly art therapy group had run for a number of years, which Alison had co-facilitated with an art therapist colleague for the previous 18 months. While the change to a cross-modality group was a departure from tradition, we wanted to work together because we had a shared interest in Jungian literature, myth and archetypal imagery. By bringing our two modalities together, we hoped to strengthen these aspects of our clinical work and extend the range of creative possibilities available to participants. We were keen to discover whether we could build on the established routines of art-making and discussion in the art therapy group, while drawing on some of the traditions of dramatherapy to strengthen the elements of story-telling and narrative. By bringing together our respective modalities we hoped to better address the distress that is an inevitable part of life on an acute ward, and together took on the challenge of introducing dramatherapy to the well-established art therapy group.

At the start of the project we revisited the traditional body of literature that informs arts therapists working with patients with psychosis, and we give a brief description of this theoretical base. In the forensic setting there are stringent safe-guards to prevent us from compromising confidentiality, and we are unable to describe individuals' clinical material. These restrictions encouraged us to focus on aspects of the group that were particularly difficult and perplexing, and we have included a series of composite vignettes based on interactions in the group, along with some of our own images made during the sessions.

During the first few weeks facilitating the art and dramatherapy group, we became increasingly aware of the challenges we faced to keep our own creativity alive within the constricted environment of the acute ward. In this chapter we describe debilitating countertransference feelings, and how myths and metaphor helped us develop our cross-modality approach and sustain the work.

In one of the first sessions, Alison made a drawing of a feather and a rock (Fig. 4.1). Months later, looking back at our artwork, it seemed to us that the image referred to attributes of Hermes: a feather from his winged sandals and a stone from one of the rocky cairns that he was believed to inhabit. On reflection, Hermes had been present all along at an unconscious level.

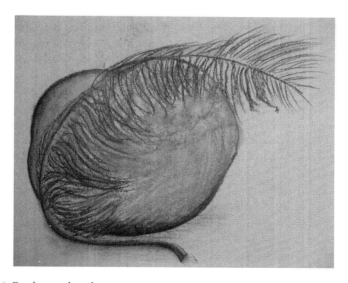

FIGURE 4.1 Feather and rock

The literature

> 'I believe one's psyche can be imaginatively stimulated only by those myths akin to one's own nature, history and personality, the myths one lives in relation to the basic complexes'
>
> *(López-Pedraza, 2010: 12)*

Our conviction that the provision of an arts psychotherapies group was essential to the wellbeing of the acute ward is supported by a literature base common to both of our modalities. There is widespread fascination with the relationship between psychosis and creativity, which has its roots in the first collections of outsider art established in the nineteenth century, and there are strong historical links between advances in the treatment of the condition and the emergence of the professions of the arts therapies (Killick and Schaverien, 1997). A substantial review of dramatherapy research for people with schizophrenia was conducted by Lambros Yotis (2006), presenting a spectrum of interventions by dramatherapists, and there has since been a Cochrane review of dramatherapy for schizophrenia or schizophrenic-like illnesses (Dent-Brown and Ruddy, 2007); art therapist Chris Wood (1997) has given a summary of the psychoanalytical theory that informs this area of work. Kleinian theory and the work of Wilfred Bion provide an understanding of the psychological structures underlying psychosis. This body of theory is the backdrop for our understanding of psychosis and the dynamic relationship between creativity and psychological transformation. The 2007 Art Therapy Clinical Practice Guideline for Working with People who are Prone to Psychotic States (Brooker et al., 2007) is a comprehensive evidence-based guide to this area of work, and The National Institute for Clinical Excellence (NICE) guidelines recommends arts therapies for people who experience psychosis (NICE, 2014).

Some troubling feelings

> I am sore afflicted with the devil's doubles, the twos, of this half-life, this twilight.
>
> *Prayer to Hermes (Creeley, 2006: 183)*

We began by co-facilitating the group without making significant changes to its established format as a supportive drop-in art therapy group. Every week we provided a 45-minute session on the ward, in an activities room housing an exercise bike, computer, music system and six chairs set around a central table. The weekly task of setting the table with the materials signalled the transformation of the room ready for the group to begin. On some days the room could be filled with noise and restless energy, while on others we sensed a menacing undercurrent. We were always vigilant and aware of the risks present on the ward, carefully monitoring any tension between the participants, and taking care to notice resentment and anger that might be expressed in the group. However, the prevailing atmosphere seemed to be of cautious, creative potential. Sometimes we were visited by patients who were floridly psychotic, but it was more usual for the group to be attended by men who were adjusting to the effects of their medication.

As we got ready to go on to the ward, it was usual for one or both of us to feel tired, 'not quite there', or not fully present. These feelings seemed to relate to a low-level, background state of apprehension and anxiety that often extended into the sessions, where, as the following example demonstrates, there were times when individuals behaved in a challenging or threatening way. In these moments they were unable to make use of the creative possibilities that we hoped to nurture:

On the first occasion that Simon joined the group he silently began to make an image. He suddenly stood up and Cathy rose from her chair to join him. He picked up his image, folded it, then tore it into pieces slowly and with what seemed to be an air of threat. He walked to the bin, threw the paper into it and walked out of the room. He did not come back.

Simon's actions had a deadening effect on us. This 'shutting down' of thought is a recognised hazard in working with this patient group, and we found it difficult to think clearly until he had left the room. Estela Welldon has described how the forensic 'patient's tendency to make sadistic attacks on his own capacity for thought and reflection is projected against the therapist's capacity to think; and it is then that the therapist feels confused, [and] numbed' (1997: 15). It is acknowledged that work with individuals with psychotic illnesses, who have 'split off' and compartmentalised parts of their psyche, evokes disturbing emotional reactions in clinicians. However, in psychoanalytic thinking, countertransference reactions are a valuable source of information about the internal psychological states of patients (Gordon and Kirtchuk, 2008). Confronted by Simon's frustration and 'stuckness', we shared the conviction that we needed to work hard to maintain our creative energy within this group, and we focussed on being open to what Simon was communicating, while at the same time remaining grounded and present for the other members of the group. We found it helpful to hold Hermes in mind, and to remember his mythic role as a catalyst for change and psychic movement (López-Pedraza, 2010). It was as if the qualities of energy and playfulness that Hermes represents had been banished from the session, and we needed to counter deadening and negative feelings, to offer inspiration and hope to the participants.

The acute admissions ward

…feels forward, finds behind the track, yet cannot stand still.

Prayer to Hermes (Creeley, 2006: 183)

On admission to the acute ward, patients were in a state of psychological crisis. Many were fearful, paranoid or had retreated into dissociated states of mind and body. There was constant concern that patients might erupt into violence, and it was necessary to hold an individual's offence index in mind in order to remain aware of risk. The daily round of medication, together with constant vigilance around safety, contributed to an underlying atmosphere of anxiety that was difficult to counter. Paradoxically, when distressed patients were brought to the relative safety of the hospital – often under duress – they were likely to experience further trauma; the tense atmosphere seemed to affect even those individuals who had initially experienced the ward as a containing and safe place. For an individual, to find themselves detained in a secure hospital is likely to be a further marker in a journey of estrangement from mainstream society, family and friends, and a hoped-for future. Most of the men had been admitted because they had committed violent acts, and whether or not they were at a stage where they were able to acknowledge the damage that they had caused, their offending history accompanied them and continued to intrude on their moment-to-moment experience. There was a sense in which they had been hermetically sealed away along with their own dangerousness.

If it provoked anxiety in an arts therapist to enter the ward, for patients finding themselves confined together in a relatively small area, it could be terrifying. At times the men would stay in their rooms, sleeping or otherwise isolating themselves from each other, the ward eerily quiet; on other occasions the shouting of confused or angry service users made the atmosphere edgy and unpredictable. There is a quality of 'gnawing anxiety' that working with forensic patients can evoke in staff (Gordon and Kirtchuk, 2008: 2). We were aware of our own anxiety around entering the ward and facilitating the group, and regularly offered support to each other around our own thoughts and feelings.

Although there was an objective at an institutional level that patients only require care on the acute admissions ward for relatively short periods of time, in practice individuals could not be moved to the other less restrictive wards until their risk of violence had decreased, which in some cases could take months or even years. When there appeared to be neither a suitable ward nor alternative placement to accommodate a person, there could be a paralysing sense of 'stuckness' associated with the individual. Metaphorically speaking, it was as if the transformational presence represented by the figure of Hermes was weak or absent.

Psychosis: a perilous realm

> Neither one nor two but a mixture walks here in me.
>
> *Prayer to Hermes (Creeley, 2006: 183)*

An air of rigidity, repetition and being 'stuck' and cut off from other people often clings to patients who experience psychosis, and Wilfred Bion names the crippling 'nameless dread' which underlies the condition (Bion, 1962, cited in Wood, 1997). The work of Jungian psychiatrist John Weir Perry (1976) informed our thinking about the nature of our work with this group of patients. He insists that the condition of psychosis is a sign that the personality needs to enter a period of transformation, and that if this is managed appropriately the individual will be able to achieve growth and change. In his view, rather than representing a self-referential state of psychological isolation, psychosis locates a person in an 'intrapsychic mythic realm'. A person in this state needs to move through a psychological and emotional process that has an archetypal and universal meaning in order to be able to reconnect with everyday life and other people. He advocates that professionals foster relatedness by entering this realm and meeting patients in their own territory (Perry, 1976).

Paul Rebillot has been a major influence in dramatherapy practice, and has left us with a vivid description of his own psychotic experience during which he found himself cut off from other people. In his words, 'every occurrence related to the mythic experience' and 'dream reality and…waking state were indistinguishable' (Rebillot, 1993: 4). Although it is common for patients experiencing psychosis to feel a strong conviction that their hallucinations and delusions make sense, it can be very difficult for professionals to acknowledge this, and to counteract the pervasive sense of meaninglessness associated with the condition. Rebillot noticed that his own progress through – and recovery from – psychosis mirrored the archetypal narrative of the 'hero's journey', which is repeated in varying forms in myths and legends across the world (Campbell, 1949).

Landscapes and imagery that related to journeys often emerged in the artwork that the men made, and again looking back at our own artwork we noticed the resonant archetypal themes in our images (Fig. 4.2). We later adopted these as our creative framework.

We found that both Perry and Rebillot encouraged us to think further about how we might hold on to a sense of hope for each participant, and provide a safe and containing space in which they could begin to find some stability and equip themselves for the task of psychological transformation. On the ward, psychosis was routinely addressed by medication, activity and distraction; in this group we aimed to provide a space where archetypal and mythic experience could be expressed

FIGURE 4.2 Track

creatively. According to Ancient Greek mythology, Hermes was responsible for disrupting established order and introducing change; with his spirit in mind we introduced poetry into the sessions, so that this new element might bring new possibilities for psychological change.

> *Cathy read a poem that she had chosen to reflect the winter months. No one looked up and the words themselves seemed to fill the room. Towards the end of the session Chris stated 'it was rubbish' but Phil said he 'liked it'. Everyone's attention returned to their artwork.*

By reading out the poem to the group, Cathy introduced a dramatherapy dynamic into the session. The temporal experience of listening to the reading, and the poem's focus on the seasons and passage of time, seemed to gently raise the possibility of movement and progression. The reading intimated a shared connection to the natural world and the elements. Cathy was conscious of the rhythm and sound of her voice as she read aloud, and she held in mind the embodied aspects of the participants' experience. Initially she chose to read poems and literature about the natural world, because she was cautious not to over-stimulate the already overburdened minds of patients with acute psychosis (Yotis, 2006: 195). However, having monitored the reactions of group members, she began to introduce fictional stories and archetypal elements, and in subsequent sessions these seemed to have a particular resonance for one of the participants:

> *Eric was an older man who had been recently admitted to the ward. In the group he made drawings with mysterious mythic themes, in chalk pastels. He listened to Cathy's reading and introduced an aspect of the narrative into his art-making. Alison commented on the similarity between Eric's image and the myth, noticing that his drawing had become more defined and more confident towards the end of the session.*

Eric augmented his own mythical framework with elements from Cathy's reading, and, by paying attention to his images, Alison validated aspects of his inner life which he had hidden from other people for a long time.

The need for a sanctuary

> . . . be here elemental.
>
> *Prayer to Hermes (Creeley, 2006: 183)*

It was clear to us that, from the moment of admission, the demands of life on the ward required patients to fit in with established routines and expectations, and that progress was equated with the ability of individuals to achieve a 'normal' way of behaving and relating. Rebillot and Perry, however, emphasise the need for individuals to take time out from everyday routines and expectations in order to negotiate and process psychotic experience. Patients in the acute ward had been removed from their previous lives and social networks, and were presented with the task of making significant personal change.

To understand more about the relationship between the group and the ward we turned to a body of theory that originated in the field of anthropology, which has a central place in dramatherapy and theatre (Hougham, 2006) and that has proved useful in art psychotherapy (Haywood, 2012). Anthropologists have written extensively about the emphasis that traditional societies place on life transitions, such as the change from adolescence to adulthood. Three distinct stages have been identified in rites of passage: in the first stage the individual is removed from their original status to enter a state of *separation*; the second stage situates the individual in a borderline in-between state of *liminality*; and the third stage, of *reincorporation*, enables the person to re-enter the social structure in a new role and with a changed status. The original concept of liminal space as the middle – psychological and temporal – stage, was subsequently extended by anthropologists to encompass the physical space in which ritual and psychological transformation takes place. Traditionally, this might be a dedicated building, a cave or a special piece of ground (Moore, 1991). In thinking about the art and dramatherapy group it seemed to us that the sessions were temporally related to the liminal stage, and that the education room, where we facilitated the sessions, represented the physical aspect of this liminal space. Liminal space is difficult to define, being 'neither here nor there' (Turner, 1967, cited in Haywood, 2012); it is both physical and psychological, external and internal, imagined and actual, individual and shared. The 'hero's journey', which was of significance to Rebillot (1993), is a symbolic description of rites of passage and a metaphor for psychological transformation, and as such involves liminal space in all of its manifestations. Thinking of the group and the sessions as a liminal space within the wider culture and physical space of the ward provided us with a means of understanding the unnerving and strangely demanding atmosphere that we associated with the group. It gave us an insight into ambiguous 'betwixt and between' feelings that the participants were likely to bring to the sessions, and in the face of these difficulties it helped us hold on to the conviction that the group made an important contribution to the culture of the ward. It was a space where the men had the opportunity to 'de-role', stepping out of social roles they may have adopted to cope with the pressures of life – and where the experience of psychosis could safely be validated and even valued for its creative potential (Nitsun et al., 1974). It allowed us to be confident that we were providing a much needed intervention.

We began the project by relying on the grounding and containing properties of art materials and art-making to provide both stability and consistency, and mark out the liminal space. Over time, we became increasingly interested in the potential for storytelling, narrative and performance to represent the possibility of change and transformation. It was as if Cathy took up the role of Hermes, the dynamic catalyst, introducing movement and other transformational elements into the sessions. For patients whose imaginative capacities had been undermined and severely depleted, this approach seemed to foster hope and creative possibility. The 'hero's journey' provided us with an imaginative framework in which to better understand and work with men on an acute ward who were likely to be either 'stuck', or poised at the beginning of a process of change.

> *Chris seemed suspended in a state of ambivalence about whether to cross the threshold into the room. Cathy said 'I brought some poems.' 'Some poems?' he asked, and walked in and sat down. Cathy read a poem about a traveller. Chris said he understood the poem and that he could relate it to his own life.*

Building a cross-modality liminal space and embracing ritual

> This mystery of night seen by day, this magic of darkness in the bright sunlight, is the realm of Hermes. . . .
>
> *(Otto, 1954, cited in López-Pedraza, 2010: 26)*

As the group settled into a routine, the theme of ritual began to take on new significance for us. Every Tuesday afternoon we would pack a small crate with the same set of art materials. It seemed that this ritual was crucial in managing the unpredictability of sessions. The risk that art materials become a danger on the ward meant that we had to remember exactly what we had taken with us. In the forensic context, the art materials are a creative resource and at the same time have the potential to be made into weapons or used to self-harm. We were careful to limit what we took in, each week choosing objects and props from Cathy's store of dramatherapy resources, such as a pack of story cards or a couple of small model animals.

As the weeks passed, we began to question our reliance on this repetitive process of preparation, and wondered if we were losing motivation. The possibility that we had become lazy seemed shameful, and we felt that in some sense we had become trapped. We identified a paradox: although we felt stuck, even 'deadened' by this weekly repetition, at an intuitive level we felt that it was in some way necessary. Once again we looked to the myth of Hermes to shed light on these contradictory feelings; oppositions and paradoxes are part of the territory of borderlines and of the unconscious. As guardian of this realm, Hermes oversees the contradictions and confusions that make psychological transformation possible (López-Pedraza, 2010). In dramatherapy it has long been recognised that ritual and theatre both involve 'special preparation' (Schrader, 2012: 36). We found that our routine helped us contain difficult feelings and unconscious emotions.

> *Chris and Phil had been patients in the ward for several weeks, and had become regular participants in the group. They had been waiting for us to open the door, and they came in and sat down. Chris immediately began drawing, settling quickly into silent expression. Phil stared at the paper. He seemed unsure about how to make a start. He seemed wary and was watching the other people in the room. Cathy initiated a conversation, 'You don't know where to start?' Phil told us he wanted something to copy and Alison*

showed him some art postcards. He chose a landscape and began to draw. The room was quiet and everyone seemed focused on the artwork.

Mindful of the potential of silence to be intimidating, Cathy offered an observation. The visual reference of the postcard seemed helpful to Phil, perhaps providing him with an initial structure. He seemed to feel anchored enough by the art materials, and the 'frame' of his blank sheet of paper, to begin to focus on his work.

Aaron arrived and sat on the exercise bike. He didn't speak, and began pedalling. Cathy showed him a postcard while he pedalled on the bike, and we began to talk with him about what was happening in the picture. Aaron said he didn't want to draw, and came to sit at the table. He picked up a pen and began to draw an abstract grid-like pattern.

There was a restless and unsettling quality to Aaron's contribution to the group. It seemed as if he had hijacked the space to give a performance which demanded the attention of everyone in the room, and the task of holding the session together for the other participants was challenging. When we reflected afterwards, it was helpful – in what we had felt to be a disruptive element of ambivalence – to bring to mind the qualities of Hermes, messenger and trickster. According to myth, it is through disruption and trickery that Hermes becomes the catalyst that shakes the established order, precipitating the need for the hero to make his journey of self-discovery.

In the closing minutes of the session we looked together at the artwork. Alison joined up some of the seemingly disparate elements in the session by suggesting to the group that parts of the images seemed to link with a poem that Cathy had read aloud.

By paying close attention to the formal qualities of the artwork, and making observations about, line, colour, materials used and 'atmosphere', we provided validation and acceptance of the psychological and emotional states of participants. We encouraged them to notice how they were feeling by wondering aloud whether they had noticed changes in their mood or focus of attention, and by acknowledging the grounding properties of the sensory aspects of art-making (Ramm, 2005).

Through participation in the group, the men had the opportunity to equip themselves with a creative focus that had a stabilising effect, supporting them to move on from the psychotic crisis that had initially led to their admission. The art materials and containing 'frame' of the paper formed a 'safe base' from which patients could interact with others in the room, and which provided the very necessary possibility of retreat. When we could – true to the spirit of Hermes – we introduced playful interventions and humour, in order to nurture imaginative flexibility and raise awareness that change was possible.

The most rewarding aspect of our cross-modality work was our combined and therefore increased ability to notice and attune to a wider spectrum of communication from the participants. Cathy was often the more proactive in offering playful and imaginative interactions, while Alison tended to pay closer attention to the artwork and potential of the art materials. We noticed that Cathy's skill in attending to posture, body language and the way participants used the space meant that she often took the role of engaging with participants who seemed restless or chose not to sit at the table. As our work together progressed, further advantages in offering a cross-modality group to these patients became apparent. While Alison concentrated on providing containment for the psychological experience and inner life emerging in the artwork, Cathy drew on her skills as a dramatherapist to introduce material and inspiration from outside the group. It seemed that by bringing the two modalities together we were able to extend the work into an extra dimension, as if the territory of art therapy expanded from the artwork and table into the room, while that of dramatherapy contracted from the performance space of the room towards the intimate territory of the table.

Final thoughts

> . . . always he is on the road between here and yonder.
>
> *(López-Pedraza, 2010: 26)*

Over the first two months the sessions went through a transition from an art therapy group to an art and dramatherapy group. The original format, which had made art materials available within a drop-in session, remained, with Cathy gradually introducing new resources. In our initial preparations for co-facilitating the group, we found it difficult to work out how to bring together our respective modalities productively, and noticed that we were battling with feelings of fatigue, which suppressed and deadened our ability to think. The resources that we added to our basic set of materials were often chosen quickly and intuitively – it seemed easier to reflect on the significance of materials and interventions at the end of sessions. We found that when one of us was feeling particularly deskilled and disempowered, the other seemed to find the energy to maintain our momentum, and in this way we were able to support each other, taking turns to assume the guiding role of Hermes.

We discovered points on which our perspectives differed, but these were usually on a matter of emphasis rather than radical differences. Reflecting on our work together, we found that on some occasions there were differences in the range of metaphors available to us; however, this provided us new possibilities and broadened our thinking. We worked together to expand our knowledge of psychosis and find new ways to think about our interventions, inspiring us and leading to greater confidence that we were providing a meaningful therapeutic framework to address the quality of distress and difficulty particular to psychosis and forensic settings. Patients who have progressed through the forensic system have let us know that they benefited from the early intervention, and remember the group well.

Thinking and writing about the cross-modality group, it seemed to us that we had embarked on a heroic and creative journey of our own. At the beginning of the project we had found it difficult to see how we could make full use of dramatherapy by introducing it to a long-established art therapy group. It was necessary for us to go through a long – both experiential and cerebral – process, and it was not until we had built a 'safe base' for ourselves, and formed our own narrative about the nature of our work together, that we felt we were facilitating a truly cross-modal group.

> Prayer to Hermes
> Hermes, god
> of crossed sticks,
> crossed existence,
> protect these feet
> I offer. Imagination
> is the wonder
> of the real, and I am
> sore afflicted with
> the devil's doubles
> the twos, of this
> half-life,
> this twilight.
> Neither one nor two
> but a mixture
> walks here
> in me –
> feels forward,
> finds behind
> the track, yet
> cannot stand
> still or be here
> elemental, be more
> or less a man,
> a woman.
> *(Creeley, 2006: 183)*

References

Brooker, J., Cullum, M., Gilroy, A., McCombe, B., Mahony, J., Ringrose, K., Russell, D., Smart, L., Zweigbergk, B. and Waldman, J. (2007). *The Use of Art Work in Art Psychotherapy with People Who Are Prone to Psychotic States: An Evidence-Based Clinical Practice Guideline*. London: Oxleas NHS Foundation Trust and Goldsmiths, University of London.

Campbell, J. (1949). *Hero With a Thousand Faces*. London: Fontana Press.

Creeley, R. (2006). *Collected Poems of Robert Creeley, 1975–2005.* Berkeley, CA: University of California Press.

Dent-Brown, K. and Ruddy, R. (2007). Drama Therapy for Schizophrenia or Schizophrenia-like Illnesses. *Cochrane Database of Systematic Reviews,* 1, pp. 1–24. doi:10.1002/14651858. CD005378.pub2.

Gordon, J. and Kirtchuk, G. (2008). *Psychic Assaults and Frightened Clinicians.* London: Karnac Books Ltd.

Haywood, S. L. (2012). Liminality, Art Therapy and Childhood Sexual Abuse. *International Journal of Art Therapy: Inscape,* 17(2), pp. 80–86.

Hougham, P. (2006). *The Atlas of Mind, Body and Spirit.* London: Gaia Books Ltd.

Killick, K. and Schaverien, J. (1997). *Art Psychotherapy and Psychosis.* London: Routledge.

López-Pedraza, R. (2010). *Hermes and His Children.* Einsiedeln, Switzerland: Daimon Verlag.

Moore, R. L. (1991). Ritual, Sacred Space, and Healing: The Psychoanalyst as Ritual Elder. In: N. Schwartz-Salant and M. Stein, eds., *Liminality and Transitional Phenomena* (Chiron Clinical Series), 1st ed. Asheville, NC: Chiron Publications, pp. 13–32.

National Institute for Health and Care Excellence (NICE) (2014). *Psychosis and Schizophrenia in Adults: Prevention and Management: NICE Guidelines [CG178].* London: NICE. [online]. Available at: https://www.nice.org.uk/guidance/cg178?unlid=606825195201631921342 [Accessed 20 June 2015].

Nitsun, M., Stapleton, J. H. and Bender, M. P. (1974). Movement and Drama Therapy with Long-stay Schizophrenics. *British Journal of Medical Psychology,* 47(2), pp. 101–119.

Perry, J. W. (1976). *Roots of Renewal in Myth and Madness: The Meaning of Psychotic Episodes.* San Francisco: Jossey-Bass Publishers.

Ramm, A. K. (2005). What Is Drawing? Bringing the Art into Art Therapy. *The International Journal of Art Therapy: Inscape,* 10(2), pp. 63–77.

Rebillot, P. (1993). *The Call to Adventure: Bringing the Hero's Journey to Daily Life.* San Francisco: Harper Collins.

Schrader, C. (2012). *Ritual Theatre: The Power of Ritual in Personal Development Groups and Clinical Practice.* London: Jessica Kingsley Publishers.

Welldon, E.V. (1997). *A Practical Guide to Forensic Psychotherapy.* London: Jessica Kingsley Publishers, p. 15.

Wood, C. (1997). Facing Fear with People Who Have a History of Psychosis. *International Journal of Art Therapy: Inscape,* 2(2), pp. 41–43.

Yotis, L. (2006). A Review of Dramatherapy Research in Schizophrenia: Methodologies and Outcomes. *Psychotherapy Research,* 16(2), pp. 190–200. doi:10.1080/10503300500268458.

5

AMBIVALENCE, BOUNDARIES, EDGES AND EXPANSION

Relatedness and collaboration in a dance movement psychotherapy and music therapy group for adults with learning disabilities

Céline Butté & Diana Whelan

I choose to meet in me the qualities that reveal to me what it is to be you, and I try them out, if only for a moment. And in so doing, I meet not only you, but another, in me. A way of expressing myself that, for example, reminds me that my gut has a voice, that my voice can go so high or so low. Thanks to you, I open up to a whole new world that only you are able to take me to. This world touches sorrow, grief, joy and bliss, and all that lives between the two. It is not my world, it is not your world, it is in fact not fixed and pre-set; instead it is dynamic, alive and emergent. It is a world that we co-create, in this moment in time, because at this moment in time, here we meet.

Diary notes, Céline, 20.3.16

Context

This chapter describes a multi-faceted piece of collaborative clinical work and research. It involves the two authors – Céline, a dance movement psychotherapist, and Diana, a music therapist – and three volunteer co-workers with varied experience of the arts therapies: Sophie, a recently qualified art psychotherapist; Janet, a dance movement therapist from overseas; and Mariska, a musician with an interest in music therapy. At the heart of this collaboration was an eight-month music and dance movement psychotherapy group offered to ten clients with learning disabilities within a day centre.

The research sought to investigate how we identify and think about meaning in the clinical work, and enabled us to reflect in some detail on this multi-layered collaborative process. In the therapeutic work with clients who have limited or no verbal language, the question of 'meaning-making' is ever present. These clients communicate their experiences in many and varied ways, often very skilfully and precisely, but the onus tends to fall on the partner in the dialogue to carefully consider and question what the communication underlying a particular behaviour may be. Creative therapeutic work invites and supports this level of non-verbal communication (Watson, 2007; Chesner, 1995; Adler, 2003).

The research followed a phenomenological methodology involving the analysis of transcripts of two focus groups attended by the therapy team. It incorporated an ongoing self-reflective process, including personal diary entries and discussions between the researchers, as encouraged by a heuristic framework (Moustakas, 1994). Quotations from the two focus groups are referenced here as FG1/FG2, followed by the research participant's initial and line number, e.g. FG1C: 230.

This chapter highlights themes that emerged from the research pertaining to experiences of collaboration, and the function of the co-working team in creating facilitative structures and a mindful culture around the work.

The therapy group

The group was established specifically for people who showed ambivalence towards making and sustaining relationships. Our use of this term was rooted in the psychoanalytic understanding of ambivalence as having co-existing 'contradictory impulses and emotions towards the same object' (Rycroft, 1995: 6).

The therapy group was deliberately located in a large communal hall in order to include individuals who did not readily move from this room during their time at the centre, but had shown interest in other creative and therapeutic groups which had previously taken place around them. Others who were referred also showed curiosity towards events happening around them, but had difficulty in sustaining engagement – some tending to place themselves on the edges, but backing away when invited to participate more directly; some observing at a distance; whilst others would move between extremes of participation and withdrawal. One member of the group had good verbal language, though was often withdrawn and silent; another was selectively mute; others had limited ability to communicate verbally; whilst about half of the members did not use words. Three members of the group were wheelchair users, the others ambulant.

Our primary intention was to establish a creative therapeutic environment within which people would have the freedom to move comfortably between engagement and withdrawal. Our intention was to support clients in understanding the implications of the choices that they made, and develop their capacity for interaction with others. We hoped that participants would gain an increased awareness of themselves and others around them, and that the group might enable playful exploration of the 'space between' (Winnicott, 1971), which might build bridges between self and other, and lead to a reduction of distress in other social situations.

As this space became established we were able to see and think more in terms of 'coming and going', in place of the dichotomy of ambivalence; this became the lens through which we then viewed the work: a shift in perspective made possible as we therapeutically supported the many movements in and out of differing qualities and degrees of relatedness, through dance, movement, music and sounds.

The team

There was a willingness in the team to explore unknown territory and to engage in a personal process of growth and learning from one another and the clients, as well as a generosity in the sharing of our own unique perspectives and insights.

It's been a kind of an evolving journey really in developing collaborative working.

FG1D: 44–46

I feel that we've come together quite organically and also set up some really strong boundaries, a really strong frame for the clients.

FG1S: 348–350

To support the co-working and inform the self-reflective research process, we established a debrief time following each group session. We would first take 10–15 minutes to individually process and reflect on our experiences in the therapy group (including the use of art, music or movement), then complete forms to describe moments in the session we identified as significant. Finally we reflected freely together on the group. In addition we aimed to meet for a 10–25-minute check-in at the start of the morning, before setting up for the group.

Boundaries for freedom: structures around the work

Collaboration: a multi-layered process of holding together

We identified multiple levels of collaborative processes. These included relating each to our self, the development of relationships with clients and with one another in the co-working team, and the facilitated interactions between clients in the group. Collaboration was also evident in our close work with staff who support clients in the different parts of the day centre, and extended into our roles beyond the group as colleagues within a wider multi-disciplinary team (Fig. 5.1).

Spaces within spaces and permeability of boundaries

Spaces which 'held' the group can be objectively located within the external environment, whilst others are more subjective and less visible. In the focus groups these formations and processes were identified as having a vital role in supporting the clinical work. The many experiences of 'coming and going' were held within these levels of space within space, evocative of the 'body, space and world of a person' elaborated upon by Thomas Fuchs (2007: 424).

The use of the hall – the being in and shaping of the physical space – was one fundamental aspect of the holding of the group (Fig. 5.1, points 2–4). Within this tangible space, three types of structures are recognisable:

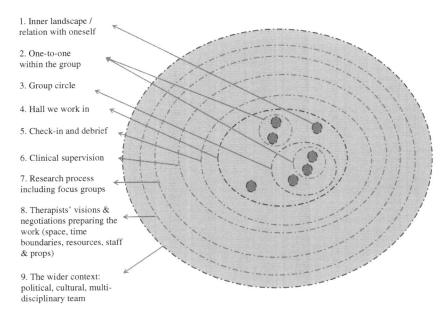

1. Inner landscape / relation with oneself

2. One-to-one within the group

3. Group circle

4. Hall we work in

5. Check-in and debrief

6. Clinical supervision

7. Research process including focus groups

8. Therapists' visions & negotiations preparing the work (space, time boundaries, resources, staff & props)

9. The wider context: political, cultural, multi-disciplinary team

FIGURE 5.1 Different levels of holding

1   A scattered beginning which consists of arriving to self (Fig. 5.1, points 1–3). During this time, the facilitators invite attention to self from wherever one is. Dyads and smaller sub-group formations may emerge and dissolve, but there is no particular invitation to gravitate towards another or to go anywhere specific in the room. It is only gradually that the facilitators invite the group to come closer together. The therapeutic intention is to offer acceptance of different sounds, rhythms, postures and places where one would sit, move or stand. This theme of acceptance was repeatedly raised in the focus group discussions. For example, Sophie spoke of her experience of a generosity and acceptance within the team which enabled us to come together strongly and work effectively in ways that might have been unfamiliar (FG2S: 787–800).

2   The traditional circle formation of so many therapy groups (Fig. 5.1, point 3). This circle within the hall created a stronger focus for the group: establishing qualities of being 'inside' and 'outside' of the circle and offering opportunities for people to explore different ways of relating with the sense of a group. This core circle within the room was there every week. It was created at the start and dismantled at the end of each session, offering a visual marker for all to recognise that for the duration of the therapy session the hall had been transformed into another type of space. It seemed to help establish cohesion between some members of the group, particularly in the early 'forming' stages (Tuckman, 1968). Some, including members of the team, experienced it as a 'secure base' (Bowlby, 1988) from which it was possible to explore and reach out more widely. For some it invited curiosity and movement towards others.

However we also recognise that for others whose familiar place in this room was outside of this territory, the circle may have felt exclusive or threatening.

3   The third is a coming together of both the above structures as they form and transform. We were always aware of those on the edges, within the wider space, those who were not present, and those who may have felt excluded by the power of the circle. We allowed ourselves to move, to varying degrees, in and out of the circle, into the wider space within the room. Music and props, too, bridged the gap, connecting across space as sounds were acknowledged and supported, and objects offered a visual and sometimes tangible link between individuals on the edges of the room and those in the inner circle. Over time the boundaries of the work seemed to expand and to enable more movement in and out of the inner circle, towards and away from the edges. These boundaries had both strength and flexibility; they sustained inclusion and presence as well as a strong awareness and tolerance of who and what was absent (Fig. 5.1, point 4). As Best states, 'to view participants within a colla-boration as mutually influencing the system can facilitate ongoing creative dialogue in a way that defining territory as either/or may not' (2000: 200).

Two of the group members drew similar images as a response to their experi-ences within the group: 'squiggles' that offer a truthful depiction of the free movement and fluidity within the sessions, represented more neatly in Fig. 5.1.

FIGURE 5.2 Sophie's drawing

FIGURE 5.3 Diana's drawing

Structures holding the team

The team members identified the check-in and debrief times as particularly important in enabling the therapeutic work (Fig. 5.1, point 5). The check-in was experienced as a valuable opportunity to acknowledge ourselves and one another so we were better able to give and receive support.

> There was an acknowledgement about where we were at, at that particular moment, and so we were aware of each other's … place in our lives … it was really, really important and I valued that very much.
>
> *FG2S: 590–598*

> And mindfully parking whatever is going on for you, parking it, so that we didn't bring it, … we were able to support each other even if … you could see one of us was struggling, there was still that support there. (others acknowledge)
>
> *FG2M: 606–611*

The debrief was experienced as essential, and Janet went so far as to say that the clinical work could not have happened without the honest sharing that took place within the team during these times (FG2J: 579).

The focus groups (Fig. 5.1, point 7), though outside of the therapeutic work itself, were also identified as contributing significantly to the collaborative process, described by Sophie as a 'time of really concentrated thinking and reflecting' (FG2S: 790–791).

Holding polarities and opposites

In considering the therapeutic frame around this group, we recognised that the paradoxical quality of therapeutic boundaries that offer edges and permit expansion was experienced particularly vividly and tangibly in this group:

> You've set up a structure that enables unpredictability.
>
> *FG1M: 1219–1220*

> It's about the structure then holding the space for things to emerge at so many different levels.
>
> *FG2D: 621–622*

> At the very beginning of our group, the holding was very strong … as a way for the client and possibly for us to be explorative … but I think towards the end those boundaries were very strong but they were able to be more malleable and … possibly more loose.
>
> *FG2S: 241–247*

The quality of the work allowed something to emerge that could not be forced. The fundamental boundaries of time, location and co-working team were set, yet we could not force a 'coming together' to happen. If 'coming together' was indeed one of the therapeutic aims, we had to let this 'with-ness' emerge.

> I guess my aim often is to try and arrive to meet … these clients, wherever they're at, whatever that is, and sometimes I haven't got a clue how I'm going to find that … and actually the whole point is … I've so enjoyed staying in the (gasp) (sings) I'm just about to do something! And playing with it.
>
> *FG1C: 485–498*

Therapeutic holding in this context can be understood as the holding together of polarising preferences by different group members, as well as those within an individual.

> This environment of 'anything's okay' was created and established from the get-go. I think that people naturally would have felt more comfortable and confident … because they knew that they were going to be held and supported.
>
> *FG2M: 79–83*

> His sounds were really connected with his deeper self and I think he was able to, touch that place within himself because of the holding of the group and the safety of the group.
>
> *FG2S: 104–107*

Responses to individuals within the group context facilitated a reaching across to each other: through the throw of a stretchy body band for example, or by the sound of the harp reflecting somebody's mood or rhythmic movement to the whole group. In these ways, new pathways were created which could bring participants together, and make differences and divergent experiences bearable.

Collaboration enabling new perspectives and experiences

Through meeting and responding to one another at all these levels (Fig. 5.1), our initial perspectives and stance towards the work transformed. For example, several members of the team described how, as the holding structures around the group became established, they were able to step back from an initial inclination to focus primarily on perceived 'positive' changes in clients and expectations for particular forms of responsiveness, and observe and see things 'for what they are', so that 'whatever happens can be present' (FG1D: 248, 252–253). Diana described her sense that this had happened especially easily in this group, and attributed this to the strength of the co-working, sharing her experience that, in being able to jointly hold this open and accepting stance, she felt a sense of ease, with neither a strong expectation or desire for particular events to occur, nor any great sense of surprise when something new occurred, akin to Bion's (1967) exhortation that therapists should approach each session 'without memory or desire'. Others also spoke of a sense of ease, and words like 'natural', 'fluid' and 'organic' were frequently used.

> There's something … that has just felt very natural and very organic … just the way as a team we've come together and been developing our co-working in a way that … the clients have brought themselves to the process.
>
> *FG1D: 251–267*

Céline spoke of how she was able, with one particular client, to shift from expecting a move from withdrawal into shared activity, to remaining with the client's experience of being on the verge of something which may or may not emerge. She described how both she and the client were then able to discover a playful quality, dancing around the question, 'maybe? maybe not?' (FG1C: 498–505). This openness to the possibility of something emergent, without knowing or even holding a strong expectation for exactly what this might be, seemed an important precursor to change in the group, reflective of Beisser's 'paradoxical theory of change', 'that change occurs when one becomes what he is, not when he tries to become what he is not' (Beisser, 1970). And as music therapist Alison Levinge (2015) describes, it is possible within the creative medium (Levinge referring specifically to music) for individuals to both reveal something of themselves and to remain hidden at the same time.

Several of the team spoke of encountering particular qualities of seeing, such as both Sophie and Céline commenting on the value of witnessing (FG1C: 103, FG1S: 407–414), and Diana developing a metaphor of 'seeing beneath a veil' from an experience within a session in which members of the team and clients had together lifted and lowered a cloth (FG1D: 1073–1082): it is only together that the veil can be lifted, as such an act is much harder to perform on one's own. This metaphor highlights the value of the collaborative work between both facilitators and clients as that which enabled this 'seeing' to happen. Barwick highlights the value of a therapeutic group in providing 'constant exposure to reported and enacted different ways of seeing, being and doing' (2014: 46), and emphasises that in order to be able to 'bear witness' we must also be able to bear exclusion and difference (ibid: 44).

Questions and anxieties around meaning and purpose within the work were explored, and we reflected on how our different individual intentions and values towards the work, and decisions about what is meaningful, might meet those of one another, becoming distilled into a shared purpose (FG1M,C,S&D: 1119–1193). These points of meeting were also experienced as challenging, giving rise to uncomfortable questions at times. As Watson emphasises 'it can be challenging for workers to examine their valued beliefs and to accept new values and theories in order to engage in a meaningful way with colleagues in collaborative work' (2008: 99). For example, Mariska described a tension between the therapeutic culture of acceptance and a more familiar target-driven approach to work and life (FG1M: 626–627). Some discomfort was also expressed around possible expectations and perceptions of the work from those in the wider cultural and political context (Fig. 5.1, point 9), perhaps reflecting our own anxieties about the value and purpose of this piece of work (FG1C,S&D: 1153–1264), and tapping into some challenging deeply-rooted social dynamics around value and exclusion in relation to disability (Sinason, 1992).

Holding on and letting go: finding, losing and re-finding

The theme of 'holding on to self' whilst relating to other is a core theme of therapeutic practice and of healthy relationships in general, yet growth and transformation includes a need to also let go. Through the work we witnessed the ebb and flow of these two fundamental processes.

> It's like the diversity and the (J:convergence), convergence, yeah.
>
> *(FG2D&J: 863–865)*

Experiences of 'losing and finding' notably included the literal experience of Céline leaving to have a baby, midway through the group. Strong expressions of anxiety within the group as Céline's impending departure approached were met sensitively as they arose. This gave way to a surge of new energy when the group returned after a break following this loss. The remaining members of the team described feeling surprised by this, and experiencing joy, relief and a sense of newness. Had the group been able to find a resilience, perhaps, a capacity to face the pain of loss, and to discover they could survive and become something new? The team described how they developed new ways of working together. Later, as the group came to its second ending and closure, the experience of absence and loss became prominent again, with literal absences and experiences of fragmentation in the group, alongside some strong manifestations of attachment to the group.

> When the goodbye happened, I really understood, 'ah, there's a lot of wisdom in this preparation process'… and I think we were okay.
> *FG2M: 385–387*

> And yet today I feel there is an absence… it's quite (J: quite emotional) yeah quite emotional.
> *FG2S: 394,403, FG2J: 402–403*

> I had this real sense though that it was ready to finish.
> *FG2M: 470–471*

For some in the team there was a need to 'let go' of certain preconceptions or assumptions about the nature of therapeutic change in order to embrace a new way of working with people. For others the therapeutic approach was much more familiar. Yet familiarity, too, breeds assumptions, and both the clinical work and the research demanded of all of us a certain willingness to let go of preconceived ideas and maintain an openness to exploring experience, as it presented itself.

> I'm learning so much. … not to assume that where I want to be is where someone else wants to be … we can so easily, I think, get caught into only seeing the world through our own eyes and … this client group is unforgiving for it.
> *FG1C: 465–477*

All the members of the team spoke in some way of experiences of losing, letting go or stepping away in order to find or re-find something important. Sophie spoke of needing to create time in the debrief to step away from the group into her own creative process, so she was then able to re-engage in thinking about the group, and when, for a while, this non-verbal processing time was overlooked, it was important for her to reclaim it. Mariska discovered a need to step back at times from trying too hard to make her experiences 'mean something' (FG1M: 594–596), whilst Janet spoke of re-finding and re-learning something she had known before: a value in 'being' rather than 'doing' (FG2J: 215–225). Notably, in the conversation within both focus groups there were times of losing and finding words which seemed to parallel a wider process, and experiences of losing and finding meaning and understanding were described at all the levels of the work, as identified in Fig. 5.1. This is an important theme in much therapy practice and supervision, where we often find ourselves having to let go of what we know or think we know, in order to find afresh what the clients need us to know, described by Mollon (1997) as a process of dreaming and waking up, creating a space to think. Perhaps there is also a qualitative change in what is then 're-found', as it is rediscovered and owned in a new, more conscious way. Roman (2016) emphasises the necessity of being able to relate to our clients from a position of not knowing or understanding. This not only allows for the clients' own experiences of not knowing or understanding to be accepted and worked with (a particularly prominent theme in work with people with learning disabilities), but also is a foundation for genuine interrelatedness with the – in some sense always unknowable – 'other'. Best also states that 'doubt ... framed as curiosity and suspense can be a powerful ally in researching one's practice' (2000: 198).

The focus group discussions explored qualities of recognising, owning and naming what we bring and where we stand, sometimes doing so in order to set it aside, sometimes in order to hold it more strongly, for the benefit of clients or for our own protection. Here we are elucidating that alongside this 'letting go' is also the experience of holding on: to therapeutic boundaries or personal preferences and needs. An example of this was identified by Mariska when she felt the need to say 'no' to a client who wanted to touch her with dirty hands. This raised some uncomfortable feelings for her, which she was able to own, as well as thinking about how the client may have experienced this encounter (FG1M: 163–207).

There were difficult moments between co-workers, too, and being able to question and challenge one another, as well as to be with one another's differences, was identified as essential to the work. Janet, for example, commented on an occasion in the debrief when another team member questioned a position she had been taking within a session, which enabled her to reflect on and adapt her practice (FG2J: 579–587). This capacity to tolerate difference was described by Mariska as something 'quite extraordinary' (FG2M: 563, 556), revealing for her a new possibility in team working.

In co-working as well as in working with clients we come up against edges in ourselves and in one another; hard and painful places, which can also become sources of transformation and growth. These two strands are also inherent in our research, where the phenomenological approach requires us to both own and make use of our personal perspectives, and to set them aside in order to focus on the meaning emerging from within another experience (Smith, Flowers and Larkin, 2009). The fact that we are researching our own experience, alongside that of others, has brought these together in a particularly vivid way.

Collaboration and collusion

The Collins English Dictionary gives three meanings to the word 'collaboration'; the first two pertain to the act of joint working or the product created from it. The third, however, is defined as 'the act of cooperating as a traitor, especially with an enemy occupying one's own country' (Collaboration, Collins English Dictionary Online). This 'treacherous' underside of collaboration reared itself when we, at times, fell into a joint collusion with a shared 'blind spot': moments when we missed, avoided or lost sight of something together. With another three co-facilitators and co-researchers, such collusion became harder as the team fostered a broader attention to the complexity of experience and plurality of meaning-making. This seemed to increase our capacity to notice and meet the diverse experiences of clients, and to hold these together in ways that could be witnessed and experienced by ourselves and the group members.

Together in stillness

A significant part of the process was our engagement with a particular form of presence in stillness (or apparent stillness), one in which the facilitator's 'sensors' were attuned to the group or a particular individual, attending to the resonances of this particular moment and encounter, first within themselves, then in time constructing a relational response. A 'therapist à l'écoute' as Sophie described, 'really listening to all that is happening at the same time… I almost feel it at a body level, you know, that sense of movement' (FG2: 319). Therapists from various disciplines have sought to describe the complexity and richness of such an embodied form of presence, with language such as 'standing on perceptive tip-toe' (Cox and Theilgard, 1987, cited in Steele, 1988: 3), and as 'compassionate presence', through which 'one learns to trust the not-knowing, not-doing, the empty space, the silence, the spaciousness of no-thing, making space for all things, for wholeness' (Lavendel, 2016).

At the end of many sessions there was a moment of suspense when we were all quiet and still, a magical and peaceful quality, something spiritual even that we all chose to stay with, if only for a few seconds. Having improvised together, come closer to ourselves and one another, in chaos and harmony; having heard that deep resonance that certain sounds made within, seen the ripples of a scarf wafting in the air, perhaps felt its touch, or heard the sounding of a bell; having given me, you and ourselves permission to be with this or that, we had fuelled something more fluid and full of possibilities (as depicted in Fig. 5.2 and 5.3 above). These were experienced as powerful intersubjective 'present moments' of the kind identified by Stern (2004) as central to the process of psychotherapy; moments of encountering something bigger than 'I', and embodying our collective psyche, as discussed at length in the Authentic Movement literature (Lavendel, 2016; Carroll, n.d.; Adler, 1999).

Conclusion

The dynamic of 'coming and going' was held at many levels in this piece of work. Becoming able to not only tolerate but value these movements 'in and out' for ourselves, enabled us to hold this perspective within and with the group. From this point, each step in or out became a step into the dance of the relationship, a movement towards or away, forming a myriad of phrases which ebb and flow, crescendo and diminuendo in the ever-evolving music of this co-created dance.

Improvised music and movement can offer a unique intermediary platform, a 'space between', an inquisitive, process-oriented attention to being who we are in movement or stillness, distinct from a goal or performance-oriented attitude. In the context of our therapy group, this stance facilitated new perspectives and experiences, a shift beyond perceived limitations. The choice made by the team members to adopt attitudes towards the work of welcoming exploration, introspection and tolerance, enabled the emergence of new meaning through the application of a gentle, inquisitive and supportive quality of presence to every moment.

Researching our collaborative practice with this client group led us to our own perceived limitations and areas of blindness, to question our beliefs and assumptions and redefine ideas of normalcy. We reflected on three possible options when working with individuals with severe learning disabilities for whom the expression of preferences may not be filtered by social norms, and for whom expressing one's self is predominantly an embodied and vocal process:

1   *Impose* our view, our way, talk at them and pull them where we want them to be.
2   *Surrender* and let them do as they please with no attempt to cultivate reciprocity, thus denying the possibility of a dynamic relationship.
3   *Compose* or seek to collaborate, to enter into a rapport that values their and our vocal and movement preferences.

Through the clinical group work, the research and co-authoring processes, we have met our own and each other's edges inquisitively. In so doing we have encountered the fragile, tenuous, enriching, enlivening and life-transforming potential inherent in consciously and mindfully turning towards collaboration.

References

Adler, J. (1999). The Collective Body in Authentic Movement. In: P. Pallaro, ed., *Authentic Movement: Essays by Mary Stark Whitehouse, Janet Adler and Joan Chodorow*. Vol. 1, 1st ed. Philadelphia: Jessica Kingsley, pp. 190–207.

Adler, J. (2003). American Dance Therapy Association 27th Annual Conference Keynote Address. From Autism to the Discipline of Authentic Movement. *American Journal of Dance Therapy*, 25(1), pp. 5–16.

Barwick, N. (2014). Core Concepts in Group Analysis: What Goes On in Groups? (Part 2). In: A. Davies, E. Richards and N. Barwick, eds., *Group Music Therapy: A Group Analytic Approach*, 1st ed. London: Routledge, pp. 36–47.

Beisser, A. (1970). *The Paradoxical Theory of Change*. [online] Available at: http://www.gestalt.org/arnie.htm [Accessed 30 July 2016].

Best, P. (2000). Theoretical Diversity and Clinical Collaboration: Reflections by a Dance/Movement Therapist. *The Arts in Psychotherapy*, 27(3), pp. 197–211.

Bion, W.R. (1967). Notes on Memory and Desire. *The Psychoanalytic Forum*, 2(3), pp. 271–280.

Bowlby, J. (1988). *A Secure Base: Clinical Applications of Attachment Theory*. London: Routledge.

Carroll, R. (n.d.). Authentic Movement: Embodying the Individual and the Collective Psyche. Essay published before 2004. [online] Available at: http://www.thinkbody.co.uk/papers/embodying.htmm [Accessed 31 Aug 2016].

Chesner, A. (1995). *Dramatherapy for People with Learning Disabilities: A World of Difference.* London: Jessica Kingsley.

Collins English Dictionary – Complete & Unabridged 10th Edition. [online] Available at: http://dictionary.reference.com/browse/collaboration [Accessed 30 Jan 2016].

Dance Therapy and Authentic Movement: Looking for Me. (1968). [film] Films Media Group, New York: Janet Adler. [online] Film Preview Available at: http://www.films.com/ecTitleDetail.aspx?TitleID=28215 [Accessed 15 Aug 2016].

Fuchs, T. (2007). Psychotherapy of the Lived Space: A Phenomenological and Ecological Concept. *American Journal of Psychotherapy*, 61(4), pp. 423–439.

Lavendel, F. (2016). Healing into Wholeness: Psychotherapy Practice Informed by the Discipline of Authentic Movement. *Body, Movement and Dance in Psychotherapy*, 0(0), pp. 1–12. [online] Available at: www.tandfonline.com [Accessed 15 Oct 2016].

Levinge, A. (2015). *The Music of Being: Music Therapy, Winnicott and the School of Object Relations.* London: Jessica Kingsley Publishers.

Mollon, P. (1997). Supervision as a Space for Thinking. In G. Shipton, ed., *Supervision of Psychotherapy and Counselling: Making a Place to Think*, 1st ed. Buckingham: Open University Press, pp. 24–34.

Moustakas, C. (1994). *Phenomenological Research Methods.* London: Sage.

Roman, T. (2016). 'Were They Better Today?' Valuing a Client's Individual Therapeutic Process within an Institution's Expectation of Positive Progress and Predictable Outcomes. *British Journal of Music Therapy*, 30(1), pp. 13–21.

Rycroft, C. (1995). *A Critical Dictionary of Psychoanalysis.* London: Penguin Books.

Sinason, V. (1992). *Mental Handicap and the Human Condition.* London: Free Association Books.

Smith, J.A., Flowers, P. and Larkin, M. (2009). *Interpretative Phenomenological Analysis.* London: Sage.

Steele, P. (1988). Foreword. *Journal of British Music Therapy*, 2(2), pp. 3–4.

Stern, D. (2004). *The Present Moment in Psychotherapy and Everyday Life.* New York: Norton.

Tuckman, B.W. (1968). Developmental Sequences in Small Groups. *Psychological Bulletin*, 63(3), pp. 387–399.

Watson, T. (2007). Music Therapy with Adults with Learning Disabilities: Sharing Stories. In: T. Watson, ed., *Music Therapy with Adults with Learning Disabilities*, 1st ed. London: Routledge, pp. 18–32.

Watson, T. (2008). Collaboration in Music Therapy with Adults with Learning Disabilities. In: K. Twyford and T. Watson, eds., *Integrated Team Working: Music Therapy as Part of Transdisciplinary and Collaborative Approaches*, 1st ed. London: Jessica Kingsley Publishers, pp. 91–123.

Winnicott, D.W. (1971). *Playing and Reality.* London: Psychology Press.

6

STRETCH MARKS

An exploration of a joint dramatherapy and music therapy group

Gillian Downie & Robin Wiltshire

Setting the scene: our emerging differences

GILLIAN: "Robin, can you help me with this scenery? We need to get set up. The chapter is due in soon!"

ROBIN: "We need to think about where we are going to put everything first, Gillian! Stop rushing ahead!"

GILLIAN: "Well, we can try out different ways of arranging it once it is on stage. We can play around with different ideas."

ROBIN: "*I like the idea of playing – but I would like to think about how it would look first. . . .*"

The dialogue above illustrates our differences. We found our shared playfulness became a starting point for our collaboration. As therapists we bring our whole selves to our work. How we are in the world impacts on the relationships we co-create with our clients and colleagues.

This chapter explores our experiences of co-facilitating a music therapy and dramatherapy cross-modality group for adults with a learning disability. We will share our rationale for the group, our different professional approaches and the ways we have worked collaboratively in using the modalities to support the group, particularly in exploring and stretching aspects of themselves.

We conclude with some thoughts around the liminal space in the context of this group and our joint working relationship.

Rationale for the group

We have both worked in learning disabilities for many years. Using our individual modalities we have noticed that over time the ability of clients to stay with emotions, sensations, thoughts and imagination can be 'stretched'. This includes stretching their quality of presence, their capacity for emotional regulation, their awareness of the present moment and their ability to be creative and enter the imagined space. We have noticed that regardless of someone's intellectual ability, their emotional structure and capacity remains intact (Sinason, 1992: 74).

We were curious to discover whether finding ways to integrate our approaches of dramatherapy and music therapy would enhance or complement this 'stretching', and interested to explore what supports clients to stay in the moment within each modality. Stern (2004: 65) highlights 'our capacities for cross-modal translation', and we were keen to explore this further.

Our backgrounds – similarities and differences

We have worked in the same arts therapies service for adults with learning disabilities within the National Health Service (NHS) for the past five years, and are in the same supervision group. For the past three years we have explored the integration of music and drama theatrically in our playback theatre[1] company and wanted to use our experience of working together in this way in the therapy group.

We differ in the way we facilitate groups: Gillian uses the ritualised structure of the Sesame Approach,[2] drawing from Jungian and Gestalt theories, while Robin's approach, informed by a psychodynamic framework, is open-ended and unstructured, taking its lead from the group. Our challenge was to find a way of offering both approaches without compromising either. Our hope was to utilise music and drama modalities equally, and meet the needs of clients in new ways.

Group structure: finding a way to collaborate

We set up the new group to run for an hour a week on an ongoing basis, with four clients. To begin with we used the Sesame structure and found that clients primarily engaged with the drama, whilst the music receded into the background. On reflection, we decided to create a space at the beginning where clients could freely improvise in music-making, which we named the Overture. This introduced them to using instruments, which supported them musically during later enactments of stories and at other points during the session. In this way we expanded our structure to include music therapy and dramatherapy more equally. Our structure was as follows:

Overture: Shared group music improvisations. This provided a non-verbal emotional barometer for the group. The quality of the musical relating seemed to be an indicator to the emerging themes developing as part of the group's process.
Warm up: Physical movement through games. Sometimes these included music and sound. They had a psychological connection to the themes emerging from the Overture and the developing group process.
Bridge in: The *bridge in* supported the themes of the story that linked with the group process. Movement, sound, mime, objects and play were used, often in the form of a ritual.

Main event: Enactment of a traditional story through movement and musical improvisation. The key role of the music was to amplify and support the emerging emotional qualities evolving in the enactment. The role of the drama offered an experience of embodiment, a felt sense of accessing the archetypes in the story. Both drama and music provided self-expression, holding and attunement.

Bridge out: Reflection on what emerged for clients during the session, through movement, music and/or words.

Ending: This included grounding, coming back into the here and now and a hand ritual.

This structure was used with flexibility and adapted to the needs of the group.

Introducing the group members

We have chosen to focus on two clients in this chapter. We will introduce Sarah and Tim, and share our clinical thinking and discussion. We write with a sense of respect for our clients, their process and their generosity in giving permission to include them in this chapter.

Sarah

Sarah was described in the referral as being unable to stand up for herself, and found relationships challenging. She isolated herself, and had anxiety about mixing with others. Her verbal communication was limited, and she tended to reply with stock phrases.

Vignette

Sarah's first session, ten weeks after the others had started the group

Sarah arrived carrying a guitar. She told us she was unable to stay for long, and none of the staff expected her to. We began by playing a ball game (she had prior experience of basketball) and noticed that she seemed to need to feel in control, telling people who to throw the ball to, and how. This need for control seemed to be also reflected in her bringing her guitar, which was the only instrument she used initially. It seemed that safety was important for Sarah. When we used imagination, she sat out, but found a role using her guitar to musically accompany the story.

To support our thinking around Sarah, Gillian brought in Greenberg's work on diagnosis. Our aim was not to use diagnoses rigidly, but to refer to them to help us think about our interactions with clients. Greenberg (1998/1975:4) warns that many people 'can have a sudden therapeutic reaction which can sometimes be avoided by a little forethought about the issues the person is dealing with.' Our reflections drew us to Greenberg's work on schizoid adaptations, where safety is a primary concern: 'To protect themselves, they have learned to construct a well-functioning public façade to hide their real self so deep inside them that even they sometimes cannot reach it' (Greenberg, 1998: 31). Sarah's way of using control in the early sessions appeared to indicate this. Greenberg (1998: 32) says that clients with schizoid adaptations have difficulties with trust, safety and intrusiveness. It was therefore important that we were predictable, so she would feel safer knowing what to expect from us. The structure of the sessions was a good way of offering this predictability.

Robin was also curious about Sarah's guitar and what she was communicating to the group by bringing it. It not only seemed to provide her with an aspect of control, but brought something of her life outside into the group, and appeared to offer her support and ease her anxiety. Sarah's use of her guitar reminded us of Winnicott's (2005) ideas around transitional objects.

Tim

Tim was referred for therapy to support his sense of identity, and address his high levels of anxiety and difficulties in relationships. Our initial experience of him was of an articulate person who was highly observant and liked to make connections. For example, he regularly commented on how the *bridge in* linked with the story; perhaps analysing the material supported him to feel safe. He also made observations about other group members, praising their achievements.

He appeared to idealise one group member in particular, constantly naming what was special about them. This led Gillian to Greenberg's writing on closet narcissism (2013: 63), where she describes how people hide their need to be special, associating this 'specialness' with an idealised other. Tim's ability to articulate what he appreciated in others seemed to raise his self-esteem. It seemed hard for him to appreciate his own worth. Greenberg says people with this adaptation can feel very unsafe when focusing on their own qualities and achievements (2013: 70). We sensed that Tim's self-esteem was fragile, and knew we had to work carefully around supporting him to own his positive qualities.

Robin was curious about Tim's anxiety, remembering Haque's (2009: 145) comments about how our differences as people can engender a sense of anxiety. He wondered about Tim's sense of self and his need to merge with others. We were reminded of Winnicott's (2005: 150) ideas around 'the separating-off of the not-me from the me' and thought of ways to support him to recognise his own qualities and differences in relation to self and other group members.

How we used the modalities to support 'stretching'

The cross-modality structure, and her previous associations with them (basketball and guitar), helped Sarah stay with her weekly therapy for the full hour, and appeared to offer her some sense of control and predictability. Over time she became involved in the drama games and musical improvisations using her guitar, and stretched the expectations of herself, staff and health professionals by staying and engaging in the sessions. In the early stages of therapy she seemed fearful of entering the imagined space offered in dramatherapy, through improvisations and story enactments. As therapy progressed she began to listen attentively to the stories and seemed enthralled by them, often using fabrics to set up the story-space, and sitting to one side with her guitar while the rest of the group enacted the story.

Stretching Sarah's ability to use the imaginative space

As dramatherapist, Gillian told the first part of *The Snow Queen*, and Sarah said she would try being the angel in the sky, with Robin's support. He supported her to choose instruments and fabrics to create the 'heavens'. She was able to play the wind chimes and glockenspiel while the goblin climbed towards her and fell slowly from the sky. The combination of using music and drama supported her to enter the imagined space, and play instruments other than her guitar. Through trying out new ways of being in the group, she was 'stretched' psychologically.

Her growth has seen a shift in her role within the group and use of music. At first, her music consisted of short surges of guitar-playing, when she would strum her guitar using open-strings, playing increasingly vigorously. These musical episodes often seemed random, and disconnected from the group's growing musical improvisation. It was almost as if she was communicating through the music, 'Here I am, what you going to do about it?' Sarah's short, abrupt musical episodes reminded Robin of Winnicott's (2005) theories relating to use of an object. Was Sarah's music her way of testing whether the group could survive her musical attacks? There seemed to be parallels to her need for control observed in the initial ball game.

By the group matching and attuning to these surges, the quality of her music changed over the weeks. It developed a rhythmic and melodic structure, and she started to use a range of different instruments including drums, cymbals, glockenspiel and xylophone. Her surges expanded to include musical phrases which became more connected and sensitive to the group's musical and dramatic improvisation. From being on the edge of the group, she grew to take a more central and integrated role. Rather than feeling the need to dominate the group improvisations, she appeared increasingly open to hearing the music of others, and this enabled her to build relationships and make an attachment to the group. It seemed that Sarah had been supported to self-regulate through the group's ability to regulate itself, providing a safe environment for a secure attachment to develop (Schumacher, 2014).

Offering Tim further holding through music

Gillian told the first part of *Jack and the Beanstalk*, where the giant in the village killed Jack's father out of jealousy, capturing the baby Jack and his mother. We enacted the story using non-verbal movement and sound. Tim chose to be Jack, and seemed to enjoy becoming a baby. He chose to lie on cushions curled up, while Robin – as his father – mimed preparing him food, and Gillian – as his mother – mimed feeding him. We sensed that this nurturing act was a tender enactment, with early reparative work. It was further 'stretched' by Robin providing music, while Tim and Gillian held hands, spun round and danced, escaping from the land where the giant was. As we spun, 'Jack' grew up in age.

In the *bridge out*, Tim said he'd loved the spinning, and felt like he'd grown up in the story. This transition from identifying with the child archetype to the young man seemed to resonate with him. Although the story, with its embodiment of child and growth, seemed healing in itself, introducing improvised music attuned to the feeling-quality present within the enactment. The music seemed to offer Tim further holding, supporting him to stay in the present and with his feelings of loss. There was an intimacy between mother (therapist) and son (client) that was sustained with Tim, a client who seemed to find focusing on his own process challenging.

Our experience of using drama and music cross-modally appeared to stretch Sarah's and Tim's capacity to stay with the moment, and stay in relation to the group. Their experiences would seem to support Stern's (2004: 65) ideas around our ability for cross-modal translation, and how the 'vitality affect' from separate modalities can connect to one another, in this case music to drama or vice versa. As a result of their cross-modal experiences, both Sarah and Tim seemed to experience a stretching of their intersubjective field (Stern, 2004: 152). As this field becomes larger, 'new paths for explicit exploration open up' (Stern, 2004: 152) and the therapeutic relationship changes. Sarah and Tim experienced new ways of relating in the group which we hope they can take into their everyday life.

We noticed how integrating music and drama offered an extra layer of containment and holding for the group and the feelings present within it. We believe that this has enabled a stretching of imagination, an increased ability to be present in the moment and a sense of group cohesion.

Working with difference across modalities

In this section we look at how we have worked with difference through the modalities, and how we used the modalities to support people to be with their difference. In thinking about this, Robin was reminded of Dalal's assertion: 'Never forget that I am the same as you, and never forget that I am different from you' (Dalal, 2011: 241). We contribute different ideas on what might interrupt clients' ability to stay with difference. Gillian explores the phenomenon of shame, and Robin considers anxiety.

Tim tended to be confluent with others, changing his description of his experience if he picked up any differences in opinion. His verbal contributions revolved around affirming others. This seemed to be his way of hiding, yet resulted in a sense of inferiority. This narcissistic wound has its source in shame (Kaufman, 1989: 25). Although shame can be useful, in that it can alert us to issues in the ways we relate to others, when extreme, shame can be paralysing. Kaufman (1989: 18) describes the effects of shame as a tortuous process, as we critically scrutinise every infinitesimal aspect of our being. As humans, we adapt our ways of being to avoid shame. Tim's deflection from self could indicate that he avoided shame by sacrificing his needs and desires, thus not developing his identity to his full potential. Perhaps in his history, difference was not valued.

Drama was Tim's strongest modality, and the oblique nature of the work appeared to support him. Tim often chose main parts, and used these to explore feelings which he might not be able to express directly. 'The 'as if' element in drama acts as a safeguard against the danger of stripping away a person's protective mask or 'false self' which, as Winnicott pointed out, is a necessary guardian self, protecting the vulnerable 'true self' from impingement and hurt' (Pearson, Smail and Watts, 2013: 49). Some of the roles he chose were characters that pleased others to the detriment of the self, for example Cinderella and Vasalissa. We sensed that he was exploring his 'pleaser' archetype in a safe way through these roles.

Exploring aspects of self through drama

When we are repeatedly shamed for being different, we learn to split off these differences. If we miss out on being validated for who we are, we adapt to fit in. Tim seemed to fear that offering his own thoughts, reflections and feelings might lead to him being shamed. Expressing difference seemed too dangerous.

In the enactment of *The Snow Queen*, Tim chose to embody the mirror. A mirror that is whole reflects back to us our image, our identity as an embodied being. In the story, the mirror is created to reflect the user in a distorted way, just as some people are offered distorted feedback throughout childhood, and beyond. Greenberg (2013: 64) suggests that wounds leading to closet narcissistic adaptations stem from being repeatedly shamed and taught to focus on the needs of others. This is a distorted mirror, a symbol of the misattunement that Tim may well have been exposed to. In the story, the mirror is carried up to the heavens because the goblin wants to humiliate the angels. Through embodying this source of humiliation, Tim was choosing, consciously or unconsciously, to explore this aspect of himself. The mirror is dropped. The fall from the grandiosity of the heavens is a long one. Tim took his time, swirling round with the support of the music, rolling and falling, then embodying the disintegration of the mirror using fabrics.

Through embodying stories, Tim discovered new aspects of self. Owning these more consciously may have been challenging, but this awareness offered him more resources and choices. Our work, through both modalities, was to recognise Tim holistically, including the emerging aspects of self: 'Deep inside of us, there is something that cries out for recognition; recognition that we exist, that we are separate and yet that we are also acknowledged as a fellow human being' (Hycner and Jacobs, 1995: 24).

Exploring aspects of self through music

Robin noticed in the musical improvisations that Tim was drawn to following others, rarely initiating the music making or influencing its feeling, mood, tempo or rhythm. Blending in with the group, he would mirror others, sometimes acting as the response to another's musical call. Being different and having his own musical voice or presence in the group seemed to be a situation which Tim avoided, in direct contrast to his use of drama and verbal material where he was more able and seemed comfortable with his differences. Dalal (2011: 241) reflects upon our conflicting desires as human beings: our need to belong and be the same, and our need to be acknowledged for our uniqueness and difference. Robin noticed that music improvisation seemed to act as a leveller for the group, and was curious about Tim's use of music and what it held for him and the group. Robin wondered whether Tim's feelings of difference in the music improvisation held some anxiety for him as it revealed an aspect of himself which he neither wanted to acknowledge nor wanted others to see. Dalal (2011: 241) talks of the potential for pity when our differences make us feel as the disabled 'other'. This seemed particularly poignant, given how skilled Tim was in the drama and verbal reflection.

Vignette

Tim finding his musical voice

Tim initiated the music, tentatively using the brushes on the drum as if hiding both his sounds and himself, and looking around to see if anyone was going to respond. Another group member joined him with an ostinato-like pattern on the temple blocks, and Sarah swiftly followed, playing the xylophone in an unstructured and atonal way. The group's music sounded disconnected and fragmented at this point. Robin joined in by playing interspersed, brusque clusters of notes on the piano, trying to link the different sounds together, yet not wanting to create any tonal or rhythmic structure. However, as soon as Robin had played a couple of clusters, Tim's response was to mirror Robin's music, copying its musical tempo and brusque style. Robin's countertransference was a sense of intrusion, as if Tim was 'clinging' to Robin's musical offering rather than developing the beginnings of his own musical world. In response to Tim's mirroring, Robin momentarily withdrew, to allow himself space to feel what Tim needed; Robin then sensed he could offer a more robust musical holding. He wanted to hear more of Tim, so offered an increasingly robust presence, to which Tim responded by becoming more musically present within the musical space. Tim then began to spontaneously explore different instruments, using the cymbal, cabassa and large hand drum. At first Robin wondered if this change of instruments was a return to passive and tentative musical play, but gradually Tim played with more force and energy, which gave him a distinct and different way of being in the group. His choice of instruments pierced through the wooden sounds created by the others, and he could be heard more autonomously, while still remaining connected to the group's music as a whole and less merged with Robin's playing. As Levinge (2015: 73) suggests, it is through musically identifying and adapting to our client's music, and connecting dynamically with both their emotional and physical being, that enables our clients to get a greater sense of who they are and – in Tim's case – risk being separate. There were times when Tim seemed to go into a shameful and anxious state. We noticed that through attuning and adapting in the music and drama we were able to reach him and support him to be more present in the group, which seemed to help him feel more self-accepting. His confidence in the drama allowed him to obliquely explore aspects of himself without judgment, in turn enabling him to try out new and different ways of being in the music.

Working collaboratively: creating the liminal space

Once upon a time, there was a land where all was ordered. The people knew what their tasks were, and when to undertake them. The Elders knew what the outcomes of those tasks would be, and how they would be carried out. There was a Great history, drawn in charts, understood by all. Every now and then, an Elder from the Above would call to the Below and share a Great Thought. This Thought would be carried on the backs of the people as they worked. One day, a young boy came to an abyss, a great Edge upon the land. An Elder called out, "Stay away from the Edge. Our world ends here!" The boy, a bold child, replied, "Does it? What would happen if I crossed the threshold?"

We are living in a culture where there is a pull to prove ourselves, yet paradoxically stay within the realms deemed acceptable. The narcissistic adaptations of perfection, competition, shame and 'not good enough' are evident everywhere including our processes explored in supervision. Writing this chapter required us to be rigorous in our exchange of theories and ideas, and the narcissistic pull to prove our worth began to creep into our work. The ideas for the chapter began to affect our perception of the needs of the group.

Smail (2010), as part of her Psyche and Soma training, teaches the art of 'listening and attending to the wisdom-teacher which lies frequently ignored and unacknowledged, within the depths of human beings'. The name she uses to relate to this inverted place is Soul. We noticed that we had stepped into the narcissistic territory, and sensed that we needed to put ego and theories aside and lean into this more soulful wisdom. We let go of our attachment to outcomes and were able to be with what emerged from the group once again. We continued to reflect on the importance of Soul.

The Soul aspect Smail (2010) refers to is 'the unknown', that which cannot be pinned down, the liminal. A liminal space can be seen as a threshold between the unconscious and consciousness, an in-between place, and – in a therapy setting – a space for processes and co-creations to emerge. On writing about liminal space, Denham-Vaughan names these polarities 'Will' and 'Grace' (Denham-Vaughan, 2010: 35). Our containing structure of the Overture and Sesame Approach, and the specific practices within them (such as melody, rhythm, embodiment and story) hold an element of predictability for the group, the building blocks from which we create the ritual, representing the 'Will'. 'Grace', the mysterious and magical quality, emerges within the containment of the therapy structure (Denham-Vaughan, 2010: 35).

As arts therapists, we aim to create a liminal space in our sessions, a threshold to the unknown. The liminal space is not predictable, but to facilitate it a strong framework is required. In experimenting with co-facilitating this group, we had to work out a way of holding on to our combined structure as we worked with two modalities. There have been times when each of us has wanted to persist with our own modality in the session, sensing opportunities for expansion. However, our respect for each other and our intention of offering a cross-modality group helped us honour the structure, and trust this to facilitate 'Grace'.

An important part of creating this liminal space has been group clinical supervision. This has been a place for thinking about our vulnerability, rivalry, competition, shame, authority and ownership of the group. Recognising and acknowledging these issues, and thinking about our differences and similarities in approach, as well as the 'in-between' that is our working relationship, has been a significant part of the group process. 'Liminal' implies crossing between the known and unknown, reflecting our own crossing between music and drama modalities, offering different perspectives of the same event. Over time we learnt to hold both perspectives equally, rather than fixing on one polarity.

Is the whole greater than the sum of the parts?

We wondered how this particular group might have responded with either dramatherapy or music therapy alone. For Sarah, the music modality was a place where she felt safe, comfortable and in control. It seemed as if music offered her a secure base (Bowlby, 1988) from which she could explore her relationship to the group. She could retreat to the music when the drama became unpredictable. Using both modalities seemed to support Sarah in stretching her way of being in the group, enabling her to take risks, hold different roles and show an increasing sensitivity and openness in relating.

For Tim, drama was a familiar place where he could draw on his repertoire of dramatic skills, and obliquely explore his process through metaphor and imagination. In contrast the improvised music was unfamiliar to Tim, but enabled him to communicate and connect with his feelings more directly. His capacity to make links raised his awareness of the connection between his music and feelings, stretching his emotional insight and development.

Many clients clearly benefit from one modality. However, our experience of interweaving two modalities has brought to light a unique third option, which may suit some clients.

The benefits we observed with this group included:

1   An ability to communicate experiences more powerfully, using both music and drama simultaneously with an emphasis on emotional impact and group dynamics.
2   Increased opportunities for creativity.
3   The opportunity to find expression in new ways, which may have otherwise been confined to one modality or not have emerged at all.

4   The chance to take risks in a new modality, while using their preferred modality as a stable base.
5   The opportunity to reveal vulnerable aspects of self more overtly and directly, leading to greater client awareness of their own processes.

Concluding thoughts

Our experience of co-working at first highlighted our differences. Paradoxically, we felt supported to stay with our differences and uniqueness when we discovered our similarities. Our shared playfulness, shared openness to include each other's differences and shared passion for developing as therapists have reaffirmed that our most important resource is ourselves.

We would like to conclude in a manner befitting our own modalities, with an extract of our own script:

ROBIN: "Little did I know when approaching this group work I'd be walking around the therapy room with a silver butterfly fabric round my waist!"
GILLIAN: "It suited you! I enjoyed your embodiments and the way you brought your instruments round with you."
ROBIN: "I liked the way you played the wind chimes with your foot – that was different! Actually, it really supported the group to reflect on difference and being themselves."
GILLIAN: "Sarah was trying to encourage me to play 'properly'."
ROBIN: "Yes, even though it was risky, it was still safe. We were able to help her think about her own need for safety, yet stretch her tolerance to stay with you being different. I can hear Tim is starting to have his own musical voice in the group. He is moving away from needing to mirror or follow others all the time."
GILLIAN: "I've noticed that too. He seems to be revealing his differences musically now. Yet there is a real sense of connectedness when the group is working together."
ROBIN: "Mmm, maybe the group has become a place for revealing sameness and difference, not just for our clients but also for you and me?"
GILLIAN: "I feel affirmed in my difference from you through this process. Before we made it so explicit, I think difference was in the shadow."
ROBIN: "Yes, I have felt challenged, but it has certainly stretched my repertoire of resources as a Music Therapist."

Notes

1   Playback Theatre is a unique form of improvised theatre enabling audiences to tell their stories. These stories are brought to life using music, drama, movement, dance and song. Gillian is an actor and Robin is the musician in the Golden Thread Playback Theatre Company.
2   The terms *warm up, bridge in, main event* and *bridge out* are taken from the ritualised Sesame structure known as "The Sesame Approach." The main event is not limited to

the use of story, but it was the most common form we used with this group (Pearson, Smail and Watts, 2013: 34–72; Pearson, 1996: 2).

References

Bowlby, J. (1988). *A Secure Base: Clinical Applications of Attachment Theory*. London: Brunner and Routledge.

Dalal, F. (2011). *Thought Paralysis: The Virtues of Discrimination*. London: Karnac.

Denham-Vaughan, S. (2010). Liminal Space and Gracious Living. *British Gestalt Journal*, 19(2), pp. 34–45.

Greenberg, E. (1998/1975). *A Brief Guide to Borderline, Narcissistic and Schizoid Disorders*. Unpublished Manuscript.

Greenberg, E. (2013). A Brief Guide to Narcissistic Personality Adaptations. In: *Diagnosis and Treatment of Personality Disorders Workshop*. Cardiff: Welsh Psychotherapy Partnership.

Haque, S. (2009). Differences, Differences, Differences: Working with Ethnic, Cultural and Religious Diversity. In: T. Cottis, ed., *Intellectual Disability, Trauma and Psychotherapy*, 1st ed. London: Routledge.

Hycner, R. and Jacobs, L. (1995). *The Healing Relationship in Gestalt Therapy*. Gouldsboro, PA: Gestalt Journal Press.

Kaufman, G. (1989). *The Psychology of Shame: Theory and Treatment of Shame-based Syndromes*. New York: Springer.

Levinge, A. (2015). *The Music of Being, Music Therapy, Winnicott and the school of Object Relations*. London: Jessica Kingsley Publishers.

Pearson, J. (1996). *Discovering the Self through Drama and Movement: The Sesame Approach*. London and Bristol: Jessica Kingsley Publishers.

Pearson, J., Smail, M. and Watts, P. (2013). *Dramatherapy with Myth and Fairytale: The Golden Stories of Sesame*. London and Philadelphia: Jessica Kingsley Publishers.

Schumacher, K. (2014). Music Therapy for Pervasive Developmental Disorders, Especially Autism. A Case Study with a Theoretical Foundation and an Evaluation Tool. In: J. Backer and J. Sutton, eds., *The Music in Music Therapy, Psychodynamic Music Therapy in Europe: Clinical, Theoretical and Research Approaches*, 1st ed. London: Jessica Kingsley Publishers, Chapter 7, pp. 107–123.

Sinason, V. (1992). *Mental Handicap and the Human Condition: New approaches from the Tavistock*. London: Fresh Association Books.

Smail, M. (2010). The Making of Psyche and Soma Training: Conditions of a Soul Pedagogy. *Sesame Journal*, 12, pp. 6–11. London: Sesame UK and International.

Stern, D. (2004). *The Present Moment in Psychotherapy and Everyday Life*. New York: Norton & Company Ltd.

Winnicott, D.W. (2005). *Playing and Reality*. London: Routledge.

7

AN INNOVATIVE COLLABORATION

Combining art and music therapy interventions for adults with learning disabilities

Megan Charles & Judith Sanoon

Introduction

We first met at a nursing home where Megan was working as a trainee art thera-pist, and Judith as a music therapist. We discovered that we had a mutual interest in each other's creative modality, and shared an appreciation for the self-development that the arts can offer.

Our work is based in a residential home for adults with learning disabilities. The home caters for long-term residents, and with an ageing population there is the added complication of dementia. Some clients move into the home when their families can no longer look after them – as Richards (2007) explains, this difficult transition can impact the clients' view of themselves, focusing on the fragility of relationships and the anticipation of loss. These are the issues that inhabit the therapy space, and are hard to articulate with this client group.

The home introduced music therapy sessions in 1998, which have been provided by Judith since 2001. Seven clients attend individual music therapy, five of them self-referred. A selection of tuned and untuned percussion instruments and lyres are pro-vided, and therapy sessions take place in a room where clients can be undisturbed. For the most part the therapy involves the use of clinical improvisation, with occasional reflective techniques such as listening to music (classical, world, jazz or recordings of improvisations) with the option to draw. Verbal discussion and reflection has a limited but important place in the therapy, which is psychodynamically informed.

Rationale

We discussed setting up an art therapy group, as we felt that skills gained in indi-vidual music therapy could be extended to clients' interactions with each other.

Our aim was to create a safe space for clients to work alongside one another, offering them a chance to develop their relationships. As O'Connor (2001, cited in Fillingham, 2007) suggested, these peer relationships may not be as valued as those in the non-learning disabled community. Interpersonal issues are often managed by the staff, and we felt that clients needed more opportunities to broaden their understanding of one another in order to begin to address these issues themselves.

Sinason (2010) highlights the variety of groups we all move in and out of throughout our lives. Some groups (for example our families) present little choice over whether we belong to them. For clients at the home, the stress of co-living with others with whom they have neither chosen to live with nor are related to, can add to difficulties they already experience. In this context group therapy can offer space for social learning, allowing group members the opportunity to explore new roles (Case and Dalley, 2006). We felt that art therapy could offer clients a safe exploration of being with and working alongside others, whilst the artwork itself could act as a safe space for clients within the group environment.

Several clients had responded to drawing in music therapy, showing a willingness to engage with art as a medium. Drawing appeared to facilitate the processing and understanding of the emotions evoked by the music, without leading to the difficulties verbal processing can present.

Phil Jones (2005) discusses the propensity in the arts therapies for the separation of the arts into different modalities, whereas in children's play and development the arts are more integrated. With this in mind, we wanted to support clients to integrate their creative expressions and experiences. Art therapy seemed to present a natural development for the work the clients had done in their music therapy sessions, but a lack of funding prevented it running alongside the existing music therapy sessions.

Art therapy group

In May 2015 we discussed working alternate weeks as a way of bringing art therapy into the home, bypassing the funding issues. Clients were consulted and the management agreed, and from September, art therapy and music therapy were held on alternate weeks. Before starting the group, and with the clients' permission, Megan sat in during the music therapy sessions. This offered her a chance to meet the clients and see how they engaged with music, and we noted their welcoming attitude to Megan and their pride in demonstrating their musical 'personalities'.

The art therapy group is open, allowing clients a choice of attending for the full duration or not, giving them a level of autonomy in an environment where personal choice can be limited. For continuity, the group – consisting of eight members, four of whom attend regularly – is held in the same space as the music therapy sessions. The group is predominantly unstructured, aside from the space set aside by Megan at the end of each session for clients to discuss the artwork. This discussion time has proved to be difficult for two regular group members, one of whom has no verbal language, the other for whom verbal language and comprehension is becoming increasingly difficult. These issues are discussed in the case vignettes.

At this early stage of the group's formation, interactions between members are predominantly confrontational and conflict-orientated. Psychotherapy group literature focuses on this conflict being mainly targeted at the therapist, and suggests that conflict, provided it is successfully negotiated, can support group cohesion (Smith, Glass and Miller, 1980). In the home we noted additional deep-rooted causes of conflict between group members: whilst the art group is new, clients have lived together for many years and have longstanding relationships with one another. As the group has developed, interpersonal tensions have surfaced, especially between two particular clients. How the artwork, therapist and group as a whole negotiated these conflicts are highlighted in the case vignettes, which also show the role music therapy plays in supporting clients to understand and process these interactions.

Joint session

We spent time providing ad hoc peer supervision for each other, discussing issues that arose within the art therapy group and how they correlated to music therapy. From this we consolidated the creative therapeutic experience into a one-off joint session, at the end of our first term of collaboration. We discussed how the joint session would work with clients and what it might mean for them and us. We explored various forms that the joint session could take, incorporating some of the experiences of individual sessions into the group. We wanted clients to explore alternative perspectives through the combined use of music and art, and to broaden their interpersonal skills. The joint session was set up similarly to the art therapy group, with various art materials in the middle of the large table for clients to use. Judith selected background music, which was played intermittently. The nature of the session was explained to clients prior to it taking place.

Case vignettes

In the following vignettes, we outline the progression from individual sessions to group therapy. All names have been changed to preserve the anonymity of clients.

Chris

Background

Chris has an acquired brain injury that has left him with short- and long-term memory problems, anxiety and agitation. He is prone to angry outbursts and verbal aggression, obsessive-compulsive tendencies and loss of executive function. Chris's outbursts perhaps communicate and reflect his awareness of and frustration with the loss of his previous, independent life. His condition means that he requires constant prompting from staff as to what to do at any given time, and he finds it hard to interact with others socially – particularly verbally – as Chris gets into verbal 'loops' and constantly repeats himself. Chris's difficulties are compounded by negative early childhood experiences. Chris has been attending music therapy since 2001, for 20 minutes a week.

Music therapy

Chris likes to arrange the instruments before starting, and spells out the therapist's name, asking "Have I got it right?" (He is dyslexic). He begins by playing short, repeated rhythmic and melodic patterns, which are both echoed and accompanied by Judith on the keyboard, providing a sense of being listened to and experiencing response. The exact repetition by the therapist of the notes Chris plays seems to have a calming effect when he is agitated. Chris's music-making seems to evolve out of an exploration both of his inner emotional world and recent events. It sometimes remains in one feeling-state, but more frequently involves the building up of tension in the music, and subsequent release, which can be repeated a number of times. Chris's facial expressions are an indicator of his response to the musical interaction, as initially it is often tense and mask-like. He sometimes smiles involuntarily, particularly near the point of release, and when a calm moment is reached he may close his eyes, with a relaxed expression. At this point Chris appears to enter into a meditative 'inner space', as opposed to being reactive to everything and everyone around him. Chris often creates a loose rondo form (e.g. ABACADAG etc.), by repeatedly returning to play certain notes and rhythms. This gives a sense of returning to the familiar in order to gain confidence to explore further. At the end of the session, Chris finds it difficult to articulate his feelings about the music we have improvised, but his mood may have changed significantly from beginning to end. When he leaves the session, often thanking Judith and shaking her hand, he enquires when the next session will be.

For Chris, music therapy allows him to share and communicate his emotional world non-verbally, to release feelings of tension and anxiety, to experience the sense of a quiet space within, and to interact with another for a sustained length of time. The use of musical form, highlighted by Roth (2014), is particularly valuable when there is a shaken sense of self, present in brain injury, which results in an altered sense of identity (Sohlberg and Mateer, 2001). However, music therapy does not provide Chris with the opportunity to interact with other clients, which he finds difficult, leaving him isolated.

Art therapy

Chris regularly attends the art therapy group and stays for the entire session. Chris has established rituals that he performs at the start of each session (much like in his music therapy sessions), which seem to help him focus on being in the space and prepare to create artwork. His rituals involve tearing the corners off his paper, followed by writing his name, the date, who else is or will attend the group, the date of the next session, and establishing the meanings and spellings of various words that he has seen or heard during the beginning of the group. After this process (which can take up to 20 minutes), Chris turns his paper over and is ready to begin. This preparation has the feel of performance art and is meticulously executed at the start of every session.

Within the group, Chris's verbal loops and compulsive actions makes it very difficult for him to engage with others, and group members (especially Tony) find it hard to tolerate Chris's repetition, often challenging Chris's behaviour in a punitive manner, which in turn exacerbates Chris's repetition. The artwork Chris creates seems to help him organise his thoughts: the back of his artwork is an overwhelming collection of overlapping writing in different sizes, colours and text styles (Fig. 7.1); this is belied by the front of his artwork (Fig. 7.2) which is often strikingly neat and ordered in appearance. Chris enjoys mixed media work and will often use collage in his artwork, which seem to echo his repetitions: the words he chooses to cut out are bound to the paper, just as his sentences are bound to the verbal loops he creates.

Chris is one of the only group members to use the space at the end of the session to talk about his artwork. He concretely describes, in meticulous detail, all elements of his work. This tends to create friction between him and other group members, particularly those that find it difficult to discuss their own artwork. There seems to be an underlying resentment, both of his ability to use the art materials confidently, and his ability to openly talk about his work. Chris is also the only client with an acquired brain injury; the other clients have been living with their disabilities from birth. This creates a marked difference in experiences for Chris and the other clients, and positions him as an outsider in the home.

FIGURE 7.1

FIGURE 7.2

Emma

Background

Emma is in her seventies and has a moderate learning difficulty combined with a history of epilepsy and depression, which has led to hospitalisation on a number of occasions. She was brought up by a foster mother before entering the home. Much of Emma's narrative revolves around the loss of this relationship, and her desire to regain it.

Music therapy

Emma asked to attend music therapy in June 2001, and she quickly developed a ritual at the beginning of the sessions, relating all the significant events of the week. Emma would then choose instruments to improvise on, playing them in a rhythmic, repetitive way. Emma was responsive to music and liked to listen and draw for part of her session. She would state what kind of music she wanted to hear and later talk about her drawing and reflect on the feelings the music had engendered. Separation plays a large part in Emma's narrative, often reverting to the moment her foster mother placed her in the home. In late 2004, following a timetable change, Emma was no longer able to attend therapy – and this proved a difficult ending for her.

In June 2013 Emma recommenced music therapy after a period of hospitalisation. She picked up from where she had left off, again with conversation as the starting point before choosing and playing instruments. Even though Emma may relate events she has really enjoyed, at some point she expresses her dissatisfaction with life by muttering almost inaudibly, giving rise to a sense of a split between what she openly reveals and what remains more hidden. Her music-making follows a similar pattern to before, but more intense, with jagged, arrhythmic motifs that are difficult to match and support, and which can continue for 10–15 minutes. Emma may mutter angry-sounding words which are not always comprehensible and are sometimes punctuated by banging the drum loudly. When Emma expresses very strong and intense feelings on the instruments, she will often let out an "aargh" as if to voice what she finds difficult to articulate in words. At these times, the quality of her playing changes to being less arrhythmic and more congruent. When Emma does eventually verbalise her feelings, she typically says that "nobody cares", or that she wants to "go home" in an angry tone of voice. The session often ends with Emma choosing songs to sing, which appears to reconnect Emma with the present, and a sense of unity – both with herself and Judith.

There is a parallel between Emma's dissociation from her aggressive feelings and Levinge's (2015) case study. Levinge discusses the consequences of a child not being able to express their 'ruthless self' through aggressive play with their caregiver. She argues that this results in the client having to hide this side of themselves, which can cause aggressive feelings to be split off from the self. For Emma, music therapy offers the opportunity to begin to reintegrate aggressive feelings in a space that she feels can tolerate them.

Art therapy

Initially, Emma did not want to attend the art therapy group. Whilst she was able to acknowledge its presence, she struggled to engage with the group or the art materials. Thinking about her strong attachment with her foster mother, as well as with the music therapy sessions and Judith, we felt that she was communicating her need for reliability and security in her relationships, elements that she doesn't experience yet in this group.

In the artwork created in the joint session (Fig. 7.3) Emma illustrates this disconnection, stating that she wanted each end of the "flower arch" to connect.

FIGURE 7.3

Tony

Background

Tony has Down's syndrome and has been resident at the home for many years. With age, Tony has become more frail and forgetful, and his thinking is often confused. There is some discussion within the team about Tony showing early signs of dementia.

Music therapy

Tony has been attending music therapy for 40 minutes a week since 2009. He had previously attended some years ago and, after a long gap, decided to return, prompted by receiving a keyboard as a Christmas present. Within the sessions Tony chose to play the keyboard, and when it came to decide what music to play, would often just say "country" or "Bill Haley", or even hold up a CD and name a track number, leaving the therapist to discern what he actually wanted. He would then ask Judith to play it on the keyboard, with accompanying 'drums' (rhythm backing). Initially he would bring along a CD of Wurlitzer music to play along to, 'hiding' his own music-making behind the CD or Judith's playing. Judith would encourage him to take the lead and create his own musical material, which had an often delicate, dreamy quality, typically played in the higher register of the keyboard. It appeared to Judith that Tony's music reflected a fragile aspect of himself which he sought to protect by keeping it hidden.

Now Tony has become frail, he tends to stay for less time, is preoccupied with his diary, and talks often about the death of his parents, his close family and his health; it is sometimes difficult to understand what he is saying. However, he is much more willing to engage with his own music, and recently suggested that he and Judith play a "lullaby", when he talked about having difficulty sleeping. The gentle nature of the music seemed attuned to how Tony was feeling. He has also become more adventurous, and lately has been mimicking his beloved marching bands with his fingers as he marches them up and down the keyboard. It is possible that the (suspected) onset of dementia has loosened his inhibitions, permitting him to express himself in a more humorous way.

Art therapy

Tony attends the group regularly, always bringing sci-fi DVDs and TV guides with him, which he uses to copy images from. As in his music therapy sessions, Tony spends time at the start looking at his diary, establishing dates for the current and next group, before beginning his artwork. He often likes to use watercolours, producing delicate and colourful results (Fig. 7.4).

Tony struggles to talk about his artwork, and when he does so he describes his work in terms of the images he has brought in as opposed to his own artwork. His

FIGURE 7.4

artwork is often aesthetically disconnected from his source material, similar to the disparity seen in his music sessions, where we perceive him as hiding himself behind the material (CDs, DVDs or magazines) he brings to therapy. This may indicate Tony's fragile sense of identity, a key factor, if as we suspect, he is developing cognitive problems in line with dementia which could further diminish his sense of self.

In the art therapy group Tony is authoritarian in manner, telling group members that they are not allowed to do certain things, or telling them that they are "being naughty". As a result of this, he often clashes with other group members. Recently, Tony has brought his feelings around his parents' death and his health into the group, which may reflect his increasing awareness of his own mortality as a result of his advancing years. This is an issue like that of his identity, that he struggles to articulate directly.

The joint session in summary

For the majority of the session, when music was playing, group members remained quiet and focused on their artwork. Silences between the music were often filled by Emma and Tony. Emma wasn't feeling well, and spent the session working while gently moaning, holding her head in her hands, and saying under her breath "I want my mum". We checked with her that she was alright to continue, and offered her the opportunity to talk – which she declined. Tony was sitting next to Emma, and put his arms around her, giving her a hug and comforting her.

In the early silences between pieces, Tony remarked that he found it difficult to concentrate, as he was thinking about the death of his parents. The group as a whole seemed to find it difficult to support Tony, and remained focused on their work, leaving the therapists to provide therapeutic holding. Interactions between the group typically occurred in the silences between music. Towards the middle of the session, Louisa, another group member, commented on Chris's artwork, saying he was "a very good artist". Later, she asked the group why Chris was cutting sections out of his artwork, which she described as a "babyish" thing to do. This triggered Chris into a frustrated, laborious cyclical monologue that he and the group found hard to manage. Towards the end of the session, Megan and Judith created a space for the group to show and discuss both their artwork and their experience of making art while listening to music. Staying present for this part of the shared space proved particularly difficult for Tony, who could not be persuaded to stay and left the room in an apparently desperate state.

The other group members were able to discuss or show the artwork they had created, and listen to one another's experiences. No one directly spoke about the experience of having music in the session, but later a client commented that is was "cool" to draw to music.

Analysis

We noticed that the combination of music therapy and art therapy in the group revealed three key properties not present in either the music or art therapy sessions alone.

1   Music facilitated a focus that had not previously been observed in the art therapy group. Some residents find it difficult to get started with the materials in the art therapy group alone; in the joint session, however, everyone began promptly, and continued to work on their art-making with an intense focus. The music seemed to act as a catalyst, enabling clients to find their creative space within the group.

2   When Tony and Emma spoke about the loss and pain they were experiencing they were met with silence from the group; these are difficult topics that often arise in the sessions and are pertinent to all the clients. In the art group the high level of verbal interaction means that the group are often too involved in their own dialogue to listen to others. In the joint session, however, we experienced the group silence – and engagement with their own artwork – as an indication that the group heard and were processing the information, but were not able to respond verbally.

Skaife and Huet (1998) write about a similar phenomenon in their case study, where an image was felt to embody something for the group that the group were not, at that time, able to acknowledge verbally. Skaife and Huet highlight how group members were absorbed in an image, despite not being able to articulate or engage verbally with the issues that the group member had brought up.

3   Music played a background role in the group, but had a significant impact, as atypically, the group worked without talking. The music appeared to have a containing effect, as the lack of conversation did not feel uncomfortable. The choice of music seemed to enable the group to become more animated when energy was flagging, and calmer, particularly after a tense moment in the group when Chris embarked on his monologue.

Challenges

In setting up our collaborative work we experienced numerous challenges. The first hurdle was securing funding for our work, which took us two years to resolve. We decided to job-share, alternating weekly sessions between music therapy and art therapy. Our belief in and enthusiasm for the potential benefits of the collaborative work outweighed the financial and time costs involved in implementing the sessions. Whilst there are many examples of cross-modality work between arts therapies, none fitted our framework. As a result, our work was without precedent, and the outcome unsure. Although we both work psychodynamically, it became clear that each modality has its own idioms, which we needed to take into account in order to appreciate the interactions between clients and modalities.

We were both aware of the impact of Judith's long-standing relationship with clients on the formation of the art therapy group. At the same time, we acknowledged that this new collaborative structure reduced their access to individual sessions. However, their response has been one of acceptance, with many asking when the next art and music therapy sessions will take place.

In analysing the joint session, we were aware that while music was playing, there was a quiet focus in the group and interaction between group members was minimal. This created mixed benefits, where music enabled a focus for art-making, but inhibited interpersonal interaction. In the art group, verbal interaction can often highlight tensions within the group and dominate sessions. Skaife (1990) discussed the conflicts that arise in art therapy groups, where verbal interaction dominates art-making, creating an uncontainable glut of material which can overwhelm the group. Whilst our objective for the group is to allow space for clients to explore their interpersonal dynamics, we were aware that this is a space that clients had not experienced previously, and could be destructive if not contained by the group. We found that while music was playing, group members were still aware of each other, but in a different way. Grocke and Wigram (2007) discussed the ability of music (when played to clients) to connect them to their socio-cultural community, providing stimulation and eliciting a relaxing effect. They also highlighted its ability to limit the expectations of interactive interpersonal experiences, an element witnessed within the joint session. Whilst verbal interaction was minimal, there was a sense that the group worked together harmoniously, which potentially could be ascribed to having music in the session. In this way we were conductors for the group interaction, interspersing music with silence, offering containment while allowing tolerable spaces for interpersonal interaction.

Benefits

Throughout our work together we have kept in close contact and shared our clinical experiences. In connecting to theories that support our work, we found that our format synced with the four levels of successful collaborative working (Twyford and Watson, 2007). Combining the *interactive* and *communicative* level, we have been able to share therapeutic aims and objectives, communicating regularly to ensure that these are aligned. On an *observational* level, Megan was able to gain insight into the clients through attending the music sessions, whilst Judith was able to observe clients in the group setting during the joint session. Working on these three levels collaboratively has enriched our understanding of the clients we work with, allowing us to work on an *integrated* level.

Facilitating a group together helped to confirm in our minds – and possibly our clients' minds – the strong links that music and art have in these therapeutic spaces. In working together, we saw how a mixed media approach can facilitate growth on a personal and interpersonal level, as discussed by Jones (2005).

Similar to the experiences of Gale and Matthews (1998) in their joint modality assessment process, the joint session gave us the opportunity to directly experience the group's engagement with both media. As well as enabling us to learn more about each other's modality, we also learnt more about the clients from different perspectives, as outlined by Watson (2008).

Thinking about the underlying issues prevalent in work with this client group (attachment, separation and loss), we thought about the impact that a considered and collaborative team can have. Dee (2012) outlines the significance of, as well as the various reasons for, early attachments being disrupted for people with learning disabilities. O'Farrell (2012) argues that it is inevitable that with poor experiences of attachment and separation, there will be a negative effect on an individual's ability to form new relationships. The collaborative approach within our work aims to support clients to utilise the therapeutic spaces to test out new roles and explore some of these issues. In the joint session, Tony and Emma were beginning to test the capacity of the group to support them, and in doing so were exploring these very issues.

As therapists working closely together, what we model in terms of our relationship to the clients, each other and the creative media, are crucial to understanding the benefits of our collaborative work. In maintaining the integrity of the music therapy sessions and the art therapy group we value the individuality of each medium, and in the joint session we attempt to demonstrate the significance of cooperation and shared aims. It is not clear what value the clients place on having both therapists holding them in mind, but it is clear in the clients' engagement that they feel able to explore the spaces offered.

Recommendations

At the heart of our work was the clear intention of providing clients with opportunities to explore and challenge their interpersonal relationships. This was borne out of a need within the residential setting. Our creative approach developed from a scarcity of resources, but as a result this work has developed into an approach that fits the needs of the clients. We don't have the opportunity to explore the impact of a more intense approach (e.g. weekly art and music therapy sessions) would have on the clients, but arguably this may be unsuitable for the long-term work that occurs with the clients.

The future

In reflecting on the collaboration, we agreed that alternating between music therapy sessions and the art therapy group, on a fortnightly basis, is a format that complements each modality and addresses our primary therapeutic objectives. The role of joint sessions was also felt to be crucial for consolidation of the work in both therapeutic settings. Moving forward, we will be punctuating our alternating sessions with a joint session at the end of each term. How we decide to integrate the media is still a work-in-progress, and we have the option of adjusting the joint group's structure to meet the clients' needs. Whilst the joint session was based around the format of the art therapy group, and evaluated on that basis, it could be possible to introduce more music therapy elements. We are still in the early stages of our collaborative work, and are excited to be able to share our journey with each other and the clients who attend our sessions.

References

Case, C. and Dalley, T. (2006). *The Handbook of Art Therapy*. Hove: Routledge, p. 231.

Dee, K. (2012). Loss, Bereavement and Learning Disabilities. In: S. Bull and K. O'Farrell, eds., *Art Therapy and Learning Disabilities*, 1st ed. London: Routledge, p. 57.

Fillingham, C. (2007). Friendship and Group Work. In: T. Watson, ed., *Music Therapy with Adults with Learning Disabilities*, 1st ed. Hove: Routledge, p. 72.

Gale, C. and Matthews, R. (1998). Journey in Joint Working. Some Reflections on an Experience of Arts Therapies Collaboration. In: M. Rees, ed., *Drawing on Difference: Art Therapy with People Who Have Learning Difficulties*, 1st ed. Hove: Routledge, pp. 168–184.

Grocke, D. and Wigram, T. (2007). *Receptive Methods in Music Therapy*. London: Jessica Kingsley Publishers, p. 179.

Jones, P. (2005). *The Arts Therapies: A Revolution in Healthcare*. Hove: Brunner-Routledge, p. 13.

Levinge, A. (2015). *The Music of Being*. London: Jessica Kingsley Publishers, p. 108.

O'Farrell, K. (2012). Learning Disabilities, Art Therapy and the Common Themes. In: S. Bull and K. O'Farrell, eds., *Art Therapy and Learning Disabilities*, 1st ed. London: Routledge, p. 13.

Richards, E. (2007). What Bit of My Head Is Talking Now? In: T. Watson, ed., *Music Therapy with Adults with Learning Disabilities*, 1st ed. Hove: Routledge, p. 61.

Roth, E.A. (2014). Clinical Improvisation in Neurologic Music Therapy. In: M.H. Thaut and V. Hoemberg, eds., *Handbook of Neurologic Music Therapy*, 1st ed. Oxford: Oxford University Press, p. 36.

Sinason, V. (2010). *Mental Handicap and the Human Condition*, rev. ed. London: Free Association Books, p. 277.

Skaife, S. (1990). Self-Determination in Group Analytic Art Therapy. *Group Analysis*, 23(3), pp. 237–244.

Skaife, S. and Huet, V. (1998). Dissonance and Harmony: Theoretical Issues in Art Psychotherapy Groups. In: S. Skaife and V. Huet, eds., *Art Psychotherapy Groups. Between Pictures and Words*, 1st ed. London: Routledge, pp. 17–43.

Smith, M. L., Glass, G. V., and Miller, T. I. (1980). *The Benefits of Psychotherapy*. Baltimore, MD: Johns Hopkins University Press

Sohlberg, M. and Mateer, C. (2001). *Cognitive Rehabilitation: An Integrated Neuropsychological Approach*. New York: The Guilford Press, p. 148.

Twyford, K. and Watson, T. (2007). Multidisciplinary Working and Collaborative Working in Music Therapy. In: T. Watson, ed., *Music Therapy with Adults with Learning Disabilities*, 1st ed. Hove: Routledge, pp. 121–132.

Watson, T. (2008). Collaboration in Music Therapy with Adults with Learning Difficulties. In: K. Twyford and T. Watson, eds., *Integrated Team Working: Music Therapy as Part of Transdisciplinary and Collaborative Approaches*, 1st ed. London: Jessica Kingsley Publishers, pp. 91–123.

8

HOLDING HOPE

Rehabilitation of Syrian refugee children through art, music and dance movement therapy

Seda S. Güney, Leyla Akca Atik & Danny S. Lundmark

Introduction

In 2014, an art therapist, a music therapist and a dance movement therapist began working together to provide services to Syrian refugee children in Istanbul, Turkey. Their aim was to help them develop coping skills following traumatic experiences caused by war and forced migration. Using the Skills for Psychological Recovery (SPR) model to synchronise themes across the arts therapies, a five-day programme was created for a maximum of sixty children between 6 and 12 years old. The therapists held meetings to discuss a curriculum that would best suit the needs of the population, and how the SPR model could be adapted within the context of the arts therapies. It was felt to be important that there was consistency in the curriculum across the modalities, helping each to reinforce the same concepts and structures. All three arts therapists found that the children benefitted from the use of a cross-modality structure, as evidenced by session observations and general feedback from the children's families, team of volunteers, translators and other professionals.

Background

In 2011, a civil war began in Syria. As a result, Turkey received a large influx of Syrian refugees, many of whom had witnessed the violence and chaos that drove them from Syria. At time of writing, 2 and a half million Syrian refugees have migrated to Turkey, of which more than half are children (Unhcr.org, 2015). Many have experienced disturbing war memories, the stress of forced migration, domestic violence, sexual abuse, as well as the deprivation of basic rights such as food, shelter, education and health care. The presence of these refugees has created tension in their host communities, as cultural and language differences have put a strain on relationships and limited resources.

War trauma and refugee status

The Syrian refugee children were dealing with the consequences of living as refugees in a neighbouring country. The children exhibited myriad psychological issues, including the effects of post-traumatic stress disorder (PTSD), grief over the loss of one or more loved ones, and issues with self-esteem and self-confidence. Many symptoms of trauma, including intense feelings of anxiety, avoidance behaviours, intrusive thoughts, nightmares and flashbacks, were common among the Syrian children (Apa.org, 2016).

Additionally, intolerance and discrimination in the host communities were a real threat to the children, as many were struggling to assimilate themselves within Turkish culture. Most of the children spoke only Arabic, resulting in a language barrier that contributed to additional problems with integration in the Turkish-speaking society. The fact that many of the children did not attend school only resulted in further isolation. Most of the children's families faced difficult socio-economic conditions, and as the number of Syrian refugees kept growing, the resources and services provided by the host government were overstretched, resulting in increasingly adverse conditions (3rpsyriacrisis.org, 2015).

In working with traumatised refugee children, it is important that their needs are met to the best of the team's ability. In line with the review of neurobiological research on trauma treatment by Streeck-Fischer and Van der Kolk (2000; Van der Kolk, 2003), in order to initiate and achieve recovery, the collaborative project needed to touch upon the fundamental needs of trauma survivors. It was important that interventions focused on handling impulsivity and aggression, problems with affect regulation, development of healthy coping skills, flexibility for specific developmental deficits, appropriate processing of trauma, reconstruction of the self, self-regulation, the need to make sense of traumatic memories and the facilitation of universality, altruism and hope.

Multi-sensory approach to trauma treatment

A multi-sensory approach to trauma was particularly important, as the effects of trauma can be perceived through bodily physical sensation, imagery and sounds (Arnsten et al., 1999). Trauma effectively shuts down regions of the brain, such as the frontal lobe and the thalamus, responsible for processing language and sensations respectively (ibid.). It simultaneously activates the limbic system – involved in the release of strong emotions such as rage and fear – and the brain stem, which governs bodily movement. Taken together, the traumatic experience triggers a strongly emotional response that is void of rationale (Van Der Werf et al., 2003). The fact that trauma is stored within the 'emotional brain', and is accessible through the senses, supports the rationale that the arts therapies, which facilitate emotional processing through auditory, visual and kinaesthetic channels (Van der Kolk and Fisler, 1995), can be effective in trauma treatment. Rhythmic participation through drumming or moving to music (Van der Kolk, 2014: 72), together with visualisation and art-making, provide a valuable multi-sensory approach to healing trauma.

Skills for Psychological Recovery (SPR) model

As a result of the need to work from a common framework, the therapists jointly built a curriculum following the Skills for Psychological Recovery (SPR) model, which was developed by the U.S. National Child and Traumatic Stress Network and the U.S. National Center for Post-Traumatic Stress Disorder (Nctsn.org, 2012). The SPR is an evidence-based model for psychosocial support that has been used in numerous post-disaster programmes, both in the U.S. and internationally. The SPR model consists of six main coping and resiliency skills:

1 Information collection and prioritisation
2 Improving problem-solving skills
3 Introducing positive activities
4 Identifying feelings, handling difficult emotions and managing reactions
5 Bringing forward healthy thinking
6 Ensuring that healthy social relations are established

The therapists collaborated and designed the curriculum with a respect for the individuality of each child and their cultural beliefs, while understanding that their needs would be different according to the nature of their trauma. With the collaboration limited to five days, each day was assigned to a different skill-set, using the SPR model as a reference, supported by child assessments and family visits. By working with one theme each day, concepts were reinforced in each group, allowing therapists to use the same topic simultaneously but through different media. The model made use of the three therapeutic modalities to support the learning experience through visual, auditory, kinaesthetic and sensory-based activities. There is evidence to show that children learn differently, with some learning better through visual stimuli, others through auditory or kinesthetic stimuli (Mahdjoubi and Akplotsyi, 2012).

Maximising the efficacy of therapeutic collaboration

Working with children with backgrounds of severe trauma, the effectiveness of these workshops depended on maintaining a positive and safe environment. In order to minimise conflict and encourage children to express themselves freely, consistent rules were established across all therapy sessions. Visual cards, movement, and voice and hand gestures were used to build and maintain a common language that would support the children to help reduce anxiety and establish clear boundaries. The use of nonverbal communication was crucial, especially considering language differences between therapists and participants – the primary language of the children was Arabic.

The team of support staff were asked to share their daily observations and questions arising out of the group with the team of therapists, allowing the therapists to follow the process of both participants and volunteers – a therapist oversaw the collection of notes and feedback for the personal and professional growth of the team. This review process helped to feed valuable information into the inter-disciplinary work of the therapists, who were able to adjust their interventions to better meet the needs of the children as a result.

Art therapy interventions

One of the most common impairments of trauma is the difficulty in managing challenging feelings, as well as a limited ability for self-expression. In a contained environment, however, through carefully tailored directives and psychoeducational processing, art therapy techniques could facilitate the identification and expression of emotions, helping the children to learn to regulate difficult emotional states. For instance, thinking in metaphorical terms, a piece of paper could act as the external container of unwanted and hard to tolerate emotions and memories. Verbal pro-cessing of the artwork could allow for the initiation of helpful thinking, the inter-ruption of negative thoughts, and initiate the construction of a defensive shield against the intrusive traumatic memories depicted on paper, by instilling hope and a sense of control. In relation to the Syrian refugee children, their drawings provided an outlet for their emotions, as they were encouraged to share their drawings, and to respond to the depicted images with new attitudes and skills.

Problem-solving skills were addressed through the use of art materials and activities. Creating an artwork requires planning, as many decisions are made in order to begin the drawing process. These include finding a starting point, choosing which colour(s) and material(s) to begin with, proceeding to develop the artwork and finally coming to an end. This process helped the children's ability to organise internal stimuli and control impulsivity, leading to higher executive functioning (Hinz, 2009). The medium itself was also important in art-making. For example, the most contained work was done with pencils, while in contrast, oil pastels pro-vided less containment. The differences lay in the physical medium, as the lines of a pencil are relatively rigid and non-flowing, while oil pastels spread across the paper with ease and are thus less controllable for the artist. The psychology behind the use of different materials fed back into the cognitive aspects of the therapy, as the art therapist encouraged direct expressions of feelings from each child. For instance, oil pastels were often used as a controlled yet fluid material to allow the emotional affect of the children to surface, and still be easily contained within the paper.

As the children were 'seen and heard' through their drawings, the personalised act of creating art helped the children to be more content and relaxed, as evidenced by their responses. Through art therapy interventions, the children were able to create a physical picture of their inner world on the paper, expressing their imagination, experiences and current state of mind. This helped not only to create an understanding of the children's inner world, but was especially important considering the language barrier between therapist and participants. In order to provide support for the children, it was important to understand the children's needs, and adjust interventions and therapeutic approaches accordingly. It was crucial that the children felt in control of their artistic process, as trauma can disrupt one's sense of control. The therapeutic art-making provided an opportunity to contain the traumatic experience within the artistic medium, helping to create a sense of control over terrifying and intrusive memories. It also encouraged active participation in the therapy process, while aiming to reduce emotional numbness and the symptoms of hyperarousal and other distressing reactions.

After completing the given directive of the day, the children often asked for free drawing time. Most of the images drawn during this period depicted the horrors they had witnessed, in varying degrees of detail, and such instances created small windows of opportunity for rekindling hope in these children. For example, one young boy made a drawing of a mosque under attack (Fig. 8.1), and when asked about his drawing, he disclosed that the 'people who were praying inside were about to die'. The therapist asked if he would be interested in helping the people in his drawing. The child said yes, however, he did not appear hopeful about it. Hearing this response, the therapist then asked if he could think of anything he would like to add to his drawing that would be helpful for the people in it. The child thought about his options carefully, and responded that he could call the neighbours to warn them, and send an ambulance to the scene. The therapist's role was to look beyond the traumatic image, trying to understand the feelings that this drawing was communicating. In this case, it was the sense of hopelessness. By

FIGURE 8.1

offering the child an opportunity to change the ending of the traumatic memory he had just depicted, the therapist offered the child a sense of hope, and encouraged a shift in his perspective by installing a sense of control over what happened in his drawing. Snyder and his colleagues (2000) provide evidence supporting the approach that hope is an essential part of psychological well-being. They describe hope as a cognitive construct based on one's motivation, which can provide the capacity to strive for more.

In another example, the Syrian children were instructed to create an imaginary sea creature. One young boy quietly drew an image of a blue sheep, along with a red rectangular house. He was invited to discuss his image with the therapist, and he explained that he had drawn a picture of a blue sheep. The therapist reminded him that the activity was about drawing sea creatures, and in response, the boy said that the blue sheep was able to breathe underneath the water. The therapist recognised the boy's ability for creative thinking and need for validation, and encouraged him to continue his work. The boy not only finished his drawing with enthusiasm, but also asked for another piece of paper, creating what would eventually be the biggest sea creature within the group. This scenario is an example of attunement, explained by Daniel Siegel (2010) as the receiving of incoming cues and streams of information in a non-judgmental manner and without self-projection. When the child sensed the therapist's attunement, he was able to feel an authentic connection, which led to a sense of trust, encouraging the child to dive deeper into the creative process, with understanding and support from the therapist to continue his creative process.

Music therapy interventions

Music therapy has been shown to help children who have experienced war trauma to express their emotions and feelings in a safe manner, while improving their self-esteem and helping them to regain a sense of purpose and personal control (Bergmann, 2002). In another study, with adult soldiers who experienced severe war trauma, Bensimon, Amir and Wolf (2008: 46) found that 'group drumming increased a sense of openness, togetherness, belonging, sharing, closeness, connected-ness, and intimacy'. The effects of war trauma seen at the start of music therapy sessions have included 'avoidance behaviours, regressive behaviours, depression, grief reactions and problems in communicating with peers' (Lang and Mcinerny, 2005: 160). As seen in the research, the social aspect of music therapy sessions was important, as the children learned to engage with one another using music.

It was a primary goal to help the children understand and transfer skills learned within sessions to their lives beyond the scope of the five-day programme. As a result, leadership activities were designed to improve self-confidence, and help the children exercise their individual creativity and assertiveness. For example, they were challenged to take turns leading the group during a conducting exercise. During the exercise, some children with less developed leadership skills were able to learn from those with greater confidence, as the therapist encouraged the parti-cipation of each child. The children were given a second chance to conduct, resulting in the opportunity to improve upon their previous performance. While there were developmental differences between the ages of the children and their ability to lead the group, the children learned from one another after the first round, and were generally more decisive and assertive when leading for the second time.

Improvisation played an important role, with the children encouraged to develop their creativity and express their emotions. During one activity, two children at a time were seated in the middle of the group's circle, each with a drum; they were asked to musically explore the space between them, responding to each other's rhythms. Sometimes needing prompting from the therapist, other times not, every pair revealed different musical interactions. After each round, the children in the centre were asked to comment on the interaction. Many children said they felt happy, and that it was fun to respond to their partner's rhythms. While there were some who were shy and opted not to participate, there were a couple of children who displayed signs of dissociation, sitting in the outer circle during the first session of the day. During a discussion with the volunteers and translators after the session, it was concluded that the passive act of watching the pairs without musical involvement had led these two children to dissociate from their surroundings. It was decided that in subsequent groups with the same activity, children in the outer circle would be handed shakers, so that they would be occupied and musically engaged. During the following two sessions that day, these interventions were implemented, and no one on the team had any further reports of children showing dissociative symptoms.

The children generally brought a chaotic energy into music sessions, which the music therapist channeled into the music-making. It was important to utilise their chaos, as it was part of the group process. By transforming this chaos into a more organised expression, group performances became more meaningful. Generally, it was necessary to adapt activities to each group, due to age-related developmental differences, as well as personal needs. For instance, a few children displayed sensitivity towards high volumes, resulting in a balancing act between matching the group's needs (who generally enjoyed playing percussion at high volumes), and keeping the volume levels controlled so as not to trigger anxiety in children with volume sensitivities. In another instance, it was realised that one vocal warm-up activity could be interpreted as sounding 'like a falling bomb', as one of the children said during the exercise. The therapist processed the comment with the group, directing the children back to the present by offering an explanation about the use of sound, and reminding them that this was a safe setting. A different vocal exercise was used in subsequent groups, to avoid a repeat of the potential trigger.

Significantly, many of the children were involved in activities that were new to them. For instance, many had never played a drum or guitar. Activities with the musical instruments were a unique and eye-opening experience for them, the instruments acting as a metaphor for opportunities in the world that they may never have experienced before. Taking into account the economic reality of their families, it was important that the children understood that they could potentially make music anywhere, at any time, without the need for traditional and costly instruments. The children were encouraged to use their voice, body-percussion, sticks, chairs, water bottles and floors to create music, in addition to the provided drums. The use of voice was also thoroughly explored; singing is deeply embedded within Syrian culture, and this appeared to be the most instinctive musical outlet for many children.

During a songwriting activity, children were asked to come together as a group to find a theme. The children in one group initially settled on the theme of animals, and, using suggestions from the group and voting for the idea that the group liked the most, the group created a song in Arabic that reflected their mixed emotions. After writing the lyrics, along with an English translation, the children were asked whether the song should be fast or slow, happy or sad. The children responded that the song should be fast and happy, and the therapist then adapted the lyrics to a musical form, using guitar and voice. The children contributed melody ideas, and the therapist organised them into a comprehensive melody which the group memorised. The lyrics were made in Arabic, and the English translation is as follows:

> The bird is sad
> The cat is happy
> The rose is wilted
> The baby is alive

Dance movement therapy interventions

> Dance/movement therapy chooses the sensorimotor level as an entry port to treat the trauma and its aftermath, and thereby directly activates the bodily resources which in turn advance the emotional and cognitive processing of the trauma.
>
> *Koch and Weidinger-von der Recke (2009: 295)*

Dance movement therapy sessions aimed to encourage creativity and safe processing of the traumatic experiences stored in the body, while supporting release and creating resources for the children. As this particular population had been exposed to chaotic environments, it was important to set appropriate boundaries. By emphasising the importance of physical personal space, a safe environment was created, which allowed the children to express themselves, while also managing the impulsiveness and aggression observed in sessions. By repeating the rules at the beginning of each session, children became aware of the importance of respecting one another's space. Turn-taking, listening, mindfulness, and an emphasis that everyone is different and moves differently were crucial for establishing group rules based on respect and acceptance. When a child's personal space was violated verbally or physically, other children warned one another that rules were being broken.

Dance movement therapy sessions included structured activities as well as time for free movement expression, where children were invited to use the space to improvise as a way of expressing thoughts and emotions. In contrast to art and music therapy sessions, children had the opportunity to be physically active in these sessions, making use of the space provided by the dance room. As a result, the sessions were very active and sometimes chaotic, the children expressing a need to release their energy through dance. As Levine (2008) notes, the discharge of frozen energy is necessary when considering the impact of traumatic experiences. Traumatic experiences seem to cause 'fight/flight/freeze' behaviours, observed in the children as aggressive outbursts, running away from the group, an inability to move when stressed, and difficulty problem-solving. By using a wide range of movements such as rolling, running, skipping, jumping, and going 'over and under', the children were encouraged to move 'from fixity to flow' (Levine, 2008: 40). Over time their range of motion developed, leading the children to find new coping mechanisms, building resilience and resources to improve their problem-solving skills.

Rhythmic movement seemed grounding for the children, and improvised dance moves encouraged a feeling of togetherness and cohesion, helping to re-establish a sense of hope and connection for even the most isolated. By mirroring and being mirrored through dance, children were encouraged to identify their feelings, and manage their responses in creative ways. In addition, the use of props such as balls, scarves, hula-hoops and stretchy materials were used to stimulate movement and encourage creative expression.

During dance movement therapy sessions, feelings of helplessness, apparent difficulty making choices, and behaviours ranging from withdrawal to hyperactivity were observed among the children. Some children had difficulty regulating their behaviours, presenting as either aggressive, or shy and withdrawn. In order to reinforce a sense of consistency and safety as well as support self-regulation, starting and ending routines were created. The use of a parachute at the end of each session helped to form an ending ritual that was predictable and calming for the group (Fig. 8.2).

FIGURE 8.2

Volunteers actively participated in the dance movement therapy sessions, supporting those children who needed one-to-one attention to engage in the activities. The translators were trained to match the therapist's voice and gestures, making the language barrier less challenging. Following the SPR model, children were invited to play, relax and experience healthy social interactions, while learning to take turns, listen, follow and lead. By having a voice, and being able to exercise choice about their movements without fear of judgment, it was observed that children regained a sense of control that had been eroded by the traumas they had experienced.

In one of the groups, two young girls were observed to be shy and reluctant to participate. They seemed to feel unsafe expressing themselves in the group, and stood next to each other for much of the movement exercises. On the third day, however, they used a hula-hoop to link up. Moving with each other and the therapist, the prop acted as a connection between the intrapersonal and interpersonal through which they were able to creatively build a relationship. The next day, they further connected through the use of hands, doing similar movements but no longer needing the hula-hoop between them. By the final day, they were more fully engaged, participating in group activities, responding to the therapist and initiating interactions with other children.

As the project progressed, the children were observed to focus, engage and relate with one another for longer periods of time. Their kinesphere (Laban, 1966) also increased: initially observed as close to the body, by the end of the week it was larger and included a full range of movement in their arms and legs. This expanded use of space and increase in movement range helped to foster their sense of belonging within the group, something that was particularly observed through the 'hello' movements, when some shy children started using larger, more expressive movements to say hello during the course of the week.

Benefits and challenges of the collaboration

Working with a highly traumatised population in a group setting

Working with a highly traumatised population, there was a need for release, reflection and self-care for both the therapists and the team. With up to twenty children to a group, it was a challenge for the therapists to pay detailed attention to the needs of specific children, and groups could easily become chaotic. For example, one child might cry because of overstimulation, another would show symptoms of withdrawal, while yet another would be asking questions with enthusiasm. As a result, the team needed to build strategies to cope with the children's varying needs.

Feedback and communication among the team

The team of volunteers and translators received trauma training from the creative arts therapists, which was a crucial part of the preparation for sessions. Individual and group supervision was used to assess and meet the needs of both the children and volunteers, while the creative arts therapists had peer supervision sessions and shared reflection notes. Emergent issues were discussed, as well as any interventions that had worked well for specific children and could help in another modality. The use of feedback between therapists and volunteers was crucial to keeping the therapists informed about what was working and any difficulties in the overall collaboration. Without this, they could not have evaluated progress, and the programme could not have been adjusted day-to-day.

Cross-modality as complementary forms of expression

The collaboration between arts therapies respected the children's different learning preferences. It was observed that papers and desks played an important role in physical containment in art therapy, drums were used to express strong emotions in music therapy, and a parachute was used to regulate the children's energy in the dance movement therapy group. The use of a combination of modalities within the same setting allowed the personal preferences of each child to be accommodated. All three therapists also saw the influence of the other therapies within their own sessions. For example, in an art therapy session a little girl drew a picture of herself and the music therapist playing a drum – acknowledging the relationship built in music therapy through art. In the dance therapy group, the children spontaneously sang and danced to the 'goodbye song' they had created in their music session. In the music therapy group, a child mentioned that he wanted to draw more pictures, reflecting the way art therapy sessions had met the child's needs.

The role of translators

Translators played a significant role in the collaboration. Consulted to obtain additional information from the children about the meanings of their expressions when necessary, translators would often include personal interpretations based on their own stories and assumptions, which could be challenging. Providing extra support and supervision for translators was crucial, where translators' interpretations and expressions could be acknowledged, and their responses to the creative process discussed.

Balancing energy levels

An aspect of the project that needed addressing was the way energy levels transitioned between the various art, music and dance movement groups. For instance, if a group of children started their day in the music or dance session, and the session ended with a high level of energy, the children went into the next session – say an art therapy session – with heightened energy levels that could lead to distraction and restlessness. Drawing on feedback from therapists and volunteers, the therapists were able to take this into consideration, and adjust the structure to ensure that energy levels were contained towards the end of sessions to smooth the transition to the next modality.

Emotional vocabulary

Significantly, the emotional vocabulary of some children was limited, and they seemed to be unaware of their own emotional state. Some experienced psychosomatic symptoms such as nausea, headaches and lack of energy, but were unable to identify and express how they were feeling. Over the course of the five-day collaboration, the children showed improved recognition of their emotions through participation and feedback. In order to consolidate these new-found skills and resources, a need for follow-up activities was identified.

Cultural differences

During the project, the team learned rudimentary Arabic in an attempt to close the cultural gap with the children, who responded positively to the team's efforts, correcting their pronunciation with laughter. The Syrian translators were extremely helpful in deciphering codes of conduct, especially regarding gender roles within Syrian society. For example, it was understood that the children perceived males as dominant figures holding authority, and women as primarily maternal figures. It was also noticed that most children were not accustomed to expressing themselves through artistic means, as their culture did not largely encourage expressive behaviour. Some of the children were initially self-conscious and shy, requiring consistent encouragement to make their own choices. Overall, the children tended to act collectively, following the actions of another, be they another child or a volunteer. As the week progressed, however, they showed more individuality and vitality in their expressions.

Limitations

The project was limited to a five-day programme, and its scope was restricted by this time frame. For instance, it was not viable to launch a comprehensive programme to explore the deeper nature of the traumas that each child had experienced, something that might have been possible if the sessions were extended over a number of weeks or months. It is believed that the efficacy of the project would have been increased had it run for longer.

Conclusion

The collaboration between art therapy, music therapy and dance movement therapy in the same setting seemed to provide significant therapeutic benefits for the participants. Through a coordinated programme that was designed to meet their specific needs, the Syrian refugee children generally responded positively to the therapeutic use of multiple art forms.

The collaboration provided not only a therapeutic, but also an educational space. Some had disclosed that they had never attended school, and most of those who did attend had not received an uninterrupted education, due to the conflict in their country. Very few had any formal exposure to art, music or dance, and for most of the children it was apparent that they had never been given a chance to express their feelings about their experiences. The collaboration aimed to close this gap, by introducing children to different artistic forms through which to express their experiences and emotions.

Overall, the team was inspired by the children's strength, resilience, sense of humour and creativity. As war and other traumatic circumstances continue to affect the lives of people around the world, it is believed that further collaborations between the arts therapies have the potential to support cognitive, emotional, physical, social and spiritual integration for those affected. It is recommended that further research is carried out in this area, looking at new ways of helping populations who have experienced war trauma and forced migration.

Acknowledgments

Maya Foundation, Project Lift, Istanbul, Turkey

References

Apa.org (2016). *American Psychological Association: Post-Traumatic Stress Disorder.* [Online] Available at: http://www.apa.org/topics/ptsd/ [Accessed 23 Apr 2016].

Arnsten, A.F., Mathew R., Ubriani, R., Tailor, J.R. and Li, B.M. (1999). Alpha-1 Noradrenergic Receptor Stimulation Impairs Prefrontal Cortical Cognitive Function. *Biological Psychiatry*, 45(1), pp. 26–31.

Bensimon, M., Amir, D. and Wolf, Y. (2008). Drumming Through Trauma: Music Therapy with Post-Traumatic Soldiers. *The Arts In Psychotherapy*, 35(1), pp. 34–48.

Bergmann, K. (2002). The Sound of Trauma: Music Therapy in a Post-War Environment. *Australian Journal of Music Therapy*, 13, pp. 3–16.

Hinz, L. (2009). *Expressive Therapies Continuum: A Framework for Using Art in Therapy.* New York, NY: Routledge.

Koch, S.C. and Weidinger-von der Recke, B. (2009). Traumatised Refugees: An Integrated Dance and Verbal Therapy Approach. *The Arts in Psychotherapy*, 36(5), pp. 289–296.

Laban, R.V. (1966). *The Language of Movement: A Guidebook to Choreutics.* Boston, MA: Plays, Inc.

Lang, L. and Mcinerny, U. (2005). Bosnia-Herzegovina: A Music Therapy Service in a Post-War Environment. In: J.P. Sutton, ed., *Music, Music Therapy and Trauma: International Perspectives*, 1st ed. London: Jessica Kingsley Publishers, pp. 153–174.

Levine, P.A. (2008). *Healing Trauma: A Pioneering Program for Restoring the Wisdom of Your Body.* Boulder, CO: Sounds True.

Levine, S.K. (2011). *Art in Action: Expressive Arts Therapy and Social Change.* London: Jessica Kingsley Publishers.

Mahdjoubi, L. and Akplotsyi, R. (2012). The Impact of Sensory Learning Modalities on Children's Sensitivity to Sensory Cues in the Perception of their School Environment. *Journal of Environmental Psychology*, 32(3), pp. 197–286.

Nctsn.org (2012). *The National Child Traumatic Stress Network: Skills for Psychological Recovery*, 1st ed. [Online] Available at: http://www.nctsn.org/sites/default/files/assets/pdfs/spr_general.pdf [Accessed 30 July 2015].

Siegel, D.J. (2010). *The Mindful Therapist: A Clinician's Guide to Mindsight and Neural Integration*. New York, NY: W.W. Norton.

Snyder, C.R., Feldman, D.B., Taylor, J.D., Schroeder, L.L. and Adams, V.H., III. (2000). The Roles of Hopeful Thinking in Preventing Problems and Enhancing Strengths. *Applied and Preventive Psychology*, 9(4), pp. 249–269.

Streeck-Fischer, A. and Van der Kolk, B.A. (2000). Down Will Come Baby, Cradle and All: Diagnostic and Therapeutic Implications of Chronic Trauma on Child Development. *Australian and New Zealand Journal of Psychiatry*, 34(6), pp. 903–918.

Unhcr.org (2015). *United Nations High Commissioner for Refugees: 2015 UNHCR Country Operations Profile: Turkey*. [online] Available at: http://www.unhcr.org/pages/49e48e0fa 7f.html [Accessed 30 July 2015].

Van der Kolk, B.A. (2003). The Neurobiology of Childhood Trauma and Abuse. *Child and Adolescent Psychiatric Clinics of North America*, 12(2), pp. 293–317.

Van der Kolk, B.A. (2014). *The Body Keeps the Score: Brain, Mind, and Body in the Healing of Trauma*. New York, NY: Viking.

Van der Kolk, B.A. and Fisler, R. (1995). Dissociation and the Fragmentary Nature of Traumatic Memories: Overview and Exploratory Study. *Journal of Traumatic Stress*, 8(4), pp. 505–525.

Van Der Werf, Y.D., Jolles, J., Witter, M.P. and Uylings, H.B. (2003). Special Issue: Contributions of Thalamic Nuclei to Declarative Memory Functioning. *Cortex*, 39(4/5), pp. 1047–1062.

3rpsyriacrisis.org (2015). *3RP Regional Refugee & Resilience Plan 2015–2016: In Response to the Syria Crisis: 2015 Annual Report*. [Online] Available at: http://www.3rpsyriacrisis.org/wp-content/uploads/2016/04/3RP-2015-Annual-Report.pdf [Accessed 23 Apr 2016].

PART II

Transdisciplinary practice and research in the arts therapies

9

REGAINING BALANCE THROUGH FAMILY ART PSYCHOTHERAPY

Katie Wilson & Yvonne Rose

This chapter describes a family's journey through family art psychotherapy within a Child and Adolescent Mental Health Service (CAMHS). Features of narrative therapy (White and Epston, 1990) and art psychotherapy were combined to create a collaborative space where stories could be explored and shared, and alternative accounts co-constructed. We will present our work with a teenage girl, Ella, and her family which took place over a period of nine months. We will describe selected therapy sessions and our observations and reflections, focusing on aspects of theory and practice which demonstrate the therapeutic enrichment of bringing these modalities together.

An Audio Image Recording (AIR) was made with the family as part of a review process to help facilitate reflective conversations about their progress in therapy. The AIR provides feedback about the family's experience of therapy and, with the family's full consent, allows us to present their voices.

Reduced resources and increased demand on services challenges us to retain qualities of innovation and creativity. Pressures on our team had begun to erode a culture of joint working, which can be perceived as an ineffective way of managing high demands on the service. We aim to show the therapeutic benefits of including a multimodal approach within clinical practice.

A way of being in narrative therapy

The narrative approach was founded by White and Epston (1990), who developed the idea that narratives are the means by which identities are shaped. Narrative therapy pays attention to the stories that we tell and that are told about us, as these stories are seen to shape how we think about ourselves and others and impact on our actions and choices in life. Narrative therapy recognises that some stories can become dominant and exert a powerful impact.

In offering a decentred position (White, 2007), narrative therapy sees the family as experts on their own lives, and places their insider knowledge at the centre of the conversation. Drawing on social constructionist theory, narrative therapy is interested in the use of language to separate the person's identity from the dominant problem (externalising). This process assists people to move away from pathologising labels, so that exceptions and competencies can be recognised (White and Epston, 1990). Reducing the influence of the dominant story creates the possibility for change.

Art psychotherapy as a means of nonverbal communication

The art psychotherapist notices, and creates space for, the interplay of multifaceted communication within an image. Art made in therapy embodies emotional expression, presenting subtle layering of meaning which may harmonise or conflict (Case and Dalley, 1992). Such multiple dimensions of expression can be hard to articulate verbally. Equally, the way in which art materials are selected and used can help the art psychotherapist to appreciate the client's inner experience. The art psychotherapist is familiar with waiting for meaning to emerge (Winnicott, 2005), and will hold in mind multiple meanings as they work to attune to the client's changing mental states.

Audio Image Recording (AIR)

Audio Image Recordings were created and developed for use in art psychotherapy as a method of identifying agents of change (Springham and Brooker, 2010). An AIR is a short film which brings together selected images made in therapy with a recorded conversation. It is a record of the client's reflections on their experience of therapy, and is usually made as they prepare to end the process. We wanted to use the same method as a means of focusing reflective conversations as a way of reviewing progress. We asked the family to choose pieces of work they had made from the start, middle and most recent points in therapy. Sharing collective and individual narratives highlighted change in the family system. Through this process, we hoped to have a clearer sense of what had been helpful to allow us to work with the family to assess the need for further therapeutic goals. With the family's consent, we have included excerpts from their AIR made in one recording during a review meeting after the tenth session of therapy. All names have been changed to protect confidentiality.

Developing a shared therapeutic language

As colleagues (Katie, art psychotherapist, and Yvonne, systemic family psychotherapist), we thought in more depth about the personal and professional qualities that we recognised in each other, and the shared foundations of our therapeutic models. We identified that perceived differences sometimes lay with a lack of understanding of the subtleties and depths of each other's therapeutic model. The process of demystifying and re-telling our theoretical structures was an essential foundation of our work together, and helped us begin to shape our therapeutic approach. Opening up difference helped us trust that within sessions we weren't going to work against each other, and would be better able to tune into the supporting structure we each brought. We were more inclined to flex – sometimes holding back, sometimes offering alternative thinking – and in doing so modelled a robust relationship.

The dominant story

Ella, 13, was living with her parents, Ben and Bronwyn, and sister Abigail, 17. Her eldest sister, Freya, 18, was studying at university in another city. The family had previous contact with CAMHS when as a young teenager Freya was diagnosed with anorexia nervosa – Ella was about 7 years old at the time. During this period the family had briefly attended family sessions but felt that it had been unhelpful, and this impacted on Ella's openness to re-engage with a family approach. When we first met Ella to assess risk she was low in mood, self-harming in the form of cutting, and struggling with her dietary intake. There was a dominant story of finding it difficult to verbalise her feelings and emotionally isolating herself, in particular from her father. Ella was setting herself very high standards academically; she strove for perfection and was finding it difficult to openly allow others to care for her.

Finding a way to come together

Our formulation recognised relational tensions, as it was the whole family experiencing distress. They seemed emotionally raw and struggling to begin a process of recovery. Battling anorexia had shattered their sense of normality, and seemed to have impacted heavily on trust and intimacy within the family. We wondered if there were untold or unclear stories about living with anorexia, and felt that beginning a healing process together would offer a space for the family to gain strength and confidence as a unit. We wanted to support a family approach, however, Ella expressed guilt about the distress her family had felt following her self-harm, and worried that this would be difficult to face with her parents. She also spoke of her concern that she would be blamed and her 'flaws exposed' if therapy took place with the family together. We wondered if a combination of art and family psychotherapy would offer the family something that was different enough from their previous experience of coming together as a family in therapy. The idea was accepted, and a therapeutic plan was formulated for two individual art psychotherapy sessions for Ella, for Yvonne to offer parallel sessions with parents, and then, for us all to work together in family art psychotherapy in the third week.

Hopes, and beginning therapy

Ella's hopes for therapy were to be able to manage attending school, not feel so 'horrific' and be better at coping with her emotions. Ella's parents' hopes were for Ella to feel secure, more happy and resilient enough to control some of her feelings instead of harming herself.

We began the first family art psychotherapy session with Ella and Bronwyn by showing where things were in the room and revisiting the agreed plan for therapy. Ella spoke about the importance of balancing time to have fun alongside more serious conversations. We suggested on this occasion that we would give an idea of what to work on, and set them each the task of making a personal tree. In providing a starting point, we hoped to contain the potential anxieties of uncertainty surrounding too little structure, and enable the family to get physically involved with the art materials. We talked about different kinds of trees, and the different stages as a tree grows, and asked Ella and Bronwyn to think of their tree as a self-portrait, suggesting that they may wish to include fantasy and magical elements. We gave them clay as a base to shape a trunk, together with a selection of twigs, bark, fir cones and seed pods and other natural materials, and invited them to make use of other art materials in the room. They worked separately, paying attention to their own work while noticing each other's. The conversation between Ella and her mum was light and playful, with a quality of nervous energy.

We structured the session to allow 30 minutes of art-making followed by time for reflection. Bronwyn described her tree as solid: a large, old oak tree which had withstood the elements. Bronwyn noted the contrast with Ella's tree, and joked about how obvious it would be to another family member which tree they had each made. Ella's tree was constructed delicately, taking to the limits the clay's ability to retain its structural integrity, and she had added sparkling string and beads (Fig. 9.1 and Fig. 9.2).

We thought about the placement of the trees on the table: how close to each other? How far apart? We asked questions about the look and feel of the terrain and landscape around the trees. Ella and her mum both acknowledged that some space was needed between the trees, as each tree had a broad canopy and required space and light to thrive. As we talked, Ella modelled a bench from clay, which she placed under her mum's tree.

Clay

We introduced clay early in the work with the intention of offering a playful and safe approach to the art-making. Clay brings solidity; it comes from the earth and through its innate qualities can absorb and contain strong emotions (Henley, 2002). It is a naturally grounding material, stimulating the senses and helping with emotional containment. Henley writes about the engagement with clay in art psychotherapy as having the effect of diminishing inhibitions, allowing repressed emotions to find expression.

FIGURE 9.1

FIGURE 9.2

How externalisation connected to working with imagery

Our directive approach of offering a theme gave Ella and her mum the opportunity to externalise and bear witness to aspects of themselves within their art-making. Exploring self-portraits through metaphor was a natural meeting point between the therapy modalities, as pictures and models can bring immediacy and life to verbal externalisations. Sharing the story of the trees created space for new narratives, as Ella and her mum jointly showed appreciation that both trees needed space to thrive. Externalising through metaphor gave the family a starting point that allowed them to bring themselves into the room in fuller and potentially unexpected ways. As we talked, the artwork and stories continued to develop, such as Ella placing a bench under her mum's tree – perhaps a place to rest and reflect. Building on this initial experience, we wanted to help the family extend their exploration of art-making by shifting to a non-directive approach. In handing over responsibility for the art, we invited the family to creatively discover how they could together take up greater agency in their own lives. To support this shift, we gave value to the processes of choosing and engaging with the art material.

Both parents attended with Ella at the second appointment. Together, they made a decision to work on a large shared picture, each gathering the paint and equipment they needed. Ella and Bronwyn chose ready-mix paint, while Ben brought tubs of finger paint to the table. Ella made the first mark, in the centre of the paper. We witnessed a high level of cooperation and sharing of space on the paper as they built on one another's colour choices and styles of mark-making. Ella playfully put a blob of red paint on her mum's nose, and Bronwyn accepted this in good humour. We witnessed ongoing tensions in the edgy jokiness between Ella and her dad.

After completing the picture, we explored the experience (Fig. 9.3). Ben said that he had not used paint for a long time, especially finger paints to make hand prints.

FIGURE 9.3

Bronwyn found the size of Ella's hand surprising and noted that she had outgrown her memory of a child's handprint. We wondered how this related to her parents seeing Ella as 'growing up'. Ella appeared uncomfortable when we explored her chosen starting point at the middle of the picture. She strongly made it clear to us that it was not her aim to be the centre of attention. We observed humour and playfulness emerging in the session, representing an area of resilience and providing a way to begin to explore events which stood outside the dominant story.

The family's reflections on the start of therapy (AIR)

Playfulness

ELLA: We all kind of contributed and I think it shows us as a family quite well … it's not really in sections unlike some of the other pieces we have done together.

YVONNE: This was the first time you came together as a three and the picture comes together as well.

BRONWYN: Yes and it's just playful isn't it, just a bit of fun.

BEN: I was quite nervous of doing 'art' in inverted commas, so poking around with finger paint was about as easy as it gets.

YVONNE: I remember that coming together was difficult as well, that idea of coming together and this marked the beginning of that.

BEN: The start of it.

BRONWYN: It did, it seemed as if it would be difficult but actually doing this wasn't at all difficult, was it? I think it just seemed very relaxed and fun so it was good.

Family art psychotherapy: middle

A dominant story continued to unfold as we heard Ben and Bronwyn express their sadness and bewilderment at once more seeking help from CAMHS. We focused on maintaining a therapeutic space that could nurture hope and allow alternative narratives to develop. By staying with and accepting the moment-to-moment experiences we hoped to validate feelings of anger, uncertainty and confusion.

Ella and Bronwyn attended the third and fourth sessions. Ben planned to attend but was held up at work. Ella showed signs of distress at the start of session, her head down and body shaky. Plasticine was quick and easily accessible and we made use of it to help regulate and contain her raw emotions.

Bronwyn told us that Ben would be feeling guilty about not being with them in therapy. She felt they could do better as parents at explaining to the girls when Ben had work commitments. Ella explained and demonstrated how she usually plays 'dinosaurs' with her dad when they need to make up.

Bronwyn told us about an incident over the weekend when they discovered alcohol in Ella's bedroom. As this was being discussed, Ella curled up and rejected comfort from her mum. In the following silence Bronwyn became tearful; she let us know this stemmed from not being able to help Ella with her distress. It felt important to support the family to stay with upset feelings and speculate about hope and a future where feelings can change and shift over time. Ella appeared calmer as we approached the end of the session, and was able to receive comforting touch from her mum.

Ella was silent throughout the fourth session. Bronwyn worked sensitively with her, communicating with gestures and signs. They worked together on a collage. Ella appeared to relax a little as she was making the picture. We tried to explore quietness and loudness within the family. We heard how quiet home will be when Abigail leaves for university in a few months. Ella let us know that she will miss her sister, as they were re-establishing their relationship.

Bronwyn and Ben came without Ella to the next session. Ella let us know she was willing to attend next week. Bronwyn and Ben chose to work with clay. We asked about the way powerful emotional content is managed within their family. Ben stated that he did not think that the family had managed this very well in the past. By the end of the session Ben had created a collection of small, finely detailed pots, and Bronwyn showed her intriguing sculpture of a head. Together we reflected on creativity – being creative and rekindling creativity within day to day life.

During the sixth session we witnessed anger and frustration as Ella expressed a flood of disgust and hopelessness. She told her parents that she felt responsible for their upset feelings and the likelihood of their relationship breaking down and ending in divorce. Bronwyn and Ben affirmed that their relationship would endure. Ella continued to fire verbal aggression towards her dad, accusing him of rejecting Freya during her struggle with anorexia. As the volatile emotional intensity built in the room, Ella expressed feelings of rejection towards family therapy, and characterised family therapists as 'making everything worse'.

Ella appeared exhausted. 'Stuckness' prevailed in the room as we worked to contain Ella's distress. We acknowledged Ella's sense of fragility and exhaustion, and suggested a short break. Katie took Ella out of the room and went to make tea for her parents. Back in the therapy room she was able to accept their help. In voicing her fears about her parents separating, Ella then bravely steered the conversations that followed which began to address the family's fundamental strengths.

Playing dinosaurs

Space was opened up as we heard about the parents' childhood experiences. Rich narratives of the strength of their love emerged alongside their resilience. An alternative story of affection between Ella and her dad, re-connecting whilst playing dinosaurs was discovered and thickened. Ella demonstrated using her hands as claws to show the 'Tyrannosaurus hugs' that she exchanged with her dad at times when it didn't feel possible to make physical contact. The tight-clawed gestures demonstrated willingness to show acceptance of each other and achieved a tentative, if wary, closeness whilst also maintaining distance. Closeness and separateness became an important theme.

Withstanding powerful emotions

Bearing and tolerating their own and others' distress seemed an important experience for the family. Ella found it difficult to emotionally regulate with her parents in the room. The brief break seemed to provide the necessary separation to then return with a renewed sense of herself. Space also enabled the parents to gather their thoughts, and process their emotions with Yvonne. The decision to take a break risked giving the message that as therapists we could not contain the emotional content of the session. It also had the potential to magnify Ella's tendency to split her feelings and projections into one 'good' and one 'bad' therapist, in the same way as we had seen Ella blame family therapy as destructive, directing her anger towards Yvonne who seemed to represent the coming together of family members.

The family's reflections on the middle of therapy (AIR)

Just playing with Plasticine

ELLA: It's good when you're not in a great mood because you can kind of punch it for a bit and then you can actually make stuff.

BEN: Very forgiving.

ELLA: Yeah.

BRONWYN: I find it really soothing just not necessarily making anything but just to manipulate. It's a bit like worry beads or something isn't it, sitting there just playing with the Plasticine.

BEN: I think that's one of the things that a lot of this has been that art defuses some of the tensions. We have had some fairly difficult sessions here. At least the art, when we were able to do it, has been able to relax things a bit.

YVONNE: And how has that helped with change do you think?

BEN: I think it has just helped us to move on. It's not anything specific, I mean we don't all rush and get the Plasticine out at home if things are hard but it has given us a chance to do something like that here.

Exploding and coming back together

BRONWYN: I think it has made me realise at least that things at one moment can seem really, really difficult but actually quite quickly, with the art that we have been doing here, within the hour you have gone from really difficult to actually it being OK, and actually having fun as well. So I think just knowing that is helpful at any time, whatever situations.

ELLA: There were a lot of emotions bubbling under the surface for a while and I think because we have been able to have, like yelling at each other times, then kind of been back to fun before we have left, I think those kind of emotions have been got out and sorted. The situation didn't need to be sorted, but they have kind of been got out of the way so that those barriers aren't between us anymore.

BEN: Exploding and coming back together.

ELLA: I mean things aren't just chilling in the air now, it's kind of gone. And I think this has reflected in our relationship at home.

BEN: Yep.

BRONWYN: Definitely.

ELLA: I think things are better at home.

BEN: More accepting of the ups and downs.

BRONWYN: A bit more open, a bit more able to show feelings and actually... perhaps particularly you two with each other that you can get angry or upset with each other, but actually that's not the end of the world you can still very quickly, often as well, move beyond that.

BEN: Yes.

ELLA: I think it's just helped us have a more open relationship, which I think also allows more space for getting on, like it allows us to have our arguments then be much closer when we are not arguing, in my personal opinion, because I would feel – I do feel – closer to you.

YVONNE: You're looking at your dad as you said that.

ELLA: Yeah.

BEN: Thank you. [pause] All that from finger paint.

ELLA: Yeah.

BRONWYN: Go finger painting.

ELLA: Magical powers.

Family art psychotherapy: approaching the end

We began to hear about positive change. Ella described how she had re-connected with her social network in school, and both parents had noticed that Ella was able to feel calm more quickly following her 'expressive moments'.

Ella demonstrated how her physical connection with her dad had changed from 'Tyrannosaurus hugs' to mini hugs using two fingers. They all worked on one large piece of paper, mostly sticking to their own areas (Fig. 9.4). Ella took up an invitation from her dad to add to his painting. She then moved to the other end of the paper to add to her mum's work. Ella was animated throughout, telling us about mythical and fantasy creatures. Ben described Bronwyn's work as an explosion, a vibrant creative burst. Ben's painting depicted a calm scene of camping in the hills. We heard that Ben and Bronwyn had recently been camping together.

FIGURE 9.4

The family's reflections approaching the end of therapy (AIR)

Separateness

YVONNE: I think the three of you have said something important about how within that picture there's more separateness around, but that you have got different thoughts about the separateness that's been expressed in that picture. Can you say a bit more about that?

BEN: I don't see it as separate, more individual, so there is more space for the individuals on that.

YVONNE: More space.

BEN: We all chose a different medium, in fact unlike this first one where we were all doing the same thing, we chose different things.

BRONWYN: Yes and I suppose it is about having that space to have your own ideas, and maybe do things a bit differently, rather than having to negotiate at the beginning. Even before we started, in the earlier pieces we would negotiate about what medium we would use, whereas last week it was just 'right, I fancy having a go at doing this, this is what I am going to do' we did our own thing, but as you say we did come together a little bit at the end with it all anyway.

ELLA: …I think that kind of shows the fact that at home it's okay to seem a bit separate, but you are still very much together.

BRONWYN: Yes.

BEN: We've read a lot into that one, haven't we?

ELLA: We're getting good. I've been practicing. [Laughter]

YVONNE: So, being separate and being individual and being together are important elements for you as a family.

BRONWYN: Yes, and I think particularly as you are growing up through teenage years it's about finding that separateness, isn't it? Finding yourself as an individual, and maybe being a bit separate from your family, but still having your family always there for you. It's kind of what you are doing in that growing-up period. And all this time we thought we were just drawing. [Laughter]

Opening up the air

YVONNE: I wonder if that kind of reflects that it's your meaning that's important here, not our meaning.

BRONWYN: Yes and I think that's been one of the pleasant surprises, and perhaps one of the things that I was quite nervous about before having never done art therapy, but actually it has been very much led by us, down to the medium we used, our ideas and even the interpretation of what we have done really.... But that was a concern, that someone else will read all these things into it that you perhaps hadn't intended at all, whereas it has been very much led by us I would say.

BEN: So it's been a facilitator hasn't it. It has given us the ability to have the conversations.

ELLA: Yes, I think it just kind of opens the air...

BRONWYN: I think because you are not just focused on what you are all saying.

BEN: You can also dive back into the painting.

BRONWYN: So it can be quite natural, for example, to have a silence while you are busy doing something, whereas if you were just sat round in a group talking silence might be uncomfortable.

YVONNE: It seems that you are thinking about the difference between having talking Family Therapy and combining the two in having Family Art Therapy, and experiencing both, because you have experienced both haven't you?

BEN: This has been just completely different.

BRONWYN: For us this really worked, whereas just the Family Therapy...

BEN: ...was too awkward.

BRONWYN: Yes it was really difficult, a really difficult thing to just sit around and try and talk, although obviously each situation is different and perhaps, you know, different circumstances mean that different things work, but for us having the combination has just been fantastic. Really good.

ELLA: I think if we had done a different kind of Family Therapy, for example just sitting and talking, I don't think that I'd have managed that. I don't think it would have really helped anything, because personally that would just be a really horrible situation for me. Not because I don't like being with people, but just because I feel very outnumbered in situations like that.

BRONWYN: There have been some quite big things, some very meaningful things said in these sessions....I think for Ella it's been maybe a safe place, or maybe a place where there is attention but not too much attention, but it's been on okay place to say things that are important.

YVONNE: There's something about sticking with it even when you're not sure about the process.

BEN: Yes, sometimes you kind of think, well, yes we came, we painted, it wasn't particularly comfortable but I don't think we actually resolved anything. It's not about coming away thinking 'right, we have solved the problem'; it's just what we have taken together, a bit of a journey.

ELLA: I feel very comfortable around everyone when I am in this room, and I think it's not necessarily about the art. It's about having a bit of fun and talking about stuff and having art there to kind of create that environment.

BEN: I agree.

YVONNE: I remember Ella, you saying that balance was important when we first met, that sense of fun and difficult conversations, so it's kind of helpful to hear that we might have got that right.

BRONWYN: I think that by its nature, young people that are coming here or children that are coming here are going through a difficult time, so it is actually lovely if you can do a session – particularly with Family Therapy combined – that can be a bit of fun as well.

AIR as outsider witness

As the family engaged in conversation during the recording for the AIR, they became an audience to one anothers' stories, retelling their journey through therapy. The structure and focus brought by the recording of the AIR resembled features of Definitional Ceremonies (Barbara Myerhoff, 1986), where an audience who are significant people in the lives of the family are invited to bear witness, in order to support the family to keep connected with their new descriptions of themselves (White, 2007). On hearing one anothers' point of view, there was another opportunity, from a stepped-back position, to make sense of their individual and relational experiences.

Collaboratively reviewing therapeutic progress alongside the family's chosen imagery brought richer descriptions into their awareness of their desires and the changes they had observed in their lives. In this process family members seemed to re-position themselves, moving from the dominant story of family conflict to a new view of separateness and coming together. Their emerging, preferred, story of 'exploding and coming back together' seemed to recognise Ella and her sister's transitional stages of adolescence, which involve both independent and dependent qualities. It was inspiring to hear their achievements, which reconnected them to their emotional commitment to each other.

After they had recorded the AIR, the family let us know that they did not need to continue with therapy, and that the process of making the AIR had felt like the completion of our work together.

Strengths of joining the modalities

Creativity, play and identity

The family placed a high value on their experience of a safe space in family art psychotherapy and being guided and supported to explore their own meaning.

Play and creativity enabled each individual's discovery of themselves, independently and as a family (Winnicott, 2005). This combined approach increased the family's creative exploration, and played an important role in providing a facilitating environment where feelings could be experienced and thought about through playful encounters.

Pace of therapy

Respectfully allowing conversations to naturally unfold supported a stance where the family was empowered to lead the therapy. This development of trusting the family to become experts in their own lives was also visible to the family. As the excerpt noted, the family were surprised that they had interpreted their own meaning from the art they had produced.

Containment

We heard from the family that being able to delve into art-making at times helped them to manage powerful feelings. The process of creating something sets up a dialogue within the self (Dalley, 1992), and through our use of reflexive questions (Tomm, 1987) about the imagery, we were able to open up space so that the family felt safe enough to begin to express their fears and share information previously 'not-yet-said' (Anderson and Goolishian, 1988). Bringing together our strengths in verbal and nonverbal approaches was a key element to bridging our therapeutic models. Integrating our models brought skillful attention to both internal dialogue and external conversations, and combined to hold a strong containing and reflective therapeutic space.

Overcoming challenges

We recognised that within the therapy room we each held a domain. Art psychotherapy provided a sense of opening up space to 'be' and to play, and to engage with art-making processes which would encourage and support reflection. As the art psychotherapist, Katie emphasised the value of art expression reaching beyond the realm of illustration of thoughts and feelings. This was playfully picked up by the family, as they joked about the 'magical powers' of finger paint.

Family psychotherapy brought systemic thinking to bear – through curiosity, narrative questions and reflexivity – encouraging the opportunity for stories to unfold so that the family could be assisted in the development of new meanings. As a systemic family psychotherapist, Yvonne wanted to ensure that we would bring our differences into the room by reflecting with each other in front of the family. Part of the process of bringing together two models was letting go of some elements of our separate practice, which was reflected in an internal dialogue developing from, 'uh oh, I would not have said that', to 'interesting, let's go further with this'. Our task of joining disciplines was eased by the fact that we both bring diversity to our individual practice. This meant that contrasting and conflicting elements within our approaches were also allowed into the room. We each recognised that this learning experience increased our focus and curiosity, as we were less able to follow our regular rhythms of practice. Sharing our modalities was in some ways exposing, and required us to wrestle with both the foundations of our approaches and our view of ourselves as clinicians. Whilst challenging, this was a refreshing experience which developed us as practitioners and affirmed our commitment to the benefits of transdisciplinary working.

References

Anderson, H. and Goolishian, H. (1988). Human Systems as Linguistic System. *Family Process*, 27(4), pp. 371–393.

Case, C. and Dalley, T. (1992). *The Handbook of Art Therapy*. London: Routledge.

Dalley, T. (1992). *An Introduction to the Use of Art as a Therapeutic Technique*. London: Routledge.

Henley, D. (2002). *Clayworks in Art Therapy*. London: Jessica Kingsley Publishers.

Springham, N. and Brooker, J. (2010). The Reflect Interview. *British Association of Art Therapists Newsbriefing*, pp. 32–35.

Tomm, K. (1987). Interventive Interviewing: Part II. Reflexive Questioning a Means to Self-Enabling. *Family Process*, 26(2), pp. 167–183.

White, M. (2007). *Maps of Narrative Practice*. London: Norton.

White, M. and Epston, D. (1990). *Narrative Therapy Means to Therapeutic End*. London: Norton.

Winnicott, D.W. (2005). *Playing and Reality*. Oxon: Routledge.

10

A TRANSDISCIPLINARY APPROACH

Working with individuals in a sex offender treatment programme

Kate Rothwell & Laura Henagulph

Introduction

When the Specialist Learning Disabilities unit opened in the East London Foundation Trust Forensic Directorate in 2009, it immediately became apparent that we would have to become more inventive in our therapeutic approaches. The complex patient population on the medium and low secure wards included those who had received diagnoses of developmental disorders, personality disorders and severe mental illness, as well as their existing learning disability. Naturally, this group also included patients who had great difficulties with both receptive and expressive language, reading and writing. We needed to adapt many interventions, but particularly those that relied on a volume of written or spoken material within a tight structure. The Sex Offender Treatment Programme (SOTP) was one such intervention. We found that combining art therapy and psychology allowed patients to access the modules in a more visceral, visual manner. In this way, the patients began to engage in the process of learning, and to internalise a way of thinking that helped to break cycles of destructive behaviour. We saw that this approach nurtured reflective function, was highly flexible and could be adapted to individual needs. The ethos of creativity and transdisciplinary working therefore became central to our practice, alongside monitoring and discussion of risk.

Evidence base

The use of arts therapies with learning disabilities has been most recently documented in the British Psychological Society's comprehensive study, 'Psychological therapies and people who have intellectual disabilities' (Beail, 2016), and describes 'A flexible, adapted and individualised approach in their work. When working with people who have limited verbal communication, adaptation can include using picture symbols and other communication aids within the therapy. Additional communicative techniques such as intensive interaction may also be used' (Beail, 2016: 93). Complex theories focused on specific work with offenders with learning disabilities is described by Hackett, Porter and Taylor (2013) and Rothwell (2008), who states 'non-verbal processes in art-making may provide an opportunity for material to surface through the work, held within the therapeutic relationship and space' (Rothwell, 2008: 118; Hackett, 2012). In the Analysis of Assimilation (Beail and Jackson, 2009) a table of seven identified stages employed by persons with intellectual disabilities is shown to begin with Warded Off, and continue through Unwanted Thoughts and Vague Awareness through to Mastery, when defenses become assimilated into the capacity to use therapeutic support to self-manage emotional responses. Beail emphasis that the accompaniment of acting-out behaviours challenges the boundaries and containment when working with the problematic material brought into session. Beail further discusses the importance of adapting psychodynamic psychotherapy work with people with intellectual disabilities (ID) stating that,

> The therapist has to work within their client's communication abilities. Therefore, the therapist must pay careful attention to the words used and attempt to identify problems from non-verbal communications, or acting out within the session. It may be appropriate to help clients communicate by suggesting words for actions or feelings. It may also help to use alternative means of communication such as drawing or using objects.
>
> *(Beail, 2016: 25)*

Beail also reported positive outcomes of psychodynamic psychotherapy for offenders who have learning disabilities (Beail, 2001; Beail, 2016: 26).

The theme of co-facilitation collaboration is considered 'a means of being transparent and to be seen as willing to share expertise and to train others up in the work with the art psychotherapist ... and for the patient to be able to see that the art psychotherapist is part of the multidisciplinary team' (Rothwell and Grandison, 2016: 190). Hughes (2007) describes a collaboration of approaches to develop new meanings and understandings supported by the 'therapeutic relationship dynamic as a tool' by incorporating art psychotherapy and cognitive behavioural therapy (CBT) (Hughes, 2007: 29). Many examples of co-collaborations and cross-disciplinary working in forensic art, drama, music and dance movement therapies are described as a means of furthering the possibility and scope of therapeutic change with offenders through case study narratives (Guarnieri and Klugman, 2016; Orlowska and Parker, 2016; Goodman and Brown, 2016; Wassall and Greener, 2016; Rothwell, 2016; Wood and Johns, 2016; O'Connell and Montague, 2016; Guarnieri et al., 2016). The dynamic configurations that enhance the therapeutic relationship with patients with highly complex presentations in both individual and group work are considered to open up opportunities for progression through adaption to therapies practiced within secure settings. Working with sex offenders with learning disabilities using a cross-disciplinary group approach for offenders usually excluded due to mental health and communication issues is explored by Chisholm, McKenzie and Murray, who offered group sessions facilitated by a male art therapist and female clinical psychologist; this closely relates to the approach discussed in this chapter and considers the importance of role identity. Benefits of conducting weekly sessions using a consistent model together, rather than at separate times and places in the week, are described in consideration of the respect, knowledge and tolerance exercised towards each clinician's differing interventions through discussion but also experience (Chisholm, McKenzie and Murray, 2000: 64). Hollins and Sinason (2000) explored the role of trauma in the lives of people with learning disabilities and highlight how this shapes interpersonal behaviour and limits communication. There is an important caveat in consideration of the clinicians' role in 'Promoting healthy lifestyles which support good mental health' (Hollins and Sinason, 2000) and recommends CBT, family therapy and psychodynamic therapy in line with the National Health Service Review of Psychotherapy (Parry, 1993).

Transdisciplinary facilitation

Every member of the multidisciplinary team interested in the Sexual Offenders Treatment Programme (SOTP) process received training on the 2012 'Sexual Offender Treatment South East Collaborative – Intellectual Disability' programme (SOTSEC-ID). The facilitators included art psychotherapists, psychologists, consultants, ward doctors, speech and language therapists, occupational therapists and nurses. Usually, four facilitators were chosen (where possible two men and two women); facilitators rotated each week to provide respite and reflective space in this challenging work. Facilitator groups always debriefed together as a foursome. This kept everyone safe, helped us to share information on the patient's emotional development and enabled us to process the transferential and countertransferential material. Facilitator groups were accountable to each other and this mitigated against any collusion in avoiding the sessions. The facilitators learned from one another; our varied approaches included psychodynamic ideas, cognitive behaviour therapy, mentalisation-based therapy and attachment-based modules to support the working theories underpinning the experiential aspects of the programme.

In this way, transdisciplinary work enabled triadic thinking: thinking together with an 'observer' always present. We used creative ways to say the unsayable. There was less opportunity for compromise and corruption and less energy taken up with forensic dynamics (such as struggling for supremacy in the group or attempting to sabotage the group). Risk behaviour within these interactions was picked up quickly and taken seriously. Reflective practice and continuous questioning maintained self-awareness and helped us to know our own vulnerabilities and strengths.

Patients could progress at their own pace. We did not wish to repeat the programme until the patient was fluent in 'SOTP-speak' but untouched by the core concepts. We aimed to observe even fleeting positive responses and adapt accordingly, working on small gains by having realistic expectations and an awareness of the patient's individual capacity. We fully acknowledged even minor changes and made them known to the patient.

We also felt that this person-centred approach ameliorated shame and therefore, crucially, the urge to reoffend. The idea of reducing shame, so prevalent and pervasive in this client group, became central to our thinking. We had observed how patients perceived the more traditional insistence on fluent verbal and written affirmations and disclosures as persecutory and shaming. This in turn dovetailed with painful beliefs about themselves and how society viewed them, already present in our patient group from a young age. The impossibility of following the programme as it was, in terms of more 'traditional' learning tools, as well as feeling guilt and shame, often led to despair and a mutinous, desperate urge to reoffend.

Art therapy preparatory work

The pathway began with the art therapy preparatory group, run solely by the art therapist and another team member (this was due to the exigencies of the service: two art therapist facilitators would be the ideal). This helped to create a core group prior to the modulated programme and introduced patients to the art materials and sensory-based learning that would be used later in the programme. The preparatory group was based around a series of positive themes in the manner of the 'Good Lives' model (Kirtchuk and Sherman, 1968; Murphy and Sinclair, 2009; Ward et al., 2004; Ward et al., 2007; Ward and Gannon, 2006: 214–223) in order to reduce shame, to create cohesion amongst the members, and to break down the 'them and us' aspect of the work as facilitators participated in art-making alongside patient.

The art therapy preparatory group involved seven to ten sessions of thematic work, after which the participants had 30-minute individual sessions in an art therapy space with materials present and work kept in personal folders. During each module participants also had set practical work, onsite café visits, and occupational therapy sessions.

The themes ran over a ten-session period. We focused on gentle, non-exposing ideas and included the following:

- Week 1: One good thing about me. / Something I like about me.
- Week 2: Someone I'd like to be like. / Five things I admire.
- Week 3: My best friend.
- Week 4: If I were a superhero.
- Week 5: My ideal home.
- Week 6: My favourite things.
- Week 7: One thing I would change about me.
- Week 8: My dream.
- Week 9: Create a character. (We used this in the next stage of group work to trial some of the more difficult processes like disclosure as an extra 'group member'.)
- Week 10: My gift to the group.

(Please note all theme titles are copyrighted.)

In the group the themes enabled group members to become familiar with each other and to explore how each person defined themselves through what they could express – and indeed, what they were defended against expressing. This preparatory work could often expose what the patient was most anxious about unveiling in the context of the SOTP, yet could be done in a way that preserved their defenses. For the art therapist, it provided a means of enabling the group to routinely use art materials, and to support group members to work creatively and non-verbally, developing a more open milieu. For facilitators who were unsure of how to work with alternative methods of communication, the themes provided a means of gently gauging how much of themselves to reveal. It also helped that the SOTP groups were held in art therapy spaces used by patients for art therapy groups. This set the scene and tone of the preparatory phase as something already familiar to them. However, for some facilitators it has been a new space that they have come to inhabit over the duration of the programme. Here, the patients are the experts and the 'hosts', demonstrating how art therapy works.

Individual transdisciplinary work

Our complex patient group included those who could not tolerate groups and those who could not be tolerated by groups. These patients had often received a diagnosis of an autistic spectrum disorder in tandem with other issues. Our service was placed in a quandary as, in general, the Ministry of Justice had made SOTP group work a condition of the care plans. In these cases, after thorough discussion with the multidisciplinary team, we decided to continue on an individual basis, attempting to incorporate the key SOTP ideas in a manner specifically tailored to the idiosyncratic learning and social communication styles of each patient. Working with one patient and two facilitators lacked the specific therapeutic powers of the group. However, we felt that there were still valuable gains to be made. The art therapist and psychologist facilitated these 'groups', which were held in the art therapy space using the same art materials and the same modules. The facilitators worked in a similar way to the larger group.

This was intensive and toxic work that frequently left the facilitators feeling overwhelmed. We debriefed extensively after sessions and attempted to hold on to the thinking; none of this would have been possible without a once-monthly psychodynamic supervision with an SOTP expert, and once-monthly super-vision at the Portman Clinic. Transdisciplinary supervision allowed for the processes at play to be recognised and explored to better understand the impact of the material on the individual facilitators. In this respect, having the art images available helped us to hold the session in mind, given the often fractured and chaotic nature of the work.

It was also necessary to look at the roles we inhabited. This was often in reference to the facilitator's actual role in the multidisciplinary team, and featured elements of the power imbalance and the projections held by the particular staff member. Often the art therapist was viewed by the patients as holding less authority than the psychologist, and certainly less than the consultant. It was also helpful to consider the family unit and how the 'child' patient related to the 'parent' facilitators – and what kind of parents the facilitators had become. Finally, we held in mind the Karpman Drama Triangle as a useful structure (Karpman, 1968). This is posited around the roles of Victim, Persecutor and Rescuer. We found that during more traditional SOTP work, these roles would become fixed over the sessions in an unhelpful way. Working as a threesome did not always guard against this and we found that, on occasion, these roles were acted out in a very concrete way. The facilitators experienced sexualised, aggressive and active offending behaviour from the patients at times. However, making the Drama Triangle structure explicit in a straightforward visual fashion gave us an opportunity again to say the unsayable and to explore why and how the shifts and calcifications happened. This developed into how it felt for all of us to inhabit each role; and, by inference, how it might feel for other people. In this way, we were able to gently touch upon aspects of 'victim empathy' without it becoming too caustic and shaming. There was a continual awareness that it was possible for all of us to inhabit all the roles at different times.

How art therapy and psychology worked together

Psychology privileged classic offending behaviour treatment approaches based on cognitive behaviour therapy (CBT) modules. This approach was well-researched and evidence-based, yet some of it clearly was not working for our patient group. The interventions generally used a tight structure that focused on maladaptive cognitions and the resultant offending behaviour. Discussion of abstract concepts and, in particular, the division between thoughts and feelings, was often oblique and puzzling for individuals with learning disabilities. We began to use art therapy to slow down and explore the components of the process piece by piece. The development of the three-way relationship enabled us to concentrate on feelings and their root causes in the context of attachment behaviour.

The sessions always started with a 'How I am feeling' drawing before addressing the material brought to the session within a loose structure, shifting between the art therapy and the psychology components of the work as required. It is important to acknowledge that this was nothing new to us; we were both familiar with aspects of each other's disciplines. Within the team, too, we actively encouraged collaboration with colleagues. It seemed unhelpful to be precious or obfuscatory about our own disciplines and we saw greater gains by sharing certain techniques and ideas, within limits (Corbett, 2014). We saw this approach as enhancing rather than diluting each other's skills. As experienced clinicians it is of course important to be confident in our own practice, as the transdisciplinary work must hold the boundaries of our chosen discipline. At times, too, working with sex offenders could be hard to bear but both patients and facilitators found the process more convivial when working together in a triangular relationship.

The two case studies have been chosen to give examples of the three-person, individual work group. Names have been anonymised.

Jason

Jason needed to work on his parallel offending. Kate, Head of Art Therapy, and Laura, a clinical psychologist, designed an individual SOTP based on the classic SOTSEC/CBT/Good Lives model, drawing in attachment theory and art therapy theory. Jason experienced problems with social communication (he was also working with speech and language therapy), which was probably part of his autism: non-verbal modules and interventions were therefore essential.

Jason found the first two sessions very hard and became very excited and aroused. He made frequent sexualised comments and attempted to touch the facilitators; this behaviour was also apparent in other contexts, culminating in Jason exposing himself and masturbating outside a session. We understood that he was trying to communicate the extreme anxiety he felt about the work but had to convey to him that this was absolutely unacceptable. We felt able to be open with him in exploring the reasons why he might behave like this. Apparently, it arose from the anxiety of being around women and the complex needs, desires and fears this evoked in him.

We developed a method of communication that helped Jason to 'mentalise', and removed the focus from him directly. By approaching topics gently and tangentially, we were able to have some valuable discussion about the root cause of Jason's behaviour, his feelings about relationships, his feelings about himself and the links between his past and present. We were also able to start perspective-taking exercises with Jason, supporting him to think about the effect of his behaviour on others. We then began more classic work around sexual development, consent and legality.

Despite this being highly complex work, Jason was able to use the approaches offered. Each session began with the three-person group drawing a picture of how they were feeling that day on a small yellow Post-it note. This was discussed and each person's feelings considered and noted. We then went on to draw from the theme. For Jason, this was initially too difficult, as his mind would wander and he would speak quickly about everything he was thinking and feeling in that moment. We would try to follow the trail and listen attentively to what he was saying, beginning to repeat his words and attempting to become involved in the dialogue, trying in this way to create a dynamic relational experience between us. The facilitators spoke to each other about Jason's flow of consciousness as a means of bringing order to our thinking, to demonstrate that we were listening and that what he said was important to us. We would also question why he needed to be abusive towards us and why he was unable to focus on the work in hand. Gradually Jason realised he was being taken seriously and being held to account. This allowed him to speak of significant experiences: a childhood pet, the pubs he frequented, the people he met and his family. Though drawing for him was very erratic, he would write down his thoughts, and it became apparent that he was higher-functioning than we had initially thought. Jason would also use the facilitator's drawings to think about his own experiences in life and to get to know the facilitators' minds. What started out as a complete tangle of undifferentiated behaviours and feelings became interspersed with thinking and moments of profound reflection where something became known. What also helped support the work was the consistency of Jason having access to the clinical psychologist on the ward most days, whereas the art therapist was part-time and less present on a daily basis. In this grouping Jason came to call the facilitators a nickname that showed he thought of us as a pair working in collaboration. At times, it also seemed that as facilitators we were interchangeable, or one and the same. This helped improve his sense of trust on the ward, enabling him to self-regulate his emotional urges to act out sexually, and find a way of expressing appropriate emotional shading towards the facilitators.

Olu

Olu was initially engaging in one-to-one art therapy while on the low secure ward with an art therapy trainee. After the trainee left, the sessions were taken over by Kate; Olu continued to work well. We went on to integrate art therapy into the SOTP work to enable Olu to access some of his difficult emotions despite his autistic spectrum disorder. Olu had a profound fear of being shamed. He was split between his religious beliefs (emanating strongly from his family) and his offending. This conflict prevented him from being able to work in a group. On two occasions the facilitators attempted to integrate Olu into a new group SOTP facilitated by the speech and language therapist, occupational therapist, psychologist, social worker and art therapist. However, Olu would act out his anxieties so aggressively it became unsafe to keep him in the group. The multidisciplinary team felt that a resistance to group work, at this point, was too strong to be overcome and that he would only get some benefit from working alone. From this point we decided to continue in the one-person group. Olu had undergone individual psychotherapy with Respond (a UK-based charity supporting people with learning disabilities) in the past, and had done extremely well on a one-to-one basis; this contributed to our decision.

Using the individual SOTP programme we designed and facilitated, Olu had built up a good relationship with each of us separately, and we were keen to place this challenging therapy in the context of containment, solidity and trust. We completed the sex education module and spoke about relationships and the expectations that accompany them; we also discussed life stages and human development, contraception, sexually transmitted infections, pregnancy, legality, consent and why people might commit sex offences. Olu became embarrassed on occasion but managed to stay with us and remained actively engaged with the sessions.

We then commenced the core of the work, drawing up a life timeline, then talking in more depth about what had happened to Olu as a child. Olu has historically found it extremely difficult to speak about the cycle of abuse, but was able to do so in the context of the sessions. We were then able to discuss his familial abuse and how this may have affected his current behaviour. There followed a short break before moving on to the final part of the work.

After the break, Olu was ready and waiting to begin working again – we had eight sessions left working as a team. The plan was to link the past and present around his offending, and try to reduce his feelings of 'badness' and lack of self-worth; then to look at the Finkelhor model (Finkelhor, 1984) in terms of practicalities, before doing the two last sessions on relapse prevention and the future. We also previewed later work on building healthy intimate relationships.

We began sessions speaking about the key work: how Olu had managed on unescorted leave when he felt attracted to someone. He assured us that he 'did not touch' but did say he had fancied people or had sexual feelings towards them. We praised him for his openness. He appeared to come to a decision and said that he wished to tell us about an incident. He later elaborated on this incident and it became clear that events had been more complex and distressing than he had at first communicated.

Olu was clearly experiencing a great deal of turmoil, while on unescorted leave, around his compulsions and his own inability to activate any internal controls. The team was highly concerned about his tendency to place himself in unsafe – and indeed illegal – situations, his suggestibility and his difficulty in refusing consent. He seemed unable to protect himself, or only able to protect himself in unhelpful and maladaptive ways. There was also a distinct lack of clarity around Olu's own role in seeking sexual contact from others, and the history and frequency of this while on unescorted leave. Unescorted leave was suspended.

We continued to work with Olu as planned, talking about safety and risk in various forms, and introduced the topic of safe and unsafe people. Using the art materials, we produced depictions of 'safe' and 'unsafe', and realised how poorly Olu understood these concepts. He portrayed a couple a 'safe' (although again the picture was unclear) but could not tell us why. Again, 'unsafe' was a concrete depiction of a person with a weapon and blood. We explored subtleties but it was clear that Olu struggled with reading whether people were threatening to him or not, and understanding whether or not he was threatening to other people. He couldn't seem to represent himself as an offender: his own self-image, as he showed throughout our work with him, was in marked contrast to how he appeared to others.

In the next session, we attempted to establish a collaborative understanding of why Olu's freedom had been restricted and what he needed to do to get unescorted leave returned. His understanding was indeed that it was about the safety of others. We opened the last session by asking Olu about his consumption of food, cigarettes and drink; we had observed and understood this as an irresistible compulsion, and hoped to make links between this and his sexual drives. Olu said that when confronted with food and drink, he felt 'desperate', and understood his feelings as 'cravings'. We made the link for him, and although it was difficult for him to hear, he remained mature and responded appropriately. We spoke about whether he can limit and monitor himself, and he stated that he needed looking after. This was a challenging session for Olu, but he also seemed relieved that we had understood him. Olu went on to work with Kate alone in art therapy to explore the 'cravings' and what he may be trying to assuage or fill up through these compulsive actions.

Olu found this process difficult, and his courage and forbearance in persevering with this work was noted. We agreed that any future relapse should be viewed in the context of how far he had come, and his newfound ability to discuss his problems and seek help in coping with them.

What works?

Largely, the benefits outweigh the challenges. Working with facilitators who are comfortable with art making and knowledgeable about various approaches enhances the opportunities of successful outcomes in forensic programmes. It is important that we use an iterative process to continually explore and adjust what works and what doesn't, given that forensic patients with a learning disability can be one of the most rejecting and resistant populations to engage in therapy.

The ethos in the service is to collaborate. We draw upon different disciplines at every opportunity to maximise resources, thinking skills and colleague support. Working alone with high-risk offenders can be risky and fraught with danger, given the lack of restraint exercised by patients who are ill-equipped to consider the consequences of their behaviour on others.

In the two case examples, the success of the work lay in the ability of the facilitators to trust one another, work together and yet be able to function independently and with respect for the other's discipline and clinical skills. When there are three or more facilitators, each from different disciplines, the need to communicate effectively in supervision and reflect openly about the work increases due to the likelihood of splitting in the group. Forensic processes are paralleled in the team, such is the depth of disturbance in the material.

The beauty of transdisciplinary work is the opportunity to learn new ways of thinking and develop new adaptions to the work. As was stated earlier, programmes had to be tailor-made so that each discipline promoted a perspective that held one piece of the jigsaw necessary to form a whole picture of the work. For example, the consultant may hold an overview, whereas the social worker is looking at the person's welfare in terms of safeguarding issues, risk to vulnerable adults and how progression is determined and understood in tribunals and parole boards. The speech and language therapist will be looking at communication skills and the occupational therapist at developing practical skills, while the psychologist has a responsibility for assessing and formulating the patient and making sure this formulation is shared by the team. The art therapist is interested in visual, unconscious communication and working with developmental and attachment processes.

When all these approaches, perspectives and disciplines are combined, a circle of support is created to provide the patient with an experience of a collaborative system where each performs their own role but is also able to be seen as part of a whole, rather like a therapeutic community but with a more distinct brief.

On reflection there are several caveats that should be highlighted in the appreciation of this working relationship. We knew that we *could* work together. It's important to know if you can work with the other facilitators. The work requires respect, a willingness to cede control to the other and, on occasion, be subsumed by the other's discipline. Trust is vital. We had to trust in the other to feel held and become fully immersed in the experience of, for example, being asked to draw, or shifting the session plans responsively. There can be nothing half-hearted about this approach, as the patient will pick up on any hesitation or resistance between the facilitators themselves. This particular patient group were often remarkably sensitive to conflicts arising between team members: hardly surprising, given their backgrounds in general.

So, while holding the duality of two disciplines, we had to operate as one mind. We had to have very effective unspoken communication. There was no room for triumphalism, dominance or unplanned leadership taking place. We had to feel comfortable enough to communicate through silence and then express our thought process openly and explicitly to safeguard against the patient becoming paranoid. To demonstrate this we would speak our thoughts aloud to each other so the patient could hear us explore any uncertainties. Over the duration of the work we found ourselves becoming more resonant, to the point that the three of us had an equal share of responsibility over what we could achieve in the session.

Conclusion

When considering an approach that would enable cognitively impaired and highly defended patients to access the SOTP, we combined art therapy and psychology to facilitate a gentle, non-exposing, iterative process. This satisfied conditions set by the Ministry of Justice and met the treatment needs of the sexually offending patient with learning disabilities. The multidisciplinary team saw patients' progress and used this to inform their decisions to grant escorted and unescorted leave. Where, previously, leave was itself perceived as a long-term goal, the patients who participated in the individualised programmes went on to be discharged into the community. We concluded that collaboration – through transdisciplinary working – promoted a highly flexible and adaptive approach to individual needs and a safe working experience for the clinicians.

References

Beail, N. (2001). Recidivism following psychodynamic psychotherapy amongst offenders with intellectual disabilities. *British Journal of Forensic Practice*, 3(1), pp. 33–37.

Beail, N. (2016). *Psychological Therapies and People Who Have Intellectual Disabilities*. Leicester: The British Psychological Society. [online] Available at: www.bps.org.uk/system/files/ Public%20files/id_therapies.pdf [Accessed 5 June 2016].

Beail, N. and Jackson, T. (2009). A psychodynamic formulation. In: P. Sturmey, ed., *Clinical Case Formulation: Varieties of Approaches*, 1st ed. New York: Wiley, Chapter 19, pp. 251–266.

Chisholm, D., McKenzie, K. and Murray, G. (2000). Working with sex offenders who have a learning disability. *Inscape*, 5(2), pp. 62–69.

Corbett, A. (2014). *Disabling Perversions: Forensic Psychotherapy with People with Intellectual Disabilities*. The Forensic Psychotherapy Monograph Series. London: Karnac Books.

Finkelhor, D. (1984). *Child Sexual Abuse: New Theory and Research*. New York: Free Press End Fragment.

Goodman, R. and Brown, E. (2016). Telling the story. In: K. Rothwell, ed., *Forensic Arts Therapies: Anthology of Practice and Research*, 1st ed. London: Free Publishing Limited.

Guarnieri, M. and Klugman, S. (2016). Trust in a forensic setting. In: K. Rothwell, ed., *Forensic Arts Therapies: Anthology of Practice and Research*, 1st ed. London: Free Publishing Limited.

Guarnieri, M., McGuire, A., Thomas, D. and Mindang, M. (2016). The internal bomb. In: K. Rothwell, ed., *Forensic Arts Therapies: Anthology of Practice and Research*, 1st ed. London: Free Publishing Limited.

Hackett, S. (2012). *Art Psychotherapy with Adult Offenders who have Intellectual and Developmental Disabilities*. PhD. Unpublished. University of Northumbria, Newcastle.

Hackett, S., Porter, J. and Taylor, J.L. (2013). The core conflictual relationship theme (CCRT) method: Testing with adult offenders who have intellectual and developmental disabilities. *Advances in Mental Health and Intellectual Disabilities*, 7(5), pp. 263–271.

Hollins, S. and Sinason, V. (2000). Psychotherapy, learning disabilities and trauma: New perspectives. *The British Journal of Psychiatry*, 176(1), pp. 32–36. doi: 10.1192/bjp.176.1.32.

Hughes, R. (2007). An enquiry into an integration of cognitive analytic therapy with art therapy. *Inscape*, 12(1), pp. 28–38. doi: 10.1080/17454830701267093.

Karpman, S. (1968). Fairy tales and script drama analysis. *Transactional Analysis Bulletin*, 26(7), pp. 39–43.

Kirtchuk, T. and Sherman, R. (1968). Goal attainment scaling: A general method of evaluating comprehensive mental health programmes. *Community Mental Health Journal*, 4(6), pp. 443–453. [online] Available at: http://www.goodlivesmodel.com/information [Accessed 5 June 2016].

Murphy, G.H. and Sinclair, N. (2009). Treatment for men with ID & sexually abusive behaviour. In: A.R. Beech, L.A. Craig and K.D. Browne, eds., *Assessment & Treatment of Sexual Offenders: A Handbook*, 1st ed. Wiley: Published Online.

O'Connell, J. and Montague, T. (2016). The 'good enough' couple. The containment of conflict and the roots of creativity in a music and art therapy group for forensic patients with intellectual disabilities and mental illness. In: K. Rothwell, ed., *Forensic Arts Therapies: Anthology of Practice and Research*, 1st ed. London: Free Publishing Limited.

Orlowska, E. and Parker, D. (2016). Embodied furies: Perversion, ambivalence and use of the body in dance movement psychotherapy. In: K. Rothwell, ed., *Forensic Arts Therapies: Anthology of Practice and Research*, 1st ed. London: Free Publishing Limited.

Parry, G. (1993). *NHS Review of Psychotherapy*. London: HMSO.

Rothwell, K. (2008). What anger? Working with acting-out behaviour in a secure setting. In: M. Liebmann, ed., *Art Therapy and Anger*, 1st ed. London: Jessica Kingsley Publishers, pp. 117–133.

Rothwell, K. (2016). Disobedient objects: Group art therapy for male patients with mild learning disabilities in a locked environment. In: K. Rothwell, ed., *Forensic Arts Therapies: Anthology of Practice and Research*, 1st ed. London: Free Publishing Limited.

Rothwell, K. and Grandison, S. (2016). Notes on service design for art psychotherapists working in time-limited group programmes on adult mental health inpatient wards. In: R. Hughes, ed., *Time-Limited Art Psychotherapy: Developments in Theory and Practice*, 1st ed. Oxon and New York: Routledge, pp. 180–194.

Ward, T. and Gannon, T.A. (2006). Rehabilitation, etiology & self-regulation: The compre-hensive good lives model of treatment for sexual offenders. *Aggression & Violent Behaviour*, 11, pp. 214–223.

Ward, T., Mann, R. and Gannon, T. (2007). *The Good Lives Model of Offender Rehabilitation: Clinical Implications*. Wellington, NZ: Victoria University of Wellington School of Psychology.

Ward, T., Bickley, J., Webster, S.D., Fisher, D., Beech, A. and Eldridge, H. (2004). *The Self-regulation Model of the Offense and Relapse Process: A Manual: Volume I: Assessment*. Victoria, BC: Pacific Psychological Assessment Corporation.

Wassall, S. and Greener, G. (2016). Inside out: Art therapy with complex female offenders. In: K. Rothwell, ed., *Forensic Arts Therapies: Anthology of Practice and Research*, 1st ed. London: Free Publishing Limited.

Wood, J. and Johns, R. (2016). Rage, resistance and repulsion: Grappling to find hope. In: K. Rothwell, ed., *Forensic Arts Therapies: Anthology of Practice and Research*, 1st ed. London: Free Publishing Limited.

11

'THE BOY WHO CRIED WOLF'

A collaborative approach to long term segregation

Emma Allen

Introduction

One cannot work in isolation with highly complex, traumatised patients with dangerous and severe psychopathologies. For those that are deemed an immediate risk to self and others, they are often psychologically isolated by illness and physically segregated from society. The high secure hospital is a collective therapist and care provider; the therapeutic relationship is multidisciplinary and a shared responsibility. Together, we adapt according to the risks we face. A collaborative, cross-disciplinary, dialectical behaviour therapy (DBT) and art psychotherapy approach to long-term segregation (LTS) in the National High Secure Learning Disability Service is one example.

Our most challenging sessions of 'pre-therapy' support is presented here where Richard, an assistant psychologist, and I worked with 'Daniel' (not his real name) while he fluctuated from being nursed in seclusion and LTS following assaults and threats to kill female staff. Daniel, 'The Boy Who Cried Wolf', often paralleled with Aesop's fable of the trickster who made false allegations, and our collaborative work took place with the support of the DBT manual: the *I Can Feel Good!: Skills Training for Working with People with Intellectual Disabilities and Emotional Problems* (Ingamells and Morrissey, 2014), combining mindfulness and image-making.

'Segregated' into themes – in the form of analysis from my own perspective – I explore a shared countertransference of powerlessness, defectiveness and shame (particularly after Daniel violently assaulted staff). I also include our joint reflections, considering the three-way relationship and dynamics. Our experience aims to identify the benefits and challenges of transdisciplinary work whilst also contributing to the sparse literature on LTS and engaging with patients through the seclusion hatch.

Daniel: the boy who cried wolf

Daniel has a long and complex history of anti-social criminal behaviour and co-morbidity of bipolar disorder, borderline personality disorder and intellectual developmental disorder (ID). Following many serious assaults and threats to kill female staff while in a medium secure unit, he was transferred to high secure services. Daniel's trauma relates to his history, offending and mental illness after suffering long and extensive family violence and abuse. After his mother died during infancy, Daniel was sexually and physically abused by his father for many years into his adolescence. Daniel was too unwell to engage in any therapy for a number of years, but was eventually referred for individual art psychotherapy by his psychologist to explore his interpersonal difficulties. Daniel could often leave people drained after talking 'at' them, going off on lengthy tangents and creating a sense of help-lessness. A non-verbal approach was considered a less threatening intervention to his communication deficits and avoidance through verbalisation. In our sessions we explored his avoidance, attention-seeking and lies, where he once told me that he was like 'The Boy Who Cried Wolf'. Daniel often made false allegations against staff and tended to delve into fantasy and exaggeration. His personality difficulties included being over-controlling, manipulative, mistrusting and testing of relationships, with an underlying fear of being abandoned, neglected and abused. Daniel seriously assaulted his female DBT therapist while in high secure and was subsequently nursed in long-term seclusion and segregation.

One-to-one art therapy: threats and endings

Daniel engaged in individual art therapy with me for a number of years, while also re-engaging in DBT with Richard. Although Daniel would project his anger towards females, paradoxically, he placed me and art therapy on a pedestal. Daniel would tell me how much he liked our sessions: me, his reports, and told me that 'you can tell the truth if you want'. Telling the truth became difficult after years of working together as I needed to tell him that I was going on planned sick leave for a number of months and that there would be a break. Although this was not an ending, Daniel found the prospect of me 'abandoning' him difficult to tolerate, and he became angry and fearful. He pushed me away, and I fell off the pedestal.

   Daniel had become very agitated with me, telling me in graphic detail how he had violently attacked his previous female therapist. He showed no remorse and seemed to enjoy scaring me, telling me that 'shit happens'. Increasingly intimi-dated, and concerned that he would attack me there and then, I strongly identified with his mother whom he blamed for his abuse. Projecting his rage at being abandoned and abused, my announcement had made him feel threatened, so he felt the need to make threats. This was the last time I saw Daniel on my own and in the same room. Our sessions were subsequently stopped, as the team became anxious that he would again attack his therapist; his corresponding treatment of DBT with Richard had also been suspended. Daniel spent many months being nursed in seclusion, where his mental state had severely deteriorated, and the risk of him hurting someone was high. When I returned from leave I was informed that Daniel had made a series of false allegations about me: that I was accusing him of touching me. A series of meetings with the ward psychologist were arranged to consider a way forward.

Proposal for combined DBT and art therapy input

Psychology and I began to plan re-establishing input. Daniel's Recovery Care Plan had indicated that he should continue with DBT for emotional regulation and improved coping and problem-solving skills; and continue with art therapy for the better understanding of feelings and improved behaviours. Daniel had responded well to a structured, directive approach in art therapy, and we considered that DBT would provide additional structure. Sessions already had to be on a two-to-one basis (two therapists to one patient) due to the possible threat of violence, but we agreed that providing both modalities in the one session would prevent Daniel 'splitting' therapists off and making serious allegations. Taking his previous assault of his female DBT therapist into account, Richard, a male DBT facilitator from the Learning Disability service who had already worked with Daniel, was recommended. We wondered if Richard and I might be able to provide 're-parenting', to ensure that previous maladaptive modes of parenting were not repeated in therapy (Livesley, 2001). In this process, the therapeutic relationship aims to provide boundaries and care that patients did not receive in childhood (Young et al., 2003). For Daniel, it would be important for me not to become the abandoning and rejecting mother, and important for Richard not to be the abusive father. Our proposal was presented to the multidisciplinary team (MDT) through both art therapy and psychology CPA reports.

Session planning and structure: adaptations and preparation

Richard and I waited many months for our input to be agreed, the priority being in re-establishing Daniel's mental health. Once we had the go-ahead from the MDT, we met to plan our sessions, and attended ward rounds together. Our initial aim was to establish contact and rapport with Daniel, repairing past relationships and engaging with him while in solitary confinement.

The ICFG manual, a modified DBT programme, is specifically designed to help those with an intellectual disability and personality disorder to identify emotions, thoughts and behaviours, increase self-awareness and reduce unwanted impulsive behaviours. We agreed to begin with the mindfulness adapted module, using experiential exercises and incorporating image-making when Daniel was more settled. Traditional DBT can be intellectually challenging; this modified programme adapts DBT to make it more accessible in managing emotional distress where 'rehearsal and repetition helps increase retention of the content' (Short, 2016).

Richard and I agreed that sessions would only go ahead with the two of us there, and that during periods of seclusion we would aim to use verbal DBT techniques to establish a three-way, safe and trusting therapeutic relationship. Increasing transdisciplinary collaboration was thought to assist in reducing incidents of seclusion, and low-key interventions to benefit coping strategies while secluded. Advice from the team was to 'take it slow' and 'not do therapy just yet', so we aimed to incorporate pre-therapy mindfulness and relaxation activities, aiming to reduce behavioural risks and alleviate content relating to past trauma. An additional aim was to continuously assess Daniel's levels of risk and mental health to feed back to the team who, at that time, only saw Daniel at the ward round and at reviews. Generally, close liaison with the MDT helps to manage risk, and differing therapeutic approaches aid the understanding and support of the work. In this case it would be important to be present at ward rounds to feed back the positivity of re-engaging with Daniel in order to help alleviate a sense of hopelessness around his case. It was important not to isolate Daniel any further, given that he already had a learning disability, which can often result in patients in feeling 'hidden'.

During this pre-therapy work, we integrated ICFG Mindfulness Practice Worksheets, repeating exercises that differentiated between a *Hot*, *Cool* and *Wise Mind* to enable learning and reduction of risk, building upon coping skills and self-reflection through 'in-the-moment' coaching. This took place through both the seclusion and quiet room hatches.

Mindfulness and sensory integration: through the seclusion hatch

Daniel was nursed in seclusion for many months without change or progress. The MDT decided it was time for us to intervene and approach him through the seclusion hatch window. Daniel had been asking after us, and was looking forward to seeing us both. The hatch was placed open for us by staff. Daniel greeted us through the window with a smile and offered his hand through the gap to shake our hands. Richard went first, and I followed, but Daniel gripped hard at my hand and wrist, not letting me go. I asked him to let go and he suddenly apologised, saying he 'didn't know what came over' him. I remember feeling a little shaken – by how possessive this felt – and left with a feeling that I couldn't ever let him down. Hyper-sensitive to feeling rejected or abandoned, Daniel often tested boundaries in dangerous ways.

Physical touch in a forensic setting is often viewed as a boundary violation, and Richard and I felt ashamed at shaking his hand, and for letting boundaries (and the rules) slip. Following this incident, a notice was put up by the seclusion room advising not to shake hands or make contact with Daniel through the hatch. The MDT's concern about my contact with him was re-ignited. This was embarrassing, as we were aware that these patients pose high risks to others, in particular by grabbing staff at the seclusion hatch; however, we were able to think about the social awkwardness of the setting and our initial anxieties, too. During long periods of seclusion, patients can often feel dehumanised (Alty and Mason, 1994; Wadeson and Carpenter, 1976) this may have been a powerful way to emotionally connect. In contrast, Daniel also expressed his fears of being touched by staff, particularly by women: 'I want to destroy all of them, but not you Emma, you are my therapist.'

We spent many sessions exploring mindfulness techniques, encouraging him to focus on more positive thoughts rather than reverting to negative tirades. Daniel often chose using the shower as a mindfulness activity he could engage in, saying he found the sound of water relaxing. I suggested listening to the sounds of an ocean drum during a mindfulness visualisation *A Walk on the Beach* was read out by Richard, guiding Daniel to 'inhale relaxation' and 'exhale the tension and tightness', while I used the drum to evoke the sounds of a calm sea (rather than a potential tsunami) and incorporate sensory integration. He sat back in his chair, resting his back on the wall and closed his eyes. Afterwards, he said he felt relaxed, but quickly reverted back to his aggressive thoughts and urges to kill. We encouraged him to keep practicing saying 'nice things' to staff and about himself – for example, pretending to be his own best friend – to increase his self-esteem and lower his risk. Daniel acknowledged it felt good to say 'nice things'.

'Squeezing the life out of women': gender, matricide and the anima

Daniel assaulted a female nurse during a rare time-out, so was again secluded. With a significant decrease in sensory input, materials and stimuli, Daniel's environment consisted of a bed with 'strong' bedding (that is tear resistant and reduces the risk of ligation), a shower and toilet, a window looking out into the hospital grounds – and a paper cup left over from his last drink. We therefore needed to be creative in coming up with ideas of coping skills for him while in seclusion. One idea was to use his paper cup as a 'stress ball', to release tension and work through his desire (expressed in a previous session) to what he would refer to as 'squeezing the life out of women' – focusing upon managing feelings of anger and rage. I suggested that maybe it was his anger that needed to be 'squeezed' out of him, and suggested he squeeze his paper cup in his fist a few times, as we talked to him about finding ways to channel and release his feelings. As he crushed the cup, it made me wonder if he was expressing his rage at his lack of nourishment, or needing to 'kill off' his need for nourishment. The intervention was made to help him focus on the present and release tension and tightness – an aim of all the guided visualisations.

Gender was another 'segregated' issue for Daniel, who was disturbingly fixated upon the idea of killing women. On a deeper, psychological level, he was perhaps trying to kill off his anima and emotionality. I often considered his relationship to the feminine alluded to his inability to nurture himself. Feminine psychological tendencies in the male psyche include the capacity for love and care, and, most crucially, his relationship to the unconscious (Jung, 1959). The character of the anima in the male psyche is heavily influenced by the mother; Daniel's absent mother may be represented as an absent, negative anima figure, that was present during times he was both suicidal and homicidal. Daniel's alienation and hatred towards women might be thought about as a rejection of a part of himself: his own feminine qualities or characteristics. Men are sometimes thought to have feelings of hatred and envy towards women who represent what they have become alienated from: feelings of warmth, security, love – all associated with femininity (Jukes, 1993; Jones, 2008). His relationship to violence seemed to be one of symbolically attacking his victim self; his vulnerabilities and sensitivity to being hurt. His relationship to women was also powerfully symbolic and life-threatening where he was unable to contain or 'segregate' his emotions. Being in seclusion may have offered Daniel a safe retreat.

Daniel often tried to shock, disgust and push us away. A difficult session took place where Daniel openly spoke of his intentions to kill women, staring at me intently through the window, and asking, 'You're thinking, "what the fuck", aren't you?' His wanting to kill women may have been a form of matricide fantasy, unconsciously wanting to kill off harmful emotions. Daniel was testing, looking for a reaction in me, and when I looked away for a moment, he seemed to jump on this, thinking he was going to be rejected by me. I told him that he wouldn't shock us away, but underneath I was feeling completely hopeless, and wanted Richard to take over the session and save me. Richard and I fought against our hopelessness, however, and attempted to explore how he pushed people away. Daniel became even more agitated, turning his back on us and shouting 'Just go, Emma!', focusing on the idea of me leaving him. I remained standing by the window, and repeated to him that we would be coming again and would see him the following week. This was just one example of a testing interaction with Daniel. It was crucial to survive these tests and prove that we were there for him, no matter what, much like a parent would. A long time later, Daniel acknowledged that he had tried to push us away and avoid dealing with his problems. He seemed pleased that we had not given up on him.

Joint reflections: parental identification

During the interview with Richard, I discovered that he hadn't been made aware of the rationale for our working together, as the ward psychologist had left the service. Richard had assumed he'd only been chosen for the work because of his gender, and that his role and participation was primarily for my safety. He had concerns about how our work would be perceived by the team: was it a last resort?

Richard also told me that initially he had tried to avoid our work becoming established, out of a dread of seeing Daniel – perhaps paralleling the patient's avoidance of conflict, where the seclusion room can be a safe retreat to incubate emotions.

Turn-taking felt similar to the parenting process, giving the other parent a break or a 'breather'. Richard, a new parent, revealed how working with Daniel seemed to mirror the difficulties he sometimes faced in bringing up a baby. At times, I felt distressed as if unable to comfort an infant. It felt exhausting to endure his tests: we had to prove that we were not the 'abandoning mother' and 'abusive father'. It seemed that the DBT exercises brought a paternal structure, with its focus on behaviour, whilst art therapy offered a more maternal focus upon emotional expression and containment (Rothwell and Hutchinson, 2011).

Being able to properly see or hear Daniel in seclusion presented difficulties of its own, along with a lack of confidentiality due to another patient being secluded next door, and our need to speak at a loud volume to be heard. Also, I found it increasingly important to consider how Richard was feeling and whether he felt involved enough. I didn't want to take over or dominate sessions; however, Daniel was hyper-sensitive to my responses and fixated on me. Sometimes, I tried to direct his attention away from me and on to Richard, and felt guilty for receiving this attention – wanting to give the 'father' a chance to feel just as important as the 'mother'. Richard admitted feeling a lack of involvement, and feeling 'no good as a therapist' (Short, 2016), and we agreed that sessions might feel more three-way if equally balanced between DBT and art therapy. I suggested that, for Daniel, image-making would help divert attention back on to himself and his emotions.

We often returned to the office feeling drained and hopeless, when writing notes and making sense of our sessions was challenging. Richard would sometimes attempt to cheer me up by showing me photographs of his baby. I often felt we were failing at our 'parenting', and reflected on Daniel's confession to being, what he called himself, an 'ex-son'. I also wondered whether Daniel's increasing fears that I would leave were unconsciously allowing the dynamics from his past to be re-enacted. It seemed that he expected to re-experience the loss of his mother, and abuse by his father. He also had unresolved grief due to years of abuse.

Assaults, abuse and allegations: lashing out and pushing away

Daniel kept referring to being 'left alone to die', and made several allegations of being abused by nursing staff. We continuously reassured him that he was being cared for. Daniel consistently found it difficult to stay in a positive frame of mind, and had the tendency to escalate quickly into negative thoughts. After one of our sessions through the quiet room hatch, Daniel violently assaulted nursing staff. This had been our first session through the hatch on the ward, and Daniel had continued to voice his fantasies of what he wanted to do to women. Daniel had sought reassurance from us both that he was being 'looked after' by staff, and we repeated positive-thinking exercises to keep him hopeful of progress. However, Daniel would quickly revert to describing violent thoughts. With this in mind, we advised staff that he should not see the female hairdresser in a situation where tools could be used as weapons, and staff agreed that his appointment shouldn't go ahead. However, as Daniel was informed of this while coming out of the locked quiet room, he started to punch staff. We witnessed this from the office and ran to the scene to restrain him; I assisted staff (while he was on the floor and couldn't see me) while Richard helped guard the other patients. Daniel was taken to his room, where he violently kicked his door and shouted obscenities at us. Violent anger can be associated with childhood abuse and deprivation, is likely to relate to past family dynamics, and affects empathy for others: a grudge against the whole world can develop, along with poor self-esteem (Liebmann, 2008). Often, when working with male offender patients, we work with both the 'boy' and the 'wolf', exploring both victim and perpetrator identities, and reaching out to both the vulnerable child and angry child. Daniel's repetitive dreams also told stories of his neglected, shameful and unwanted parts of himself that were lurking in his unconscious world. Through sharing stories and dreams with us through the hatch, he was no longer alone with these images, and his identification with 'The Boy Who Cried Wolf' could be interpreted as being the story of his internal world, or inner experiences of how he had coped. Stories are a useful metaphor for exploring anger (Liebmann, 2008), where acting out and projection are common primitive defences. Daniel often described a nightmare of rescuing a little boy and girl from an abandoned children's home. Our 'parenting' had perhaps helped him to connect to his more vulnerable self.

Joint reflections: powerlessness

I didn't want us to become the bad guys and get blamed – I did not see that coming.
Richard Short (interview), 2016

Our anxiety level was raised after Daniel assaulted staff. We thought we might be blamed or held responsible, and our sessions closed down. To our relief and surprise, these sessions continued to be considered helpful by the MDT, and seen as a useful way to keep them updated on his mental state. We had expected the criticism that we were making things worse. Powerlessness is one of the most expressed forms of anger and violence from those that have an invalidated sense of self through severe deprivation, abuse and trauma and, for Daniel, is often represented through his acts of violence.

We had to continuously reflect upon our own sense of powerlessness in the high secure setting, in the MDT and when working directly with Daniel. We often felt 'de-skilled' due to already having to further simplify the manual which felt quite removed from formalised DBT and art therapy, feeling powerless at how to help him.

Image-making, through the quiet room hatch

After a few weeks of periodically having time out of long-term segregation, Daniel was introduced to using art materials. We offered him a box of pastels, passing his chosen colour through the hatch one at a time. The quiet room was easier for image-making than the seclusion room, due to a table being attached to either side of the hatch, providing room to work on. Offering materials felt like providing him food: a form of nourishment and care that was harder for him to reject or attack. He referred to his first image as being 'safe', and told us that making the image had made him feel 'good and relaxed'. He made an image entitled *Emotions*, (Fig. 11.1); he admitted that he didn't really know what these emotions were, but could identify how the colours made him feel, saying he found it easier to describe

FIGURE 11.1

how he was feeling through colours, such as the 'emotional blue' and 'suicidal red', that he told us there was 'hardly any of' in the images he had made for us. The two mountainous shapes seemed to indicate his unpredictable, 'up and down' emotional state, and gave us clues as to his mental state behind the hatch.

The *Feelings in My Body* (Fig. 11.2) exercise (Francis, 2012), helped Daniel to learn what an emotion was, and to see how he experienced them. His 'suicidal red' pastel was focused around the centre of the body, continuing out to each hand. We identi-fied that his fear and anger was at his core, influencing his potential to lash out. Naming the colour 'suicidal red' (possibly referring to his anger and fear) allowed him to metaphorically 'kill off' feelings that were too unbearable to manage, instead of being violent. Combining art therapy and DBT is thought to be particularly effective for those who are emotionally dysregulated; coordinating the two can reinforce learning skills, using both sides of the brain and body (Heckwolf et al., 2014).

We continued to structure sessions with ICFG mindfulness practice worksheets, followed by image-making. Just as sessions began to find their flow, and images were starting to be referred to as having 'no fear', Richard had to announce he would be leaving to start his clinical training.

Breaks, and fears of abandonment

Daniel was informed that Richard would be replaced by another male DBT facil-itator, and we suggested a short 'break'. We were not sure how he would respond or feel, as he'd been more concerned by the prospect of my leaving, and I hoped this wouldn't impede his progress or be a setback. Daniel initially said he was pleased for Richard to be getting a 'better job', but admitted he felt sad, too. I initially thought he'd handled this well, but then Daniel proceeded to tell us how he'd known 'already', as staff had been laughing outside his room, saying that both

FIGURE 11.2

of us were leaving, and that he was 'thinking of doing a new therapy anyway'. Daniel maintained it was true, even though we suggested this might be imagined. Daniel's interpretation may have also come from his need to remain in control, and at the same time to test out if he was going to be left by both of us. It seemed he needed to reject us before feeling rejected.

We suggested the use of a worksheet to think about thoughts, feelings, and behaviours around endings. Daniel was able to use the worksheets to explore underlying fears of being abandoned, telling us that he didn't want to be 'left to die'. He was reassured that sessions would not be ending, but that there would be a break, to give time for another facilitator to be identified. Daniel asked if he could have one-to-one art therapy with me, but we advised him that we didn't think this the best way forward, considering the past. I told Daniel I didn't want him to deteriorate like last time, and to trust us that he was not being abandoned or rejected. He agreed he would try to cope this time, and accepted our rationale for continuing joint therapy. Daniel then wrote down on paper, 'Richard is leaving but Emma is not leaving'. Our three-way relationship had offered a unique opportunity to support Daniel with unresolved bereavement and loss: a prominent theme for individuals with learning disabilities, when the patient's existence can be

FIGURE 11.3

validated by knowing that another cares if they live or die. Offering art materials not only offered hope, but allowed him to feel human again.

Daniel was then asked to make an image expressing his feelings about endings. Daniel was able to name emotions: 'annoyed', 'uptight', 'angry' and 'upset' (Fig. 11.3). His image depicts three crosses, symbolic of the family dynamic of mother, father and son. Daniel asked if the three of us could 'all be in the same room' for our last session. Rothwell (2016) considers that patients with a learning disability, when trusted and respected, are less likely to be violent, and this made me wonder if this might be true for him. We therefore asked staff if we could hold our last session in the same room together.

Our last session with Richard in the dining room

Our last session with Richard took place in the dining room, with a team of nursing staff sitting outside, observing. Daniel spoke of knowing that his mother's death and childhood abuse had 'affected everything' and expressed a wish to 'work on everything now'; he was told, however, that future treatment with another DBT therapist would follow the same, careful pace. Daniel said goodbye to Richard, and was presented with a certificate of attendance, that he had specifically requested, and which he proudly showed to staff as he was led back to his room.

Concluding reflections

Daniel's traumatic history, characterised by violence, abuse, loss, mental disorder and criminality, had had a huge impact on his ability to trust and be trusted. Our transdisciplinary approach allowed us to offer a 're-parenting' process for Daniel's 'victim' and 'perpetrator' identities. Working with both the 'boy' and the 'wolf', we jointly survived the tests, the attempts to shock or push us away, and the ongoing allegations and threats of violence.

Applying DBT and art therapy simultaneously provided emotional regulation and reinforcement of practicing, accepting and changing. DBT strengthens and enhances art therapy by maintaining a structure, while the image-making of art therapy provided sensory input, mindfulness in action, and a safe container for Daniel's unmanageable emotions. DBT techniques helped focus on the positive, distracting him from his homicidal expressions and incorporating mindfulness provided an important common ground for us both as practitioners. Overall, however, it was our joint therapeutic relationship, and our offering of a secure and trusting attachment that helped re-engage Daniel into therapy and out of the seclusion suite. Our close liaison, and exploration of countertransference allowed for a deeper understanding, and flexibility in approaching the dark territory of Daniel's inner world.

Forensic work, particularly through the seclusion hatch, should never be carried out in isolation; our turn-taking helped assist us through complex, challenging projections, threats of violence and allegation, and reduced the risk of Daniel becoming overly fixated on me. We learnt that initial early planning would have been helpful in alleviating any feelings of invalidation or assumptions on our part about our roles: Richard was not a 'security guard', but brought 'fatherly' structure into the context of unsafe projections onto the maternal. Imagery offered a safe container, allowing Daniel to unconsciously re-integrate a more harmonious relationship to the feminine: his emotionality. Our shared countertransference of hopelessness was counterbalanced by a sharing of more positive attachments and parental experience. Richard openly shared his parallel experience of parenting, comparing it to our 'parenting' for Daniel – which allowed us to feel less isolated in our hopelessness, and helped alleviate powerful parental projections. Together, we supported each other over the complexities of working with what at times felt like a distressed infant, and when Richard showed me photographs of his own baby, he offered a sense of rebirth, and hope that a new life could be born within Daniel, if we helped to nourish it.

By repairing ruptured relationships, we found a way for us to connect and start again. Daniel's fears of abandonment and being left to die paralleled our own fears of the work being suspended. It felt important for Daniel to begin to trust again and be trusted; to re-emerge out of isolation and to know he was being 'held in mind' while likewise 'held' in seclusion. Our three-way therapeutic relationship had offered an alternative sense of containment to that offered by seclusion.

Acknowledgments

My thanks go to Richard Short for contributing through an interview. Richard worked as an assistant psychologist at Rampton Hospital for the last five years and has now commenced his doctorate in clinical psychology. I also wish to thank 'Daniel' for his consent to the work.

References

Alty, A. and Mason, T. (1994). *Seclusion and Mental Health: A Break with the Past.* London: Chapman & Hall.

Francis, L. (2012). *Feelings Are Something You Feel in Your Body. Colour the Places You Feel Your Feelings.* [online] Creative Connections. Available at: www.CreativeConnections. org.uk/ [Accessed 23 Sep. 2016].

Heckwolf, J., Bergland, M.C. and Mouratidis, M. (2014). Coordinating Principles of Art Therapy and DBT. *The Arts in Psychotherapy*, 41(4), pp. 329–335.

Ingamells, B. and Morrissey, C. (2014). *I Can Feel Good!: Skills Training for Working with People with Intellectual Disabilities and Emotional Problems.* Hove: Pavilion Publishing and Media Ltd.

Jones, D.W. (2008). *Understanding Criminal Behaviour: Psychosocial Approaches to Criminality.* London: Willan Publishing.

Jukes, A. (1993). *Why Men Hate Women.* London: Free Association Books.

Jung, C.G. (1959). *The Archetypes & the Collective Unconscious*, 2nd ed. London: Routledge.

Liebmann, M. (2008). *Art Therapy and Anger.* London: Jessica Kingsley Publishers.

Livesley, W.J. (2001). *Handbook of Personality Disorders: Theory, Research & Treatment.* New York: Guilford Press.

Rothwell, K. (2016). Disobedient Objects: Group Art Therapy for Male Patients with Mild Learning Disabilities in A Locked Environment. In: K. Rothwell, ed., *Forensic Arts Therapies, Anthology of Practice and Research*, 1st ed. London: Free Publishing Limited, Chapter 13.

Rothwell, K. and Hutchinson, L. (2011). Hiding and Being Seen: The Story of One Woman's Development through Art Therapy and Dialectical Behavioural Therapy in a Forensic Context. *ATOL: Art Therapy Online*, 1(2). [online] Available at: http://ojs.gold. ac.uk/index.php/atol/article/view/274 [Accessed 23 Sep. 2016]

Short, R. (2016). Interview, in person.

Wadeson, H. and Carpenter, W.T. (1976). Impact of the Seclusion Room Experience. *The Journal of Nervous and Mental Disease*, 163(5), pp. 318–328.

Young, J.E., Klosko, J.S. and Weishaar, M.E. (2003). *Schema Therapy: A Practitioner's Guide.* New York: Guildford Press.

12

LEFTOVERS

Exploring body image

Camilla F. Matthews

'If I could lose another four pounds, I might like myself,' Trudy said.

'Trudy', like many people, subscribed to the illusion that restricting her food intake and disciplining her body would put her in control of her life. Distracting herself by focusing on narrow and structured tasks to alter her body shape afforded temporary relief from chaotic and painful feelings and felt more manageable than addressing the complexities of relationships. For many years Trudy had overridden communications from her body when she felt tired or physically weak, and was unable to identify whether she was hungry or full. In childhood, food had been refused if she had been 'demanding' or argued, and now her taut demeanour was a physical manifestation of her unheard voice and denied neediness.

'Susan' had a belief that she had 'no body but lived behind her eyes'. Her desire to not eat repeatedly collapsed into binges of forbidden foods. Her mother had used food as a reward or comforter, and she believed that this had generated confusion about her bodily sensations. She could perceive the parallel between her enmeshed bond with her mother and her vacillating relationship with food, and was fearful of addressing her interpersonal issues directly, believing herself utterly inadequate to the task. Anxiety about stabilising her eating patterns reflected her paradoxical investment in perceiving herself as overweight (Orbach, 1978).

Definitions of body image

Schilder (1935: 27) described body image as 'the picture of our own body which we form in our mind'. To this definition has been added the notion of the body as a psychological experience (Fisher and Cleveland, 1957), which includes the attitudes and feelings of individuals towards their bodies (Kolb, 1959). Bruch (1973) includes cognitive awareness of the bodily self, the accuracy in recognising bodily stimuli, the sense of control of one's bodily functions and one's rating of the desirability of one's body by others. Totenbier (1994) suggests that the formation of this image is based on reception of sensations coming from skin, viscera and muscles, and includes a sense of body unity, position and posture. Our body image is crucial in the development of our concept of self, and is the psychological blueprint for the organisation of our social behaviour, contributing to the formation of our object relations.

Body image and eating disorders

A significant feature of any eating disorder is having a self-evaluation that is very reliant on one's perception of body weight and shape. Body image disturbance is categorised as either distortion or disturbance. Distortion is when an individual believes that her body's shape, structure or weight differs significantly from the image seen by other people or in a mirror. A person with body image disturbance accurately assesses body size but experiences extreme dislike for her body, as a whole or of specific parts. Compared to other variables, body image difficulties appear to be among the most important prognostic factors (Button, 1993; Bruch, 1973). No substantial or lasting recovery is achieved without addressing the body image disturbance.

Theoretical issues and considerations

Bruch considered the 'outstanding deficiency' (1973: 282) to be a difficulty perceiving body stimuli, along with evidence of weakness in body boundaries and depersonalisation. This she attributed to inaccuracies in the reciprocal feedback patterns in the transactions between caregiver and child. Kohut (1971) suggested that disruptions in the capacity to self-soothe and modulate body tension are part of a defect in the development of a cohesive self, which may later present as an eating problem. Selby (1987) and Levens (1994) consider key issues to be around dependency and independence, with eating compulsively – or restricting intake – as a bid to control what is outside oneself, in an act of both helplessness and power. Similarly, Gaddini (1982) relates eating to a concrete attempt to protect against the terror of separation, whilst starvation he equates to a defence against the recognition of an object and an outside world.

Kearney-Cooke and Striegal-Moore (1997) also postulate two possible pathways to the development of body image disturbance: internalisation and projection. Internalisation is a progressive process whereby a combination of key events and/or significant relationships leave a person with a strong 'charge' around their bodies, and with internalised negative representations of their physical selves. Projection as a process focuses on early personality development, particularly the differentiation of the self from the world as the sense of body boundary is formed. The unique closeness of the body to the individual's identity maximises the likelihood that the body reflects and shares in the person's most important preoccupations, becoming a 'screen' on which one projects one's most intense concerns. Consequently, over-whelming internal states or interpersonal struggles that they feel inadequately equipped to deal with, are projected onto it. Perceiving their bodies as changeable, the out-of-control feelings are projected onto concerns of weight, shape and size, providing an illusion of a means of restoring order. The efforts expended afford temporary relief from aversive emotional states by offering distraction which constricts cognitive focus onto a structured task that appears manageable.

Grogan (1999) found evidence that perceived confidence, self-esteem and a sense of control and choice were key issues in a positive self-image. She found that discussion groups which promoted a sense of agency in relation to cultural norms, dieting and promoting positive strategies, were sufficient to produce significant changes in the women's body satisfaction scores.

The key issues around body image disturbance have incorporated perceptual, physical, cognitive, emotional, behavioural and interpersonal dimensions which point to a multimodal approach to therapeutic treatment.

The context of the group

This group was part of a National Health Service (NHS) community-based eating disorder recovery programme. It was available to those clients who had completed their primary treatment and whose eating disorder had stabilised. They had there-fore made a secure attachment to the unit, had confidence in our treatment and had learnt to work in groups, sharing information and some difficult feelings.

My co-therapist, Ingrid, was an experienced psychologist who was competent working both cognitively and dynamically and was trained in dialectical behaviour therapy (DBT). We were both members of the multi-disciplinary team, and had co-facilitated eating disorder recovery groups together in the past. The aim of the group was for participants to increase their acceptance of a realistic body image. This would hopefully be achieved through identification of their prevailing attitudes towards their bodies, and by exploring the events and experiences that had structured this 'picture'. The second aspect was to overcome attitudes and behaviours that maintain their disturbance, and develop alternative beliefs about themselves and their bodies.

From the literature on treatment of body-image disturbance we gleaned a range of cognitive tools: diary keeping, questionnaires, desensitisation techniques, relaxa-tion and grounding techniques, visual imagery and guided fantasy to uncover long established negative beliefs. From DBT we utilised mindfulness and meditation, and incorporated a robust attitude to 'therapy sabotaging behaviours' such as non-completion of homework, absences and lateness. From the arts therapies we employed expressive and directive techniques such as body tracing, dance move-ment, self-portraits, mask-making and sculpture, used in conjunction with verbal psychotherapy interventions.

Using the above information we drafted a 12-week programme utilising a range of techniques. Over time we found strong resistance to desensitisation, discovering that mindfulness was more meaningful than relaxation and enabled the development of a crucial 'observer' self to emerge. We generated our own subjects for image-making, and found that as groups developed their own life, members preferred to depict their internal worlds without direction from the therapists.

The pre-group

Prospective group members were invited to attend an experiential 'pre-group', enabling them to have a 'live' experience of using less familiar techniques of mindfulness, movement, guided imagery and art materials. Information about the boundaries and structure of the group were given along with the goals of treatment. Members were advised that participating meant actively taking on the challenge of changing their body image, and a commitment to taking care of their bodies. They were instructed that there was an expectation of undertaking homework as well as keeping data logs and a journal, alongside attending. At this point a number of questionnaires were completed, highlighting features or areas of their bodies that aroused negative feelings which precipitated situations and automatic thoughts pertaining to their appearance. These helped to establish the picture women held in their minds about their bodies, and highlight areas to work on. A mindfulness exercise moved into a kinetic grounding technique, with gentle movements exploring where the body touched a surface.

Group members were then asked to use art materials to depict 'thin', 'fat', 'lumpy', 'curvy' and 'slender', with a 5-minute time limit on each picture. This enabled group members to experiment with the materials and discover their respective properties, as well as generating significant discussion. Women discovered their connections with 'fat' as being 'out of control', 'greedy', 'lazy and ugly', but also discovered some positive associations with 'maternal', 'gentle' and 'non-threatening'. Similarly, 'thin' was experienced negatively as being 'cold', 'competitive', 'mean' and 'rigid'. Lumpy was associated with 'cellulite' and 'fat', whilst 'curvy' posed a dilemma, as it connected with 'femininity', 'sexuality' and 'desire', which for most group members held problematic contradictions. Following this experience, group members decided whether to commit themselves to attending the programme.

Starting the group programme

Sessions 1–4

The group was structured to last for two hours with a flexible coffee break. A format evolved: an initial 'check in'; follow-up of homework; mindfulness or guided imagery; presenting the theme of the session; coffee break; and art therapy, followed by discussion. At their first session, participants were given a relaxation/ mindfulness CD, log books to monitor distressing thoughts and feelings provoked in relation to body image, a journal for writing or drawing between sessions and a file to keep handouts in.

Guided imagery helped participants to gain a fuller awareness of their bodies in three dimensions, and examine any memories or associations aroused. It was also used to evoke significant stages in development, and the concomitant affective arousal and beliefs. Information, presentations and discussions focused on 'components of body image', the 'psychology of physical appearance' and issues of culture, education and religion. Mindfulness exercises attempted to establish a capacity to notice and tolerate feelings and thoughts without distracting, dissociating or retreating back into obsessional eating disordered reverie. Fuelled by the dissatisfaction activated by the questionnaires and the previous guided imagery, group members unleashed vitriol on their self-portraits, adding written lists of disliked attributes onto the page. Their internal blue-prints were depicted with concrete realism, indicating a level of accuracy for how their bodies appeared in the world, but heralded and embellished with tremendous self-hate.

Debbie ruthlessly noted every imperfection with arrows highlighting any surplus flesh (Fig. 12.1), while Trudy depicted a twisted blue figure, contorted and angular. She noted how cold her extremities get, with 'icy feet and hands', always feeling 'empty inside', and told the group about early deprivation, recalling eating tiny pieces of her brother's mattress. Ellen's image focused strongly on her thighs, which she contemptuously described as being 'massive and blubbery'. She said that she constantly fantasised about surgery, and that sexual intimacy with her husband was very rare. She added that she kept chocolate bars in her attic, so that the task of accessing them provided some potential thinking time, instead of simply eating them and propelling the familiar cycle. We noted a parallel in the group process: therapy providing time to reflect, while also invoking intimacy, that might incite a desire to flee. Susan related to Ellen, and spoke of feeling inherently untouchable. She loathed her fleshy fallibility, and spoke of hating having a body. Her image was heavy, and depicted lines of undulating fat (Fig. 12.2). She spoke of a lack of perceptual discrimination, having previously felt as though her body blurred and blended into the environment. She described nebulous sensations of an unpleasant environment in her memory, but without the ability to grasp specific details. She noted that in the past, speaking like this would have taken her into a panic attack.

Carol's image was of a muscular figure, not a caricature but more consciously positive. The outline was strongly defined and seemed rooted to the ground, with splayed flat feet; the figure was wearing a bikini. Next to the drawing, copious criticisms were scribbled in pink felt tip. Carol connected the sense of solidity with the polished wooden floor at work where she was a fitness instructor. The confident figure – juxtaposed with the pink words of criticism – appeared to reflect the ambivalent experience of actively inviting attention whilst fearing censure. In parallel, Carol's emerging investment in maintaining her belief system about her body, weight and shape potentially separated her from the rest of the group, making her a target for projection and scapegoating. As therapists, we invited the ambivalence to be acknowledged by all participants, highlighting the seduction of familiar belief systems and the frightening voyage of discovery into something new.

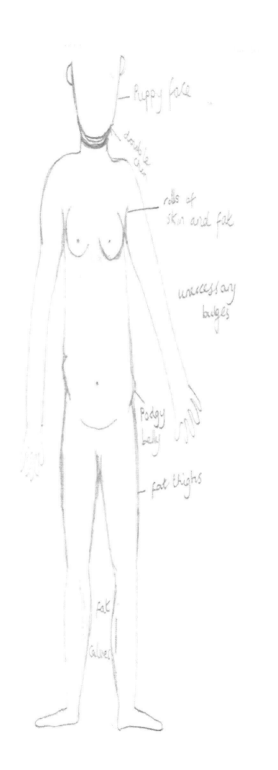

Puppy face

double chin

rolls of skin and fat

unnecessary bulges

Podgy belly

fat thighs

fat calves

FIGURE 12.1

FIGURE 12.2

Drawing round each other's bodies on large sheets of paper was a challenge of intimacy and reality-checking. The group prevaricated, glued to their seats in terror and silence. Cautiously, Debbie, Trudy and Carol discussed their fears of being too large, and 'too much' for others. Trudy feared she would 'block out the light' with her immense neediness and insatiable hunger. Debbie and Carol empathised, recalling the importance they felt of subjugating their needs to others. Susan and Ellen feared the task would inspire rejection in the other person, doubting that physical closeness could be tolerated. Susan said wildly, 'What if I smell?' and the others laughed with her, and started to negotiate who would lie down first to be drawn round.

In the process of drawing onto the resulting life size figures, various organs and areas of the body were identified as pertinent to actual events, and others as significant locations of psychosomatic distress. Carol highlighted her throat as a vulnerable area, and talked about the benefits of repeated tonsillitis as a child, as it facilitated rare tenderness from her mother. Debbie drew the ghost of a foetus in her womb, telling the group about a termination she had felt coerced into, and how her father had refused to touch her in the preceding months, but had hugged her after the operation. The group honoured these disclosures in silence, until Ellen finally suggested cutting her figure out. The others followed suit, and at Ellen's suggestion each briefly danced with their paper 'body', united with themselves for a moment before the session's end.

Collages made with magazine images elicited discussion about the social advantages of attractiveness, and cultural concepts of beauty. Carol brought in her nursery recollections of the fate of Cinderella, whilst Trudy identified with the Ugly Sisters, talking about the roles ascribed to her and her sister, and the fierce sporting competition they were encouraged to engage in; set up to be adversaries, she had experienced neither support nor closeness with her sister. The disadvantages of being attractive were expressed as being perceived as self-centred and unreliable, and treated with envy or as mindless sex objects. The group noticed how the socialisation of the meaning of the body went beyond magazine ads, film and television, and was conveyed in their interactions with peers, parents and others in the form of self-consciousness and generalised expectations of acceptance or judgements.

Outside in

Sessions 5–8

Various cognitive tools were taught, and their use encouraged in order to monitor and investigate body image distress between sessions. ABC's (antecedents, behaviours and consequences) were introduced to help analyse events and slow them down, along with diary sheets and worksheets aimed to encourage compassionate rational challenges. Examples of distorted perceptions of body size, internal dialogues and negative body talk were explored through presentations, work sheets and discussion, in a bid to challenge dichotomous thinking.

The concept of mindfulness was explained, and models of 'being' (when one is fully present in the moment) and 'driven' (when one is preoccupied by doing and activity) were explored. Additional homework included sharing important photos and undertaking self-care activities such as massage, bubble baths or spa treatments.

Art activities included family portraits and developmental time lines that charted important events from birth to the present day. As group members mapped their development, it became apparent that their lack of early nurturance and acceptance had been translated onto their bodies. For Carol, Trudy and Debbie this meant that if they were 'good enough' (thin enough), they would be loved. Early experiences of being put on diets as youngsters were tearfully discussed, and the concomitant sense of humiliation and shame shared in the group. Carol told the group about her nickname 'the whale', and her memory of the school nurse calling her out of class to be weighed, while Trudy told the group that in her teenage years both the fridge and freezer were padlocked in response to her binges. Ellen shared her confusion that her mother restricted her diet whereas her grandmother, who lived with them, insisted that she drank raw eggs whipped in milk for breakfast each morning.

Group members moved from literal depictions of their bodies to more evocative images associated with childhood memories. It became clear that negative parental 'voices' had been absorbed in the creation of highly critical beliefs about themselves. Ellen had been described as 'selfish' and 'thoughtless' when she became distressed and reluctant to physically care for her ailing grandmother or change her dressings, and Trudy was told she was 'manipulative' and 'attention seeking' when she was upset by school bullies. A negative self-image served to protect idealised parents. It was easier for Trudy to conceive of herself as 'demanding' rather than feel the loneliness generated by her mother's detached unavailability. Susan resonated with Trudy's description, and talked of her own mother's recurrent depression – and earnest attempts to bring her to life through achievements and good behaviour. Debbie recognised in her own images the fearful nature of her home life during school years, and talked about her father's alcohol use and occasional violence. Discarding the strong public veneer of his respectability, she recognised the burden of inconsistency that her father had created, and her internalised denial of it as a problem (Fig. 12.3).

Carol felt that teachers at school had consistently ignored her as a person because she was obese. As a teenager her mother had seduced her boyfriends, but now she

FIGURE 12.3

held the admiring gaze of women watching her body while she instructed them. She was able to identify that she wanted to be the centre of attention in a positive way, and to be 'seen'. A group member congratulated her on changing her life around, and this statement of approbation enabled Carol to glimpse a potentially destructive sense of victory, where she took on the role of her mother in relation to other women. At other times Carol struggled to participate in the group discussion, and her attention was directed to finding split ends in her hair, or touching her face. At these moments, we tried to help Carol notice what feelings she had disengaged from, and what this meant to her. She discovered that, in part, she switched her attention to her appearance when she felt different from, excluded by or envious of the other group members. However, these members were able to help her reconnect with them, and to include her different view as part of the whole group perspective.

As painful experiences and conflicts were revealed in the group, members articulated the compulsion to return to their eating disorder, to cut off from their feelings and reactivate the belief that controlling their bodies was the answer. The therapists affirmed that such feelings were usual at this stage of the process, and we dedicated time to practising grounding techniques, developing a 'safe place' that group members could visualise and bring to mind, as well as highlighting the positive gains that group members had stated, such as increased confidence and self-regard, and a sense of success.

Inside out

Sessions 9–12

Group members were encouraged to maintain their use of logs and journals and instructed to use desensitisation. The group continued to work on emerging memories from childhood, and help each other problem solve around current situations where their body image difficulties were likely to be activated. It was noticeable over the ensuing weeks that, with the exception of Carol, the artwork depicted an increasing integration of 'good' and 'bad' elements represented on one page, rather than as polarised extremes. Group members no longer required themes or direction for their art work, but were able to free associate on paper.

Ellen worked on a series of grotesque images prompted by vivid dreams she was experiencing. These evoked disturbing thoughts regarding her uncle, who lived with them and had dementia. She believed she had discovered memories of boundaries being transgressed by inappropriate touching, and feelings of being scared and alone. Dismissed by her mother but encouraged by the group, Ellen spoke to a cousin about the experiences, who validated them, sharing similar experiences and trauma of her own.

Several group members felt that they were negatively regarded by their mothers for being 'Daddy's girl'. This dynamic was communicated in teenage years through competitive comments and overt criticism. Preserving a negative self-image thus protected them from further envious attack. Trudy recalled her mother shouting 'Fat c★★t!' out of the window when she successfully applied for a promotion at work. There were strong feelings that fulfilling one's potential was equivalent to damaging 'mum', or being oppressive or dominating towards others. There seemed to be a lack of having being endorsed as a woman, or the ability to use power benignly. As anger swelled in the group, it mobilised a desire for action and change. Group members helped each other rehearse interacting with family, friends and colleagues differently, and encouraged increased self-assertion.

One of the women in Carol's fitness class had commented on her stretch marks, and Carol had felt annihilated. This gave rise to a conversation about perfectionism and the value of being able to accept being ordinary or 'good enough'. Trudy spoke of a family wedding looming, and her desire to be herself rather than compromise her integrity in a bid for 'membership'. She wondered if, following her group experience, it might be possible to interact with her sister without rivalry, but to meet valuing their differences. She observed that her sister had also suffered from the family role ascribed to her.

Susan worked through a series of images involving religious symbols regarding her mother. She lamented her core belief that she was unlovable, derived from her mother's inability to bond or respond intuitively to her and her evolving personality; she felt fundamentally attacked by the person who should protect and support her. Her art work went from depictions of Madonna to 'sacrificed child', to hurt and angry pictures of jagged explosive shapes, and she commented that it felt more powerful to be angry than hurt. She noted that her mother too denied a fury, a fury at her own restricted education and lost opportunities.

Carol's images seemed to reflect a continuing affirmation of herself, and attempts at visibility; she depicted herself twice as Superwoman, and made other images where her name filled the page, in bright colours or with glitter. She said she enjoyed putting herself centre-stage in the image, and had reasserted herself.

Debbie had worked on a series of images which seemed to have their own momentum. The first was a 'mud/s★★t' construction, made out of soaked paper and paint. The next three images had colours and shapes emerging from the 'mud/s★★t' chaos. Then three bean-shaped pods were painted and glued onto paper with green encasing swirls. Finally, out of a mound of soaked paper and glue, a lotus flower blossom emerged. Surprised by her own process, Debbie told us that she did have gifts and value: she had something to offer the world that she did not want to conceal or sabotage anymore.

Ending

As the group met for its final session, and members reviewed their artwork and the journey it represented, there were strong feelings of celebration for the supportive milieu they had created and the attachments they had made. There was also sadness about losing this environment, and anxiety about maintaining their achievements. All group members had increased their understanding of themselves, and had come to identify significant themes and triggers. They had met their internal worlds through a variety of media, and could hold internal dialogues.

Transdisciplinary working

Yalom (1995) suggests that co-therapists must learn to exploit each other's strengths. Coming from different modalities, we each brought our own skills and characteristics. I had over twenty years' experience of working as an art therapist with eating disorders, and was skilled working at psychological depth with trauma. Ingrid had many years of experience holding boundaries with people with personality difficulties, and was rigorous with adherence to the programme and completion of tasks. I discovered that, to communicate mindfulness in a meaningful way, one had to teach from an internal, lived experience of it.

Importantly, we had a mutual respect for each other and our differences, and could model this to the group participants. We had a shared desire to create a psychological space for the exploration of the issues underlying the eating disordered symptoms, which superseded any competitive feelings. Consequently, we worked well with holding different facets of the transference and any splitting that occurred. At worst I felt that robust pursuit of incomplete homework delayed and stultified the group; at best we responded to the resonances being amplified in the work of the group with intuitive ease.

Conclusion

Translation from the physical body to the mental representation of the body – and then to attitudes and behaviours towards the body – is a complex and emotionally charged developmental process. Once a negative body image is formed it serves a powerful maintenance function, which determines what is noticed and remembered about experiences.

The multimodal aspects of this treatment ensured that the cognitive elements were channelled and complemented by the exploration and expression of emotions. The movement between modalities permitted accessing material within an individual's threshold of tolerance, and allowed movement between thinking and feeling, culminating in behaviour change and an increased sense of choice and agency. It is well documented that arousal of feelings must be complemented by cognitive reconstruction to facilitate change (Ryle and Kerr, 2002). Mindfulness helped individuals develop skills for tension release and stress reduction, alongside the vital capacity to observe thoughts and feelings from an increasingly neutral perspective.

Structured feedback questionnaires showed substantive improvements in participant ratings of body image satisfaction, and the qualitative feedback questionnaires cited many changes in attitudes towards themselves, relationships and general wellbeing. Expressing feelings and developing assertiveness skills were identified as key areas to be developed, alongside learning to trust others in mutual respect and responsibility.

As therapists our backgrounds and skills were complementary. Together we created a holding environment that enabled group members to explore the impact of others' perceptions of their bodies, and how they in turn had projected and internalised emotions and meaning onto their bodies. The opportunity to experience their bodies as a positive object enabled a healthier process of separation and individuation to occur.

Acknowledgements

This piece of writing grew from a smaller article published in *Therapy Today*, December 2006, Vol 17/Issue 10. Reproduced with kind permission of the publishers.

References

Bruch, H. (1973). *Eating Disorders: Obesity, Anorexia Nervosa, and the Person Within*. New York: Basic Books.

Button, E. (1993). *Eating Disorders: Personal Construct Therapy and Change*. Chichester: Wiley.

Fisher, S. and Cleveland, S.E. (1957). An Approach to Physiological Reactivity in Terms of a Body Image Schema. *Psychological Review*, 64(1), pp. 26–37.

Gaddini, E. (1982). Early Defensive Fantasies and their Psychoanalytic Processes. *The International Journal of Psychoanalysis*, 63(3), pp. 379–388.

Grogan, S. (1999). *Body Image*. London: Routledge.

Kearney-Cooke, A. and Striegal-Moore, R. (1997). The Etiology and Treatment of Body Image Disturbance. In: D. Garner and P. Garfinkel, eds., *Handbook of Treatment for Eating Disorders*, 1st ed. Blackwell: Guilford Press.

Kohut, H. (1971). *The Analysis of the Self*. London: The University of Chicago Press, Ltd.

Kolb, L.C. (1959). The Body Image in Schizophrenic Reaction. In: A. Auerbach, ed., *Schizophrenia: An Integrated Approach*, 1st ed. New York: Ronald Press, pp. 87–97.

Levens, M. (1994). *Eating Disorder and Magical Control of the Body: Treatment Through Art Therapy*. London: Routledge.

Orbach, S. (1978). *Fat Is a Feminist Issue*. London: Arrow Books.

Ryle, A. and Kerr, I. (2002). *Introducing Cognitive Analytic Therapy: Principles & Practice*. Chichester: Wiley & Sons.

Schilder, P. (1935). *The Image and Appearance of the Human Body*. New York: Psychology Press.

Selby, T. (1987). Compulsive Eating: Issues in the Therapy Relationship. In: M. Lawrence, ed., *Fed Up and Hungry: Women, Oppression and Food*. London: Women's Press.

Totenbier, S.L. (1994). A New Way of Working with Body Image in Therapy, Incorporating Dance/Movement Therapy methodology. In: D. Dokter, ed., *Arts Therapies and Clients with Eating Disorders: Fragile Board*, 1st ed. London: Jessica Kingsley Publishers, Chapter 13, pp. 193–207.

Yalom, I.D. (1995). *The Theory and Practice of Group Psychotherapy*. London: Basic Books.

13

ALMOST PARADISE

A creative arts collaboration helping US veterans recover from homelessness

Lisa Peacock

A growing number of people in the US are learning about the impact of the arts therapies.[1] It is a gradual ascent. Few people understand that it is a psychotherapeutic practice – using arts in psychotherapy. People confuse art *as* therapy for art *in* therapy. The US lags behind the UK in the creative arts, in terms of the number of practitioners, institutional settings incorporating creative arts and, uniquely, insurance companies reimbursing for services. So, in retrospect it is miraculous that dramatherapy, art therapy, music therapy, writing and poetry therapy, yoga therapy, mindfulness of breathing, a men's group, and healing retreats are the heart of a therapeutic model of care in a conservative Midwestern state. Inspired by UK strategies to help people recover from homelessness, this integrated programme was designed to support veterans' recovery. Currently, this programme operates in four transitional housing residences, one transition-in-place housing project helping more than a hundred veterans each month.

This chapter introduces the voices and experiences of some of the arts therapists engaged in this work that began in 2012. In this chapter you will learn a little about the challenges this population presents and what inspired a British dramatherapist to create a collaborative environment, using a variety of creative arts therapies. You will read about structures that supported regular collaboration among the therapists, hear the voices of practitioners, understand the impact of their collaborative efforts, discover challenges that arose, and learn about collaborations that grew out of the programme.

The population

Recent figures show a rapid decline in veteran homelessness in the US, with a 17 per cent decrease from January 2015 to January 2016 alone, indicating that the overall rate has declined by nearly half (47 per cent) since President Obama's initiative to end veteran homelessness took effect in 2010 (NCHV, 2016). Presently there are less than 40,000 veterans experiencing homelessness on a given night. This is according to point-in-time counts, where on one night the US Department of Housing and Urban Development (USHUD) conducts a national count to estimate the total number of people who are homeless. Debates continue on the most effective way to permanently resolve this problem – a topic worthy of its own book.

David Peacock, MA, HCPC, is a UK veteran and dramatherapist, who envisioned this programme of care as therapeutic programme director.[2] He arrived in the Midwest with a lifetime of personal and professional experience working with people with addictions as well as those recovering from homelessness. 'Homelessness is a very complex condition with multiple causes and therefore very challenging to fix,' said Peacock. 'A man may be suffering from trauma and therefore become addicted to alcohol or drugs. This impacts on relationships and might result in divorce. Here, in this Midwest state, if a man falls behind on his child support payments, he loses his driver's license. Imagine trying to maintain your job without a car in an area where public transportation is subpar at best. It's a self-defeating cycle.'

Creating and supporting a collaborative environment

A 2005 study by the Mental Health Foundation of Scotland found that taking part in arts and drama-based therapies improved participants' self-esteem, communication skills and social interaction (Mental Health Foundation, 2006). The arts therapies provide an opportunity for participants to find their voice, appreciate their unique contributions, and become empowered; characteristics that may help veterans recover from homelessness and transition into the civilian community, post-service. When one's self-esteem is strengthened, one's ability to connect to others increases. It is also an invitation to think creatively, using one's imagination, often a casualty of post-traumatic stress (Van der Kolk, 2014; Tick, 2005).

Northfield Military Hospital in Birmingham, England in the early 1940s saw the emergence of the therapeutic community model of care. It was the first effort to combine psychiatry with group psychotherapy refocusing attention on the relationships within the group, and redefining patients as participants actively engaged in their own treatments and recovery (Harrison, 2000). Here, the work of Wilfred Bion and John Rickman is instructive even if their intervention was short lived – after only six weeks, military authorities shut down this powerful and dynamic experiment as it was not approved. Bion and Rickman believed the curative elements in group therapy are in dealing with intra-group dynamics and exploring the here and now – that is, the content of relationships in the group itself. Vinogradov and Yalom (1989) point out that group psychotherapy provides an environment where group members interact with each other as well as the therapist. This makes group psychotherapy an ideal tool for veterans who are re-socialised into the brotherhood of military service.

'It was very challenging to put in a therapeutic community model of care in the US,' Peacock said. 'The UK is ahead of the US by about thirty years in the way the arts therapies are incorporated into treatment and how addictions are addressed.' Peacock set up the residences with few but firmly applied rules: no alcohol or drug use, no racism, and no homophobia. At the heart of the programme is a 12-week menu of arts therapies that provide daily opportunities to connect with one's life story and choices that impact one's life journey. 'The programme provides each veteran with time to relax, relate and heal, before working on finding a job and housing. Regular meetings with a support worker to update a nine-area psycho-social support plan address these basics,' Peacock explained. 'This side supports the work of the creative arts therapists by addressing practical matters. Without these two types of support, veterans are often doomed to make the same choices and engage in the same behaviours that brought them to a condition of homelessness.'

'Initially, myself and the director of veterans programming met with the creative arts therapists in clinical meetings so that I could communicate my vision to them and they could meet and network with each other,' Peacock said. 'After the first couple of months of programming I brought the therapists back together to identify the recurring themes in groups and set a schedule, so that therapists worked on the same issue in the same week for continuity of care.' Peacock was inspired by the Rudolph Steiner philosophy of teaching that emphasises the role of imagination in learning, integrating the intellectual, practical and artistic development of students (Steiner.edu, 2016). This is why he chose such an expansive array of therapies. Working collaboratively, therapeutic staff identified these recurring themes, worked together to group them, and discussed a logical order – walking in the shoes of the veterans. Here is what they created:

- Homelessness
- Identity
- Family relations
- Mental health/substance abuse
- Anger/fear/trust
- Grief and depression
- Isolation/loneliness and self-esteem
- Service and the warrior's ethos
- Stress/pressure
- Future life
- Your new home
- Independence/spiritual journey

After the final theme is addressed, the groups return to focus on the first theme. In this way, with ongoing enrollment, a man who entered the therapeutic pro-gramme at any time will have the chance to explore all of the themes over the twelve weeks. Peacock encouraged therapists to use this characteristic to their advantage, asking more long-term group members – elders in the community – to share their wisdom and lead by example for newer group members, a way to begin to rebuild or strengthen esteem.

Some of the recruited arts therapists, while experienced clinicians, had never worked with veterans. Peacock invited therapists to staff trainings and staff retreats to educate them about this population.[3] This immediately sparked collaborations between therapists. Peacock was a resource – a sounding board – when therapists had challenges in their group with a person or the group as a whole. 'Ultimately the therapists found their own solutions, but needed the support of someone to talk to,' Peacock said. Furthermore, the author offered additional support, based on her previous work with veterans and family members. This typically took place in the form of phone conversations and emails, due to the considerable distance among the various programmes.

The following sections share the voices and experiences of many of the arts therapists involved in the programme.

A dramatherapist's view (the author)

Dramatherapy offers a whole-body experience, thereby providing a possible gateway to whole-body healing; that is, connecting the mind, body, and spirit (Emunah, 1994; Jennings, 1996; Rogers, 2016). Trauma is experienced in the body; experienced trauma alters the way the emotional brain functions due to stress hormones (Van der Kolk, 2014). Therefore, activating the physical component is an essential part of the healing process (whether trauma is experienced in military service or childhood, for example). Twenty years ago Greta Schnee (1996) pointed out that *social disengagement* is the central challenge for people who are homeless and mentally ill. Disengagement leads to mistrust, fear, and suspicion. Apathy and negativity become their daily diet. However, Schnee argues, dramatherapy has the potential to help them re-engage through interaction and creativity, and take the initial steps toward socialisation.

I practice dramatherapy according to Renée Emunah's (1994) five-phase dramatherapy process that incorporates opening rituals, warm-up exercises, an enactment (or main therapeutic focus), processing, and closing rituals. This is similar to Sue Jennings' (1996) embodiment, projection, and role enactment (EPR) developmental paradigm.

As the resident dramatherapist working with this population, my first task is to gain participants' trust. This is addressed in a variety of ways, such as creating group alliances where group members set the guidelines for behaviour in the group. So, for example, swearing may be okay in one group, but not in another. One alliance called for 25 pushups to be performed by anyone entering the therapy space who let the heavy fire doors slam. Another alliance suggests a group member leaves the room if he needs to fart. This idea came from a group with a few members recently incarcerated, where farting is used as a weapon to disrespect enemies. The author shared with the other therapists the importance of creating a group alliance and they followed suit. We noticed that by members taking an active role in shaping the group's behaviour, they became more invested in it.

The group might continue with a simple warm-up activity, such as enjoying a butterscotch hard candy and sharing personal reflections on the first time they had done so. This sensory connection to life-story would allow the theme of love relationships to arise, leading to sharing a play-script or fable to work with – at 'arm's length' to one's own life story – and helping group members explore the relationships among the characters developed in the session. Through scene-work or collaborative writing and sharing in the group setting, veterans could gain new personal insight, be affirmed by others, and/or realise that others share their experience. It is the dynamics of art creation in the group setting – the collaboration, negotiation, problem solving, and acceptance – that are the tools of healing. To paraphrase Shakespeare's *Hamlet*, 'the play is not the thing – the *thing* is the act of creation (Absoluteshakespeare.com, 2016).

During processing, participants always have the opportunity to 'pass' instead of sharing, which meets participants where they are at – not imposing expectations, accepting all forms of participation as engagement, and thereby communicating no judgment. So it becomes more likely group members will stop judging themselves – another way to enhance self-esteem. These tools are familiar to all arts therapists and while the way these elements are explored may vary in form, their purpose is the same.

It is part of my practice to inform other therapists of salient issues that arise during the group. Occasionally I make suggestions to other therapists. For example, in one residence, when the dramatherapy group worked on a play and 'finding a sense of belonging' arose as a salient theme, I shared this with the other therapists. The art therapist went on to explore this using an exercise on the four-core emotions, and the music therapist provided songs and song-writing exercises on this theme. I followed up these groups by using the poem 'Where I'm From', by George Ella Lyons (1996) in the writing and poetry therapy group, where group members were invited to write their own version and share it – or not – in whatever way they felt comfortable. Finally, Peacock led a men's group where the 'arm's-length' approach is put aside, and direct addressing of the theme is offered. So, by the end of the week veteran participants may have gained a sense of who they are by:

- Reconnecting to childhood experiences
- Identifying ties to others in their families and communities
- Identifying emotions and how these are expressed, both positively and negatively
- Writing songs associated with watershed moments in their lives
- Developing a sense of their life journey
- Their responsibility or part in creating their life journey, including becoming homeless

This is akin to the Steiner (Steiner.edu, 2016) method of teaching and social change where experiential work in the arts is an integral part of the learning process.

Over time I've learned:

1   Be prepared with a plan.
2   Be prepared to throw out the plan.
3   Know that participants will find what they need.

This humanistic approach to psychotherapy supports the client, as he or she finds their own answer by empowering them to discover their own potential (Rogers, 2016).

An art therapy intern's view

Cheryl Pete, MA, art therapist and licensed professional counsellor, was the programme's first art therapy student intern. Describing her first impressions of the programme, Pete said, 'It was so arts-focused and so change-oriented – an idea of a therapeutic community where it's not just one session a week, but where the entire structure of the programme is designed around the therapies. There were other therapists to collaborate with and learn from. It was very exciting.'

Speaking about the collaborative process, Pete said, 'It was such a supportive environment… working with different therapists helped me understand that there are many ways to approach the same challenge.' Pete trained with the art therapist, Stefanie Workman, the dramatherapist (the author, who also ran the writing and poetry therapy group), and Peacock, who ran the men's and life skills groups. Pete met Sarah Zajac, the music therapist, at her first monthly staff training (each month Peacock led a staff training to help educate all staff and to build community), and this rapport developed into a friendship where conversations on practice regularly occurred. Each month Peacock led a staff training to help educate all staff and to build the community.

Veterans, who became fully engaged in the art-making process, came up with the idea of an open studio, Pete recalled. 'Veterans went from making art because "someone told me I have to do it" to "I'm doing this because I want to express something." The open studio was a lot about holding the space, too. It wasn't uncommon for me to have guys come in just to talk. There was something about having time set aside that created a safe place.' By the time Pete's internship ended, the open studio was such an entrenched part of that residence's culture that the author continued to hold an open studio for over a year.

'Art therapy is essential for people who have experienced trauma,' Pete emphasised. 'It is able to access and heal emotions and experiences in ways that traditional counselling cannot. Because of what I have witnessed art do for the people I work with, I see myself as an art therapist first and a counsellor second.' Pete is now the resident art therapist at the newest residence. She regularly confers with the author on how her groups are going, and discusses challenges to developing a therapeutic relationship with veterans when the population is more fluid.

An art therapist's view

Stefanie Workman, MA, ATR-BC, offered art therapy at the initial residence, which was converted to the therapeutic community model. Speaking about the initial converted programme, Workman recalled the initial resistance to the expressive therapy groups. 'Not everyone was enthusiastic about being in the groups; there were a lot of challenges to overcoming the initial hostility of some residents who previously were not required to attend any type of therapeutic programming.' Workman discussed these challenges with the author and together they developed strategies for gaining trust.

At the new residence it was very different. When residents first arrived they were informed about the programme and began the groups immediately, so there was no transition period. 'The therapies were explained to the veterans beforehand,' Workman remembered. 'They were aware of the benefit of using art in the context of a therapy session and how it was beneficial, so there was no hostility or resistance.'

Speaking about the 12-week programme by themes, Workman talked about the value of having the structure while retaining flexibility to adapt to the client group. 'We had some overarching themes and similar overarching goals. I tended to loosely pick from the twelve themes based on what the veterans brought to the group.' Workman would check in with the author, too, when challenges occurred or to discuss ways to motivate veterans to participate in extra-curricular projects, such as an art museum tour to inspire the creation of art for the first veterans' art show.

A music therapist's view

Music therapist Sarah Zajac, MT-BC, was hired because of her ability to be calm under pressure, her desire to learn, and her enthusiasm for the collaborative process. 'I loved the idea of having so many different therapies and different ideas at the table,' Zajac said. 'I felt it created a 360-degree support system for our veterans and therapists. Everyone had a different skill and no one could fall through the cracks – not everyone responds to music therapy, but then there is dramatherapy and art therapy.' As Malchiodi (2005) notes, being able to use a variety of expressive forms is helpful when working with clients, so they can find a form they feel most comfortable with, and communicate effectively and authentically. 'I witnessed veterans find support with whatever suited them best,' Zajac echoed. 'The collaborative format was unique and refreshing. I was being supported as well. I was not this lone arts therapist against the world, which is what it feels like sometimes. Music therapists commonly joke about how much we are defending our validity, and in this type of environment I did not have to do that.'

Zajac attended some of the staff trainings and retreats, because veterans were a new population for her and she wanted to learn all she could. This helped Zajac confer with Peacock to learn more about the population, effective techniques, and discuss challenges she faced. 'I knew he always had my back,' Zajac said. Zajac spoke about the value of experiencing the trainings in the role of a participant rather than facilitator, which enabled her to stand in the shoes of the veteran clients and experience it for herself. 'These trainings also helped educate me about the practices and techniques used in the other therapies, which was helpful in case – in a session – the conversation included what occurred in another therapy group.'

Reflecting on what it was like to work as part of a weekly therapeutic programme, Zajac said it helped not to practice in isolation. 'I could always talk to someone about an issue I had with a group member; I could learn how others managed challenging behaviour, and I could also offer support by sharing my experience with another therapist. For example, I spoke with Lisa [the author] over the phone and together we devised strategies for focusing the groups or dealing with a challenging client.'

Zajac also learned that she had to practice in the moment. 'One day I planned to cover The Warrior Ethos – a set of principles by which a service member lives. These include 'I will always place the mission first; I will never accept defeat; I will never quit; and: I will never leave a fallen comrade behind.' The evening before my session there was a shooting in Texas on a military base by a service member, so when the veteran residents arrived for the group, they did not want to talk about The Warrior Ethos. Instead, I followed the Iso Principle, a technique where the music therapist chooses music and activities that match the clients' current emotions or energy level and gradually brings them to a different emotion or energy level (Heiderscheit and Madson, 2015). The goal in this example was to gradually bring the veterans away from negative emotions by the end of the session. We started with a high-energy exercise and at the end of the session I used guided imagery and breathing'. These are effective interventions to achieve relaxation (Chou and Lin, 2006); it slows the heart rate, brings one's focus to the 'here and now', promotes body awareness, and aids in sleep. Zajak contacted the author about this change, so that appropriate adjustments could be made in the next day's writing and poetry therapy group.

A therapeutic yoga teacher's view

Dae Evans, a registered yoga teacher, certified in Therapeutic Yoga, offered yoga five days a week for the first six weeks just after one of the residences opened. It was scheduled between mindfulness of breathing and the creative arts therapeutic programming. Therapeutic Yoga is not a rigorous, athletic practice. 'It's a slow practice that is mindful of intentional movement,' Evans explains. 'Each session began with a focus on the breath, relaxation techniques, loosening and lengthening of the muscles, and then strengthening of the muscles concluding with meditation time. Residents were invited to not take risks that may cause injury and to pause or take a break when they felt the need.'

'Initially there were clinical meetings with all arts therapeutic staff attending,' Evans recalls. 'Passing along information from one therapist to another was helpful, especially when a resident was having a difficult time, or if an event such as a medical emergency occurred that changed the energy of the house.' Evans also recalls how insight was gained by learning how a resident's demeanour and participation changed from one therapeutic session to another.

When Evans offered yoga therapy on a day that was followed by dramatherapy or writing and poetry therapy, the author checked in with Evans by phone to find out if anyone appeared negatively activated or anything else significant had occurred in the session. The author then incorporated this knowledge into warm-up activities in her session. For example, a slow race activity, where the slowest person crossing the room wins, helped bring attention to the breath. Any remaining feelings connected to the therapeutic yoga group might be brought up by a group member. When the author realised how challenging it was to offer yoga to the veterans (for example, a couple of veterans thought it was a religious practice, and refused to participate), the author began attending these groups together with another therapist, in support of Evans, for self-care, and to tangibly represent the concept of partnership in healing.

Weekend retreats

The programme partnered with Red Bird Trauma Recovery Center, a 60-acre retreat center run by Shianne Eagleheart, LICDC, CS, ICCS, a Native American medicine woman from the Seneca tribe, who has worked for more than 30 years with people who have experienced trauma and/or people in recovery. Once every three months, veterans from one of the residences travel there to spend the weekend connecting with nature, relaxing, and engaging in the Earth Medicine and healing ceremonies offered by Eagleheart. Activities include participating in a healing lodge, talking circles, making art such as a drum or ceremonial shield, and optional working meditation such as chopping wood or building a trail.

In September 2015, nearly three years after the programme started, a Welcome Home Veterans Retreat was planned by Peacock and Eagleheart – another creative collaboration – and attended by more than 70 veteran residents and former residents, nearly all of the creative arts therapists and a few support staff. A special ceremony welcomed home all veterans. Many in the programme had never received a proper acknowledgment for their service. Having most of the creative arts therapy staff (dramatherapist, art therapist, music therapist, and therapeutic yoga instructor) participate in this ceremony spoke volumes to the veteran participants.

After the Welcome Home Retreat, therapists decided to focus group sessions in the following week on its effects – to explore and expand the partnership feeling that had permeated the event. Pete mentioned the calmer affect of veterans who had attended this retreat, compared to before their participation.

Staff retreats and trainings at Red Bird Center offered several benefits. They allowed staff members and therapists an opportunity for self-care and connection outside of the residences, and provided an opportunity to address professional challenges, as well as personal issues that can lead to countertransference. 'During these retreats,' Pete recalled, 'I witnessed therapists and staff members – from kitchen staff to programme managers – taking the opportunity to address emotions related to their work, gaining hands-on experience of the creative arts therapies, developing a deeper understanding of each other's roles in the organisation, and discovering commonalities in their workplace experience. Furthermore, therapists had a chance to interact and share ideas with other creative arts therapists – a rarity in the field.'

'Getting to know and learn from David [Peacock] led to some life-changing experiences,' Evans said. 'David's activities helped me further understand the trauma and symptoms of veterans; the empathy, therapy, and professional boundaries necessary to effectively help them; and also the self-care required to shoulder the sadness, pain, and sometimes feelings of hopelessness. David and Lisa [Peacock] understand that clinical healers need support among themselves,' Evans concluded. 'The individual and group connections they facilitate promote loving, intellectual, self-actualizing and happy healers who are determined to help those in need.'

Collaborations that went beyond the programme

Sharing art created in the groups – with the veterans' permission – offered opportunities to educate the community about the power of the creative arts therapies. The author organised these events, including:

- Framing and displaying some of the therapeutic art in the residences, to honour the veteran artists and prepare for an Open House.
- Organising a performance of veterans' art.
- Organising museum shows in a couple of cities, accompanied by experiential workshops, for college students and community members.
- Planning a veterans' art show for Veterans' Day with a talkback featuring veteran artists.

Such events required art to be selected, framed, displayed in a storytelling fashion with appropriate explanatory labels, then removed and stored or displayed elsewhere – all steps that the therapists came together to perform. These projects mirrored the group processes of collaboration, problem solving, acceptance, witnessing and honouring.

At the start of the programme, Peacock knew it would be important to measure the impact of this model of care that incorporated creative arts therapies. The author found a community health programme survey measuring empowerment of people served, and a partnership with a professor at a local university helped take this research to the next level. Initial indications are that positive effects on participants include increased self-esteem and optimism about the future.

The author also invited one of the art therapists to assist her at a resource event for female veterans and children – two populations the programme didn't serve.

Memory boxes were created and stories shared,[4] leading to a collection of materials to bring this activity back to the veterans at the residences.

Benefits and challenges

As to the impact of a model of care that incorporates several creative arts therapies, there is some evidence that the programme fosters long-term stability among veterans. In 2013, when the national average of veteran residents in transitional housing programmes moving into permanent housing (who are still in that housing one year later) was 68 per cent, this programme achieved a rate of 90 per cent; it is now 95 per cent.

However, initial funding support melted away, as the nonprofit organisation's priorities changed. The administration had never bought into the continuity-of-care or creative arts therapy ethos, and Peacock resigned in late 2015. Nonetheless this programme existed for nearly three years in the form described above. The creative arts therapeutic staff who remain work hard to stay connected and continue to share their experience and knowledge with one another even as the programme itself declines: residences have just one or three groups a week at present. In any form, however, it is a privilege and honour to serve those who have served our country.

Final thoughts

Veterans recovering from homelessness may be at the lowest point in their lives, and working with them requires respect for and honouring of their service. In addition, learning how different creative arts therapists strove to engage this population was helpful for all involved; therapists helped each other work through challenges encountered and shared the ideas that worked most effectively. The Veterans Administration does not currently offer many creative arts therapies to veterans – maybe a single art therapy group each week, along with its traditional regime of talking therapies and medication. So, working outside these confines offers veterans greater freedom of choice. Also, Malchiodi (2005) points out that with the growing US trend toward brief therapeutic encounters, combining therapeutic forms is increasingly important.

Perhaps a testament to the success of the collaboration was the friendships that formed amongst practitioners. These relationships inspired the author to set up a monthly creative arts therapy self-care group for these therapists and other professionals in the area. This is a time to share experience and wisdom, and nourish spirits that tend to so many others.

While rates of maintaining independent housing one year later increased tremendously – more than 20 per cent higher than prior to this programme – the personal impact on the veterans was clear at the first Welcome Home Veterans Retreat where previous residents came back to share their experience and inspire current residents by speaking of their renewed family relationships, confidence, and independence.

Notes

1 Commonly referred to as 'expressive arts therapies' or 'creative arts therapies' in the US.
2 David Peacock is the husband of the author. Hereafter *the author* refers to Lisa Peacock, the author of this chapter and *Peacock* refers to David Peacock, the therapeutic programme director.
3 The author did not attend these as Peacock's work and trainings were kept separate from the author's to eliminate any potential bias.
4 For more on this see vetartproject.com (2016).

References

Absoluteshakespeare.com (2016). *Hamlet*, Act II, Scene II. [online] Available at: http://absoluteshakespeare.com/trivia/quotes/quotes.htm [Accessed 6 Dec. 2016].

Chou, M.H. and Lin, M.F. (2006). Exploring the Listening Experiences During Guided Imagery and Music Therapy of Outpatients with Depression. *Journal of Nursing Research*, 14(2), pp. 93–102.

Emunah, R. (1994). *Acting for Real: Dramatherapy Process, Technique, and Performance*. New York: Brunner/Mazel, Inc.

Fisher, L.B., Overholser, J.C., Ridley, J., Braden, A. and Rosoff, C. (2015). From the Outside Looking In: Sense of Belonging, Depression, and Suicide Risk. *Psychiatry*, 78(1), pp. 29–41.

Harrison, T. (2000). *Bion, Rickman, Foulkes and the Northfield Experiments: Advancing on a Different Front*. London: Jessica Kingsley Publishers.

Heiderscheit, A. and Madson, A. (2015). Use of the Iso Principle as a Central Method in Mood Management: A Music Psychotherapy Clinical Case Study. *Music Therapy Perspective*, 33(10), pp. 45–52.

Jennings, S.E. (1996). Brief Dramatherapy: The Healing Power of the Dramatized Here and Now. In: A. Gersie, ed., *Dramatic Approaches to Brief Therapy*, 1st ed. London: Jessica Kingsley Publishers, pp. 201–215.

Lyons, G.E. (1996). Where I'm From. In: D. Murphy, ed., *The United States of Poetry*, 1st ed. New York: Harry N. Abrams, Inc., p. 23.

Malchiodi, C.A. (2005). Expressive Therapies: History, Theory, and Practice. In: C.A. Malchiodi, ed., *Expressive Therapies*, 1st ed. New York: Guilford Publications, Chapter 1.

Mental Health Foundation (2006). *Arts, Creativity and Mental Health Initiative. Executive Summary of the Findings of Four Arts Therapies Trial Services, 2003–2005*. Glasgow: Mental Health Foundation, pp. 1–12.

NCHV (2016). *HUD, VA, USICH Announce 17 Percent Decrease in Veteran Homelessness in Past Year*. [online] Available at: http://nchv.org/index.php/news/headline_article/hud_va_usich_announce_17_percent_decrease_in_veteran_homelessness_in_past_y/ [Accessed 5 Aug. 2016].

Rogers, N. (2016). Person-Centered Expressive Arts Therapy: A Path to Wholeness. In: J.A. Rubin, ed., *Approaches to Art Therapy: Theory and Technique*, 3rd ed. London: Routledge.

Schnee, G. (1996). Dramatherapy in the Treatment of the Homeless Mentally Ill: Treating Interpersonal Disengagement. *The Arts in Psychotherapy*, 23(1), pp. 53–60.

Steiner.edu (2016). *What is Waldorf Education*. [online] Available at: http://steiner.edu/what-is-waldorf-education/ [Accessed 29 Mar. 2016].

Tick, E. (2005). *War and the Soul: Healing Our Nation's Veterans from Post-Traumatic Stress Disorder*. Wheaton, IL: Quest Books.

Van der Kolk, B. (2014). *The Body Keeps the Score: Brain, Mind, and Body in the Healing of Trauma*. New York: Viking.

Vetartproject.com (2016). *Vet Art Project*. [online] Available at: http://www.vetartproject.com/ [Accessed 30 July 2016].

Vinogradov, S. and Yalom, I.D. (1989). *Concise Guide to Group Psychotherapy*. Washington, DC: American Psychiatric Press, Inc.

ACKNOWLEDGEMENTS

First of all, our gratitude goes to our authors for their imaginative and diverse contributions, each finding their own way to put into words that which so often takes place beyond words; we appreciate their openness to our suggestions and comments. We would also like to thank our clients and research participants who spoke so eloquently of their experiences, inspiring us to create this book. Finally, our thanks go to Tessa Watson – who wrote our foreword – for her encouraging words, and to Jonny Shapiro for his invaluable contribution to the copy editing.

INDEX

abandonment 140, 142, 145, 147–50
abuse 133–4, 140–41, 144–6, 161
acting-out behaviours 127
acute admissions ward 45–6
acute mental health settings 30–41; *see also* staying connected
adaptations 141–2
ADMP UK *see* Association for Dance Movement Psychotherapy UK
adults with learning disabilities 55–68, 81–94
affect attunement xiii, 77
AIR *see* Audio Image Recording
alienation 42, 143–4
allegations 145–6
'almost paradise' 165–77
altruism 96
ambivalence 50, 55–68
Amir, D. 100
analysing data 38–9
Analysis of Assimilation 127
anima 143–4
anorexia nervosa 113, 118
apathy 168
apprehension 45
art psychotherapy 15–29, 42–54, 81–108, 111–25, 141; combined with DBT 141; combined with dramatherapy 42–54; combined with music therapy 81–94; and Down's syndrome 88–9; family 111–25; with moderate learning disability 87; refugee children rehabilitation 95–108; use in anger management 84–6

art therapy group 82–3
assault 145–6
Association for Dance Movement Psychotherapy UK xviii
attachment 12, 20, 73, 77, 87, 92–3, 128, 131–5, 150, 154, 162
attunement xiii, 20, 52, 71, 75–77, 100, 112
Audio Image Recording 111–12, 117, 119–23; as outsider witness 123
authentic movement 66
autism spectrum disorder 132–5

balancing energy levels 105–6
Barwick, N. 63
Beail, N. 127
bearing witness 63
beginning therapy 32, 114–17; clay 114–15; playfulness 117; working with imagery 116–17
being one's self 20–21
Beisser, A. 62
belonging 25–6
benefits of collaboration xviii–xix, 92, 104–6, 175
Bensimon, M. 100
bereavement 148
Best, P. xix, 20, 40, 59, 65
binge eating 159–60; *see also* body image
Bion, W. 44, 46, 62, 166
bipolar disorder 21, 35, 140
body image 152–64; conclusion 163–4; definitions of 152–3; and eating disorders 153; ending 162–3; group context 154–5;

inside out 161–2; outside in 159–61; pre-group 155; starting group programme 155–9; theoretical issues/considerations 153–4; transdisciplinary working 163
body language 9
borderline personality disorder 140–41
boundaries 55–68; for freedom 55–62; permeability of 57–60
'boy who cried wolf' 139–51; *see also* long term segregation
brain injury 83–6; art therapy 84–6; background 83–4; music therapy 84
breaks 147–9
'brick mother' 4
British Psychological Society 126–7
Bruch, H. 152–3
building liminal space 50–52

CAMHS *see* Child and Adolescent Mental Health Service
Care Programme Approach 6
case vignettes: Chris 83–6; Daniel 140, 149–50; Ella 113; Emma 86–7; Jason 132–3; Ms C, 25–6; Ms A 22–3; Ms B 23–5; Olu 133–5; Sarah 71–3; 'the band' 9–11; Tim 72–4, 76–7; Tony 88–9
Cattanach, A. 31
CBT *see* cognitive behavioural therapy
challenges of collaboration xviii–xix, 91, 104–6, 175; balancing energy levels 105–6; complementary forms of expression 105; emotional vocabulary 106; feedback 104–5; role of translators 205; working with trauma 104
change-focused experience 170
chaos 101, 152, 162
Child and Adolescent Mental Health Service 111–25
Chisholm, D. 128
civil war 95–6
clay 114–15
Cochrane review 44
co-morbidity 140
cognitive behavioural therapy 127–8, 131–2
cognitive impairment 136
cognitive reconstruction 163
coherence 20, 83, 129
collaboration 55–68
collective experience 18–19
collusion 65–6
combining therapies 15–41, 69–94; art psychotherapy/music therapy 81–94; dance movement/art psychotherapy 15–29; DBT/art psychotherapy 141; dramatherapy/music therapy 69–80;

music therapy/dance movement psychotherapy 30–41
comfort food 152
comfort zone 33–4
coming back together 119–20
'coming and going' 56–8, 61, 66–7
community women's group 15–29
compartmentalisation 45
compassion 19, 66
complementarity of music and movement 32–3, 40
complementary forms of expression 105
complementing modalities 93
compulsive eating 153; *see also* body image
confidentiality 43
connection 30–41
connectivity 23–5
containment 98–100, 124
corrective recapitulation 3–4
countertransference xxi, 43, 45, 76, 128, 139, 150, 173; *see also* transference
cravings 134–5
creating collaborative environment 166–8
creative arts collaboration 165–77; art therapist's view 171; art therapy intern's view 170; benefits and challenges 175; collaboration beyond programme 174–5; conclusion 175; creating/supporting collaborative environment 166–8; dramatherapist's view 168–70; music therapist's view 171–2; population 165–6; therapeutic yoga teacher's view 172–3; weekend retreats 173–4
Creative Connection 16–17
creative spaces 42–54
creativity 123–4
Creeley, Robert 42–3
Crickmay, C. 18
criminality 149–50
cross-modality practice 1–108; ambivalence vs. expansion 55–68; Family Awareness Group 3–14; holding hope 95–108; innovative collaboration 81–94; Moving Colour 15–29; rupture vs. nurture 42–54; staying connected 30–41; stretch marks 69–80
cultural differences 106

Dalal, F. 74, 76
dance movement psychotherapy 15–41, 55–68, 95–108; combined with art psychotherapy 15–29; combined with music therapy 30–41, 55–68; refugee children rehabilitation 95–108
data collection tools 35

DBT *see* dialectical behaviour therapy
de-roling 49
deeper connections 34
Definitional Ceremonies 123
definitions of body image 152–3
dehumanisation 142
dementia 88, 161
Denham-Vaughan, S. 77
depression 21, 86–7
developing shared therapeutic language
 112–13
dialectical behaviour therapy xx,
 139–51, 154
dichotomy of ambivalence 56
difference across modalities 74–6
disabled 'other' 76
disconnection 23–5
discrimination 96
dissociation 5
distortion 153
disturbance 153–4
dominant story 113
Down's syndrome 88–9; art therapy 88–9;
 background 88; music therapy 88
dramatherapy 42–54, 69–80, 165–77;
 combined with art psychotherapy 42–54;
 combined with music therapy 69–80
drawing 82, 98–9
dual facilitation process 19–20; enabling the
 group 19–20
dynamic of 'coming and going' 66–7
dysfunctional patterns 3–4, 11–13, 23–4

Eagleheart, S. 173
eating disorders 153, 159–63; *see also* body
 image
edges *see* boundaries
efficacy of therapeutic collaboration 97–8
embodied exploration 18–19
embracing ritual 50–52
emerging differences 69
emotional brain 96–7
emotional vocabulary 106
empathy 131, 158
Emunah, R. 168
enabling group members 19–20
enabling new perspectives 62–3
enabling therapists 20–21
end of therapy 120–23, 162–3; opening up
 the air 122–3; separateness 121–2
endings 140–41
engagement 11–13, 56
epilepsy 86–7
Epston, D. 111
executive functioning 98

expansion 55–68
exploding 119–20
exploration of combined groups 69–80
exploring aspects of self 75–6; through
 drama 75; through music 75–6
exploring body image 152–64; *see also* body
 image
expressing self through music 75–6
externalisation and imagery 116–17

facilitating engagement 11–13
facing rupture 42–54; *see also* rupture
fallibility 156
false self 75
family art psychotherapy 111–25; *see also*
 regaining balance
Family Awareness Group 3–14; clinical
 vignette 9–11; conclusion 13; discussion
 11–13; family history 4; introduction
 3–4; overview 6–9; rationale for
 co-working 5; therapeutic approach 5–6
family history 3–5
family reflections; end of therapy 121–32;
 middle of therapy 119–20; start of
 therapy 117
fatigue 52–3
fear 32
Fearn, M.C. xiv
fears of abandonment 140, 142, 145,
 147–50
feedback 26–7, 104–5
fight/flight/freeze behaviours 103
Fillingham, C. 82
filtering of experience 15–17, 27–8
finding 63–5
finding way to collaboration 70–71
Finkelhor model 134
forced migration 95–6, 107
fostering personal narrative 18; importance
 of improvisation 18
foundation of psychotherapeutic theory
 27–8
Foundation Trust Forensic Directorate 126
freedom 57–62; holding polarities 61–2;
 holding together 57; permeability of
 boundaries 57–60; structures holding
 team 60
from fixity to flow 103
Fuchs, T. 57
further holding 73–4

Gaddini, E. 153
Gale, C. 92
gender 143–4
Gestalt theory 70

going beyond the programme 174–5
good enough family 13
Good Lives model 129, 132
'good therapist, bad therapist' 119
Greenberg, E. 71–2, 75
Grocke, D. 91
Grogan, S. 154
group dynamics 4–5
group feedback 26–7, 114
group frame fostering of narrative 18
group structure 70–71
guardian self 75
guide to good practice xvi–xxv; challenges of collaboration xviii–xix; professions in arts therapies xvii–xviii; terminology xvi–xvii

Hackett, S. 127
Hamlet 169
Haque, S. 72
Hayes, J. 19–20
hero's journey 49–50
high security hospital 3–14; *see also* Family Awareness Group
holding hope 95–108; art therapy interventions 98–100; background 95–6; benefits/challenges of collaboration 104–6; conclusion 106–7; cultural differences 106; dance movement therapy interventions 102–4; introduction 95; limitations 106; maximising efficacy 97–8; multi-sensory approach to trauma 96–7; music therapy interventions 100–102; Skills for Psychological Recovery model 97; war trauma/refugee status 96
holding on 63–5
holding together 57
holding the unspoken 22–3
Hollins, S. 128
homelessness 165–77
homophobia 167
hopelessness 99–100, 142, 144, 174
hopes 114
how art therapy and psychology work together 131
Huet, V. 90
Hughes, R. 127
human rights 95–6
hyper-sensitivity 142

I Can Feel Good! 139
ID *see* intellectual disabilities
idealised 'other' 4
identities of arts therapies xvii–xviii

identity 123–4
image-making 146–7
impact of arts therapies 165–6
impact of mental disorder 11–13, 15–17
importance of improvisation 18
improvisation 15–18, 32–4, 100–101
individual transdisciplinary work 130–32
inhibition 37, 88, 114
innovative collaboration 81–94, 111; analysis 90–91; art therapy group 82–3; benefits 92; case vignettes 83–9; challenges 91; conclusion 93; joint session 83, 89–90; rationale 81–2; recommendations 92–3
inpatient settings 31–2
inside out 161–2
intellectual disabilities 127–8, 140–41; *see also* learning disabilities
interpersonal connection 29, 91–2
interplay between music and movement 32–3, 40
interventions 81–94, 98–104; art therapy 98–100; dance movement therapy 102–4; music therapy 100–102
intrapsychic mythic realm 46–8; *see also* psychosis
intuition 19, 52–3
Iso Principle 172
isolation 71–3; first session 71–2; using imaginative space 73

Jack and the Beanstalk 73–4
Jackson, T. 127
Jennings, S. 168
joining modalities 123–5
joint reflections 144–6
joint sessions 83, 89–90
Jones, P. 82, 92
Jung, C. 70

Karpman Drama Triangle 131
Kaufman, G. 74
Kearney-Cooke, A. 153
kinesphere 104
Klein, M. 44
Kohut, H. 153

Larkin, Philip 9
lashing out/pushing away 145–6
layering of experience 15–17, 27–8
learning disabilities 126–38
leftovers 152–64; *see also* body image
letting go 63–5
Levens, M. 153
Levine, S.K. 103
Levinge, A. 62, 76–7, 87

liminal space 49–52, 77–8
liminality 49
limitations 106
literature 44
locating embodied exploration 18–19
long term segregation 139–51; case vignette
   140; combined DBT and art therapy 141;
   conclusion 149–50; fears of abandonment
   147–9; image-making 146–7;
   introduction 139; lashing out/pushing
   away 145–6; last session 149; mindfulness
   142–3; one-to-one therapy 140–41;
   parental identification 144–5;
   powerlessness 146; session planning/
   structure 141–2; 'squeezing life out of
   women' 143–4
losing 63–5
low life point 175
LTS *see* long term segregation
Lyons, G.E. 169

McKenzie, K. 128
Malchiodi, C.A. 171, 175
matricide 143–4
Matthews, R. 92
mature dependence 8, 13
Maudsley Hospital 4
maximising efficacy 97–8
meaning-making 55–6
means of nonverbal communication 112
medium secure forensic hospital 42–54
Mental Health Foundation of Scotland 166
mental health recovery 11–13
mentalisation 132
middle of therapy 117–20; exploding/
   coming back together 119–20; playing
   dinosaurs 118–19; playing with Plasticine
   119; withstanding powerful emotions 119
mindfulness 102, 142–3, 147, 154–6, 163
mixed-media approach 16–17
modalities for co-working 5
moderate learning difficulty 86–7; art
   therapy 87; background 86; music
   therapy 86–7
Mollon, P. 64
Moving Colour 15–29; client themes 21–6;
   conclusion 27–38; dual facilitation
   process 19–20; enabling therapists 20–21;
   fostering personal narratives 18; group
   feedback 26–7; introduction 15–17;
   locating embodied exploration 18–19;
   unfolding shape of the group 17–18
moving towards depressive position 13
multi-faceted collaboration 55–7;
   therapeutic team 57; therapy group 56

multi-layered process of holding together 57
multi-sensory approach to trauma treatment
   96–7
Murray, G. 128
music therapy 30–41, 55–108; combined
   with art psychotherapy 81–94; combined
   with dance movement psychotherapy
   30–41, 55–68; combined with
   dramatherapy 69–80; and Down's
   syndrome 88; with moderate learning
   disability 86–7; refugee children
   rehabilitation 95–108; relatedness and
   collaboration 55–68; use in anger
   management 84

nameless dread 46–7
narcissism 74
narrative therapy 34–5, 111–12
narratives of Family Awareness Group 3–4
National Health Service xviii, 15–29, 70,
   128, 139, 154–5
National Institute for Clinical Excellence
   16, 44
need for sanctuary 48–50
new perspectives 62–3
NHS *see* National Health Service
NICE *see* National Institute for Clinical
   Excellence
nonverbal communication 27–8, 31–2, 56,
   73–4, 82–4, 87, 97–8, 112, 127, 132, 140
not what it says on the tin 3–14; *see also*
   Family Awareness Group
nurturing creative space 42–54; *see also*
   rupture

Obama, Barack 165–6
obsessive-compulsion disorder 83–4
O'Connor, R. xiv
O'Farrell, K. 92
one-to-one art therapy 133, 140–41, 148
opening up air 122–3
opposites 61–2
'other' 4, 65, 76
outside in 159–61
outsider witness 123
'outstanding deficiency' 153
overcoming challenges 124–5

pace of therapy 124
parallel offending 132–3
paranoid–schizoid thinking 13
parental identification 144–5
parent–child dyad 10–11, 131
participants' voices 35–8
pathologising labels 112

Peacock, D. 166–75
perfectionism 162; *see also* body image
perilous realm 46–8
permeability of boundaries 57–60
Perry, J.W. 46–8
personal narrative 18
Pete, C. 170, 174
physicality 18–19
Plasticine 117, 119
play 6–9, 18–20, 123–4
playback theatre 70
playfulness 69, 117
playing dinosaurs 118–19
playing with Plasticine 119
polarities 61–2
Porter, J. 127
Portman Clinic 130
post-traumatic stress disorder 96–7, 166; *see also* trauma
potential space 19–20
powerful emotions 119
powerlessness 146
Prayer to Hermes 42–3
pre-group experience 155
preparations for sessions 141–2
preparatory work for art therapy 129–30
presentation of case material 21–6;
    connectivity/disconnection 23–5; holding the unspoken 22–3; separation/belonging 25–6
projection xiv, 6, 13, 25, 130, 146, 150–56, 168
properties of combined therapies 90–91
psychodynamic psychotherapy 127
psychological isolation 46–7
psychosis 42, 44–9, 52–3
PTSD *see* post-traumatic stress disorder

qualitative methodology 34–5
quiet room hatch 146–7

racism 167
Rampton Hospital 150
rationale for co-working 5, 31, 69–70, 81–2
re-finding 63–5
re-parenting dynamics xix, 141, 150
Rebillot, P. 47–9
recommendations for research 39–40, 92–3
recovering from homelessness 165–77
recovery-focused model 16
Red Bird Trauma Recovery Center 173
refugee rehabilitation 95–108
refugee status 86
regaining balance 111–25; AIR as outsider witness 123; approaching the end 120;

Audio Image Recording 112; beginning therapy 114–17; being in narrative therapy 111–12; coming together 113; dominant story 113; family art psychotherapy 117–19; family reflections on end of therapy 121–3; family reflections on middle of therapy 119–20; family reflections on start of therapy 117; nonverbal communication 113; shared therapeutic language 112–13; strengths of joining modalities 123–5
rehabilitation 95–108
reincorporation 49
rejection 22
relatedness 46–7, 55–68; boundaries for freedom 57–62; collaboration/collusion 65–6; conclusion 66–7; context 55–7; holding on, letting go 63–5; new perspectives 62–3; together in stillness 66
reoffending 129
resilience 117
Respond 133
responding to music therapy 171–2
Rey, H. 4
Rickman, J. 166
ritual 19, 31, 34, 50–52, 84–5; embracing 50–52
Rogers, N. 16–17
role of translators 105
Roman, T. 65
Roth, E.A. 84
Rothwell, K. 127, 149
rupture 42–54; acute admissions ward 45–6; building liminal space 50–52; conclusion 52–3; introduction 42–3; literature 44; need for sanctuary 48–50; psychosis 46–8; troubling feelings 44–5
ruthless self 87

sanctuary 48–50
scapegoating 22–3
Schaverin, J. 18–19
Schilder, P. 152
schizoid adaptations 71–2
schizophrenia 21, 23, 35, 44
Schnee, Greta 168
seclusion hatch 142–3
secure base 58, 78
segregation 139–51; *see also* long term segregation
Selby, T. 153
self-assertion 162
self-awareness 39
self-care 173
self-confidence 21, 23, 96, 100

self-development 81
self-discovery 50
self-esteem 72, 96, 100, 143, 154, 166
self-evaluation 153
self-expression 26–8, 75, 98; through
    drama 75
self-harming 113–14
self-locating 23
self-perception 23–4
self-projection 100
self-regulation 96, 133
self-soothing 153
self-worth 134
sense of identity 72–4, 84–5, 89, 123–4;
    holding through music 73–4
sense of 'in between' 22
sense of self xiii, 84–5
sensory integration 142–3
separateness 121–3
separation 25–6, 49, 86–7
serious play 4
service user population 31–2
Sesame Approach 70
session planning 141–2
severe psychopathology 139
Sex Offender Treatment Programme
    126–38; art therapy preparatory work
    129–30; art therapy and psychology
    working together 131; case vignettes
    132–5; conclusion 136; evidence base
    126–8; individual transdisciplinary work
    130–31; introduction 126;
    transdisciplinary facilitation 128–9; what
    works 135–6
sexualised transference 10
shame 25, 74–8, 129, 133
shared therapeutic language 112–13
shifting positions 19–20
Siegel, D. 100
significant therapeutic benefit 106–7
silence 89–90
Sinason, V. 82, 128
Skaife, S. 90–91
Skills for Psychological Recovery model 95,
    97, 104
Smail, M. 77
Snow Queen 73, 75
Snyder, C.R. 100
social disengagement 168
SOTP *see* Sex Offender Treatment
    Programme
'SOTP-speak' 128–9
spaces within spaces 56–60, 66–7
specialness 72
specific groups 56

specific teams 57
spinning 74
splitting xviii, 13, 45, 75, 86–7, 119,
    141, 163
spontaneity 38
SPR *see* Skills for Psychological Recovery
    model
'squeezing life out of women' 143–4
starting group programme 155–62; sessions
    1–4 155–9; sessions 5–8 159–61; sessions
    9–12 161–2
status of refugees 96
staying connected 30–41; conclusion 40;
    context of approach 31–2; data collection
    tools 35; deeper connection 34; fears/
    beginnings 32; findings 38–9; interplay
    between music and movement 32–3;
    methodology 34–5; out of comfort zone
    33–4; participants' voices 35–8; rationale
    for combined approach 31;
    recommendations for research 39–40
staying with differences 79
Steiner, R. 167, 169
stepping outside comfort zone 33–4
Stern, D. xiii, 66, 70, 74
stillness 66
Strange, J. xiv
Streeck-Fischer, A. 96
strength of joining modalities 123–5;
    containment 124; creativity/play/identity
    123–4; overcoming challenges 124–5;
    pace of therapy 124
stress 143–4
stretching 69–80; conclusion 79; creating
    liminal space 77–8; emerging differences
    69; group structure 70–71; introducing
    group members 71–2; rationale for group
    69–70; similarities/differences 70; using
    modalities 72–4; vignette 76–7; whole
    greater than sum 78–9; working with
    difference 74–6
Striegal-Moore, R. 153
structure of sessions 141–2
structures around work 57–62
structures holding the team 60
stuckness 26, 38, 44–6, 118
substance misuse 5, 8, 166
supporting collaborative environment 166–8
supporting stretching 72–4
surrender 67
'swimming alongside' 20
Syria 95–108

taboo 7
Taylor, J.L. 127

terminology xvi–xvii
theoretical issues on body image 153–4
Theory of Play 19–20
therapeutic approach 5–6
therapeutic boundaries 61–2
therapeutic community model 171
therapeutic yoga 172–3
therapy sabotaging behaviour 154
thinking power 6
'This Be the Verse' 9
threats 140–41
together in stillness 66
Totenbier, S.L. 153
transdisciplinary approach 126–38
transdisciplinary facilitation 128–9
transdisciplinary practice 109–177; almost
    paradise 165–77; leftovers 152–64;
    regaining balance 111–25; 'the boy who
    cried wolf' 139–51; transdisciplinary
    approach 126–38
transdisciplinary working 163
transference xiv, xviii–xxi, 10, 19–20, 163;
    see also countertransference
transforming experiences 62–3
transitional object 8, 72–3
transitioning 25, 39
translation from physical to mental body
    image 163–4
trauma 3–5, 46, 95–100, 104–7, 128,
    139–51, 163, 168, 173–4
treatment of trauma 96–7
tribal gatherings 34
troubling feelings 44–5
true self 75
trying again 27–8
Tufnell, M. 18
Turkey 95–108
Twyford, K. xiv

unfolding shape of group 17–18
unknown 77–8
unspoken 22–3
US Department of Housing and Urban
    Development 166
US veterans 165–77

use of clay 114–15
USHUD see US Department of Housing
    and Urban Development
using imaginative space 73
using modalities to support stretching 72–4

Van der Kolk, B.A. 96
verbal 'loops' 84–5
veteran populations 165–6
victim empathy 131
Vinogradov, S. 166
violent crimes 3–7
vitality affect 74
vulnerability 6–7, 77–8, 144

war trauma 96, 100, 107
Watson, T. xiv, 63, 92
way of being 111–12
weekend retreats 173–4
Welldon, E. 45
what interventions work 135–6
'Where I'm From' 169
White, M. 111
whole greater than sum of parts 78–9
whole-body experience 168–70
whole-body healing 168
Wigram, T. 91
Winnicott, D.W. xiii, 18–20, 56, 72–3, 75
withstanding powerful emotions 119
Wolf, Y. 100
Wood, C. 44
working backgrounds 70
working collaboratively 77–8
working with difference 74–6; exploring self
    through drama 75; exploring self through
    music 75–6
working with imagery 116–17
working with individuals 126–38
working with traumatised population 104
Workman, S. 170–71

Yalom, I. 3–4, 163, 166
Yotis, L. 44

Zajac, S. 170–72